Czeslaw Milosz

NATIVE REALM
A SEARCH FOR SELF-DEFINITION

Translated from the Polish
by Catherine S. Leach

UNIVERSITY OF CALIFORNIA PRESS
BERKELEY, LOS ANGELES, LONDON

University of California Press
Berkeley and Los Angeles, California
University of California Press Ltd.
London, England

First California Paperback Edition 1981
ISBN 0-520-04474-6

Library of Congress Catalog Card Number 68-17807

2 3 4 5 6 7 8 9

Contents

Introduction

———◆———

THE IDEA FOR THIS BOOK came to me, I guess, one day in August, several years ago, in Mrs. Helen Naef's home on Lake Geneva. I say "guess" because impulses of this kind flash through one's mind and soon afterward, to all appearances, are forgotten. They crystallize somewhere below the surface, and it is only much later that one becomes aware of a well-defined aim. But let me begin by describing the locale.

The vineyards on the hillsides of Lake Geneva have a good southern exposure. Below, along the lake shore, runs the highway and the electric lines of the Geneva-Lausanne railroad. Across the expanse of water (which always looks smooth from the hills) you can see the Alps, sometimes clearly, sometimes only in outline, depending on the weather. There is a little gate to the garden, which pushes open, and after dinner you walk over the parched earth, in the furrows between the grapevines, and snip off the ripest bunches for dessert. A wooden arcade, two stories high, casts its shadow along the two inside house walls, which enclose a garden and the courtyard. Its boards creak underfoot. Those boards and some floors of red, slightly worn-down brick had already prepared me for something. It all began, though, in the attic. There, I discovered an old chest painted green with red flowers and a similarly painted canopy bed, which had served generations of Swiss peasants. I felt a brief pang of regret then that I was dumb. Because dumbness is not just physical, and the apparent ease of a conversation in French can mask a gaze that is fixed elsewhere. The fragrance of that attic was familiar, as if it came from the corners of my childhood, but the country where I was born was far away, and for my companions my behavior was like a jack-in-the-box's, governed by some mysterious mechanism. Even our mutual taste for old furniture, which somehow retained the presence of bygone persons, concealed a fundamental difference in tone. If I wanted to explain what those pieces of furniture meant to me, what figures they brought to mind, I would have to go back, arduously, to the very beginning and entangle myself in dates, histories of institutions, battles, and customs.

The revolving globe of the earth has become very small, and, geographically speaking, there are no longer any un-colored areas on it. In Western Europe, however, it is enough to have come from the largely untraveled territories in the East or North to be regarded as a visitor from Septentrion, about which only one thing is known: it is cold. Standing beside the canopy bed, I felt both a native and a foreigner. Undoubtedly I could call Europe my home, but it was a home that refused to acknowledge itself as a whole; instead, as if on the strength of some self-imposed taboo, it classified its popula-tion into two categories: members of the family (quarrelsome but respectable) and poor relations. How many times I had remained silent because, having come from those foggy expanses that books, even textbooks, rarely provide information about (or, if they do, provide false), I would have had to start from scratch! Now there was the added anguish of renunciation. No, I will never imitate those who rub out their traces, disown the past and are dead, although they pretend they are alive with the help of mental acrobatics. My roots are in the East; that is certain. Even if it is difficult or painful to explain who I am, nevertheless I must try.

The first germ of this book, then, was the desire to bring Europe closer to the Europeans. Today, I would define my aim differently. There is a new organ, which we may call the telescopic eye, that perceives simultaneously not only different

points of the globe but also different moments of time; the
motion picture created it in all my contemporaries. And I,
more often than my contemporaries, had to make use of it,
tossed as I was by circumstances from one civilization into
another, from high-pressure areas into low, and vice versa. From
the Russian Revolution of 1917 seen through the eyes of a child
and a foreigner, to New Mexico and the coast of California,
all the way to the old house on Lake Geneva, I have wandered
through zones of storm and calm, heat and cold. New images
canceled out none of the old and, strictly speaking, I do not
see them in chronological order as if on a strip of film, but
in parallel, colliding with one another, overlapping. The pressure
from this reality I have swallowed has made it necessary for
me to connect the marchland of Europe where I was born, with
its mixture of languages, religions, and traditions, not only to
the rest of the continent but to our whole age—which has
long since become intercontinental.

So I decided to write a book about an Eastern European,
born more or less when crowds in London and Paris were
cheering the first aviators; about a man who cannot be fitted into
stereotypes like the German *Ordnung* or the Russian *âme slave.*
Such an undertaking is far from easy, because the penchant for
general but unproven notions is deeply rooted in all of us. Not
only the reader but also the author, in attempting to make the
characteristics of countries and peoples concrete, hesitates between simplification and the many-sidedness of truth. So it is
not at all a case of my having plenty of material that needs
only "touching up" to make it acceptable to popular taste. I
am beginning a quest, a voyage into the heart of my own, yet
not only my own, past.

Perhaps these words sound a bit too scholarly. My literary
interests do indeed often take me to the frontiers of anthropology, history, and sociology, but I do not claim to be learned.
Curiosity about the world, the passion itself, escapes classifica-
tion. Two Chinese girls who pass, laughing, along a street
below an elevated-railway station in New York, followed by

the eyes of the passengers waiting above; a Soviet officer, a native of Tbifisi, drinking tea with his little finger stuck out as a sign of good manners, while the heavy artillery fire of the 1945 winter offensive rumbles beyond the window; the ermine and the golden chain of His Magnificence, the Rector of my university (which preserved its medieval ceremonies); a press photo from a conference at the Kremlin with the profile of a friend of my early youth among the dignitaries— each experience branches into a series of associations, demands to be given permanency, to be linked up with the whole. In abstract art, curiosity is not the basic drive behind the drafts- man's work, but you do find it wherever an exact recording of the link of a bracelet, the clasp on a dress, the carriage of a head has seemed worth the artist's effort. Perhaps, of all that I have ever read about painting, Baudelaire's short essay on Constantin Güys has pleased me the most. His eulogy of crinolines, powder, and rouge is very wise, because one can get at man only obliquely, only through the constant masquerade that is the extension of himself at a given moment, through his historical existence. This does not mean that I would like my writing to be as close as possible to genre painting or to forego a discussion of ideological quarrels. That would be a very meager portrait of a concrete time and place. All I can say is that, being attracted rather to that special realm where fashions, news of the day, changes of opinion and creed are all somehow linked up, I mistrust the probings into the sub- conscious that are so honored in our day. I am not competent in this area and am even afraid of it, for in this anticlassical procedure it is easy to lose all sense of measure.

If I want to show what a man who comes from the East of Europe is like, what can I do but tell about myself? Of course, I could invent a fictional character and put together a biography out of the observations I have made of myself and others. But involuntarily I would choose details that suit a preconception: that is, I would reject what seems to me atypical. Without the controls of reality to inhibit me, I would be without a ballast, like a balloon. And, in spite of everything, a ballast is useful. So it is better for me to stick to what is mine and to work only with the material I have experienced firsthand.

"A diary: that part of our life we can talk about without blushing." Ambrose Bierce's aphorism should discourage lovers of sincerity. Obviously complete candor is impossible, and the more its semblances are preserved, the greater the role contrivance plays. In pretending to unattainable truth, we perpetrate a lie, since we exclude those things that show us in an unfavorable light. Even if, as happens today, some authors find self-flagellation delectable and, for fear of sounding false, stress their acts of madness and error, we can be sure that they exercise some sort of self-censorship and that even they never "get to the bottom." There is nothing degrading in our fundamental incapacity to lay bare all the particulars of our fate. If it were any different, if that chaotic richness, in the presence of which our faculties are like a circle of lantern light in the darkness, did not exist, we would not constantly be aspiring to form achieved by a process of elimination, and probably the art of writing would disappear. It is enough that we realize to what extent thought and word are incommensurable with reality. Then it is possible to set one's limits consciously.

The vision of a small patch on the globe to which I owe everything suggests where I should draw the line. A three-year-old's love for his aunt or jealousy toward his father take up so much room in autobiographical writings because everything else, for instance the history of a country or a national group, is treated as something "normal" and, therefore, of little interest to the narrator. But another method is possible. Instead of thrusting the individual into the foreground, one can focus attention on the background, looking upon oneself as a sociological phenomenon. Inner experience, as it is preserved in the memory, will then be evaluated in the perspective of the changes one's milieu has undergone. The passing over of certain periods important for oneself, but requiring too personal an explanation, will be a token of respect for those undergrounds that exist in all of us and that are better left in peace. Yet one can avoid the dryness of a scholarly treatise because the outside world will be colored by memory and subjective judgment. My intention is to stay within these bounds, although I cannot promise beforehand what the outcome will be.

Place of Birth

——————◆——————

FOR MANY CENTURIES, while kingdoms rose and fell along the
shores of the Mediterranean and countless generations handed
down their refined pleasures and vices, my native land was a
virgin forest whose only visitors were the few Viking ships
that landed on the coast. Situated beyond the compass of maps,
it was more legendary than real. For that matter, chroniclers
have never given much attention to the tiny peninsula that can
be found today by running one's finger along the map from
Copenhagen across the northernmost edge of Germany and
Poland. Its distance from the beaten track helped to keep it one
of the most isolated enclaves, where time flowed more slowly
than elsewhere. Surely, though, by the time Plato was writing his
dialogues, my country had joined the round of international
trading. Pieces of transparent amber with a petrified insect inside came from there. The amber passed from hand to hand
as an article of barter among primitive tribes, and traveled a
long way by land—along the Dnieper as far as the Black Sea—
before reaching the Greek archipelago. Its discovery at excava-
tion sites has enabled us to reconstruct the main vertical lines—
from south to north—along which certain of our acquisitions
from the Bronze and Iron Ages moved.

This was the only sign of habitation that came from the
wooded region on the Baltic until the end of the Middle Ages,
when the forest dwellers became a scandal for Christianity. As
long as all minds were preoccupied with the spread of the
True Faith, and the main theme of chivalric songs and legends

was the struggle with the infidel, it is no wonder that those provinces, which the light of the Gospel had never penetrated, stirred up fears and reminded men of their unfulfilled duty. Europe, too, had her redskins, who served notice of their presence in constant armed attacks, appearing unexpectedly and just as suddenly withdrawing to their inaccessible retreats. To the neighboring Slavs, their language was incomprehensible; the level of their technical knowledge, if measured by their armaments, was inferior to that of their adversaries. Their bows, spears, and leather-covered shields had to stand up against suits of armor and the lance, but their swiftness of maneuver made up for this shortcoming. It was during this epoch that the generic name for these tribes first made its appearance: "Litwa," or Lithuanians. To what extent they could be called barbarians or savages it is hard to determine, owing to the inadequacies of written sources and the biased judgments of the Christians. They had a rather complicated religious organization supported by a hierarchy of priests. Gradually, as they extended the boundaries of their possessions, they organized themselves into a state. In the year 1226, the Polish prince of Mazovia, as a defense measure against the Lithuanian raids, called in the Teutonic Order of the Knights of the Cross and allowed them to settle in the territory later known as East Prussia. From that moment, the Lithuanians' main enemies were knights from various Western countries, who looked something like tanks and who wore over their armor white capes emblazoned with a black cross.

All that happened a long time ago, but Europe has retained the memory of her struggle with the last pagans of the Western world in her collective consciousness—true, the memory is hazy, but it is conspicuous enough in certain modern Catholic catechisms. For example, in *Christenfibel*, the work of Pieper and Raskop, two German theologians, we read: "But during this second period, new peoples entered the Church's orbit: beginning with the thirteenth century, Teutonic Knights conducted battles and skirmishes on the frontiers of the West in the name of the Church and the Empire. They subdued the Prussians, battled with the Lithuanians, penetrated to Latvia and Estonia, and pushed on as far as Peipus Lake."

How much the accident of our birthplace can separate us from the set of opinions held elsewhere may be worth noting here. Even the most primeval tragedies of a people endure because they are given permanence by proverbs, folk songs, whatever is handed down by word of mouth, and later they become the stuff of a nation's literature. The image of an exterior darkness, of peripheries, where only zealous missionaries ventured, was so firmly rooted in the minds of the two German theologians that they thought it fitting to set it forth along with the truths of the Faith. But in my childhood I was shown a completely different picture. The epic of the Christian mission was, in effect, an epic of murder, violence, and banditry, and for a long time the black cross remained the symbol of an evil worse than the plague. All my sympathies, therefore, went out to the "noble savages" who defended their freedom and knew why they defended it: because wherever the Teutonic Knights were victorious, there they built their castles and transformed the local population into a herd of slaves toiling for the profit of the Order.

The books that recounted the heroism of these pagans and described places with familiar-sounding names fell into the hands of my companions and myself at an age when our initial reactions were being formed and they must have left a deep psychic imprint. The consequence of such reading was surely an instinctive loathing for violence disguised as ideology and a skeptical attitude toward the apologetics of all "civilizers."

The ability of certain ethnic groups to organize themselves into states is something of an enigma. Under the sign of their black crosses, the Order subjugated Prussians and Letts, but it could not put down the Lithuanians, who were linguistically akin to these two groups. Pressured on their western flank by the Roman Christians (Poles and the Knights of the Cross), the Lithuanians sought only to uphold the *status quo*, while all their expansionist thrust was directed toward the East, toward the domains of those Christians who had accepted their religion from Byzantium—the princes of Novgorod, Tver, Moscow, and Kiev. The gods worshiped under sacred oaks proved to be more powerful than the Byzantine deity, and thus arose one of Europe's strangest political organisms: the Grand Duchy of Lithuania. At the zenith of its development, it reached as far as the environs of Moscow; on one side it touched the Baltic, on the other the Black Sea, it even made a vassal state out of Bessarabia, but the small Baltic tribe that lent its name to the Duchy did not attempt to impose its own ways on those who recognized its suzerainty. On the contrary, it practiced a deference so great that, as a consequence of marriages with Ruthenian princesses, the court of the Grand Duke oscillated between fidelity to the ancient pagan rite and acceptance of the Gospel copied down by the Kievan monks.

The greatest danger was from the Order of the Knights of the Cross; and Poland, which also felt threatened because of the increasing power of its protégés, was the only possible ally against it. The intricate strategy of Polish and Lithuanian diplomats—the former searching for access to the East, the latter submitting to necessity—brought about the marriage of the Grand Duke of Lithuania with the Polish Queen Hedwig (Jadwiga)* and, little by little, prepared the two states for unification. Hedwig, daughter of the ruling house of Anjou, entered history as a special kind of saint: by espousing the pagan leader she sacrificed her personal happiness to the higher cause of Catholicism. What the sword of the Order could not achieve was accomplished through marriage: a mass baptism of the Lithuanians took place on the riverbanks in the year 1386 by decree of the Grand Duke. The last pagans in Europe had ceased to be a scandal for the Faithful.

For young nations, facts pertaining to such a distant era are

* She was twelve years old. (Tr.)

merely dates in a textbook. In the milieu where I grew up, the "problem of the Union" was not only talked about frequently, it could even provoke passionate controversy. Supporters of the Union would point out the exceptional character of such a peaceful march of civilization and would contrast Polish methods with the brutal tactics of the Teutons. Their adversaries saw in the Union an exceptionally guileful commercial transaction because the Grand Duchy of Lithuania brought to the Commonwealth an area three times larger than the Polish kingdom. And, if we compare it to the union between England and Scotland, for Lithuanians as for Scotsmen it meant the gradual dying out of their language. Lithuanian patriots, whose animated discussions I remember, more often than not were ignorant of the language of their ancestors.

At any rate, the Commonwealth was immense, and for a long time neither the Germans nor the Muscovites could compete with it. In 1410, the united forces of Poland and Lithuania routed the Teutonic Knights during the Battle of Grunwald and Tannenberg. And later, when Ivan the Terrible ruled in the Kremlin, his army suffered defeat after defeat at the hands of the king of the "Republic" (as it was called then). But in the eighteenth century the internal decay of the double state, which occupied the whole middle of Europe, opened the way for Russian encroachments and thus radically affected the balance of power in Europe.

The Commonwealth was not a national state. The projection of nationalism, which was a relatively late concept, into the past leads to such absurdities as the quarrel over whether Copernicus was a German or a Pole. The language of the enlightened was Latin, which, in written literature, began to give way to Polish at the time of the Reformation. But the Statutes of the Grand Duchy were set down in an Eastern Slavic dialect, which proves that its ethnic core had fused with the mass of peoples subordinate to it. A considerable number of city dwellers used German in everyday life, even though colonists usually underwent assimilation in the course of a couple of generations. The Jews brought with them a deformed German, and Caucasian merchants Armenian. In this melting pot, a gradual settling of elements took place: Polish became more and more synonymous with the "language of culture," that is, the language of the ruling class; Lithuanian and the dialects that later came to be classified as Ukrainian and Byelorussian passed into the category of "folk speech." The idea of nation, however, was not connected with language. Loyalties were based on regional attachments.

The Commonwealth could not claim religious homogeneity. It was cut in two by the line between Catholicism and Orthodoxy—not, thanks to one of the Vatican's largest undertakings, a very neat line. The undertaking, which was only partially successful, attempted to mend the schism by a policy of mutual concessions. The Byzantine Christians were to retain the Greek ritual, and so were not obliged to introduce Latin. They were required, however, to accept the ecclesiastical hierarchy with the Pope in Rome as its head. This was the origin of the Greek Catholic (Uniate) Church, established in the year 1596. It was to become a church of martyrs from the moment the territory where it had implanted itself was taken over by Russia. The czar saw it as a greater threat than Catholicism and suppressed it by police methods.

The Catholic half of the Commonwealth remained faithful to Rome, though not without rebellions or internal splits. For a few decades, the teachings of Luther, Zwingli, and Calvin seemed to have gained the upper hand over the Papacy. The Protestant movement tended to be more radical here than elsewhere, giving rise to numerous groups of Anti-Trinitarians. In addition, the Commonwealth possessed the greatest concentration of Jews on the continent of Europe; so great, in fact, that the majority of Jews today, no matter where they may be living, can say that their fathers or grandfathers once had their home on the banks of the Vistula, the Neman, or the Dnieper.

I am trying to keep historical details to a minimum. They are necessary, however, if I am to place my native province in a wider framework. While reading Shakespeare, I have to ask myself how the ethnically Lithuanian part of the Commonwealth, which touched the Baltic, looked at the time Queen Elizabeth was ruling England.

I can presume that the masts of the nimble ships chasing after Spanish galleons around Jamaica and Barbados were mostly from my country. Records kept by shipping firms in the port of Danzig show that England was well supplied with a certain commodity that also came from the region where I was born; namely, live bears. Today this sounds like strange cargo. The fate of these cousins of mine, forced into the role of gladiators at "bear gardens" or torturers for mangling criminals, appears to have been no more enviable than that of the bulls in the *corridas*. If overseas trade consisted of natural products of this kind, the Lithuanian forests must have been scarcely touched by the axe, and the changeover from a system of simple farming to an export economy must have only just begun. As for the local population, testimonies left by contemporaries reveal that a sincere Christianity did not deter the Lithuanians from offering sacrifices to numerous gods and goddesses (just in case).

To be truthful, I must admit that my region did not produce a single figure who swayed the world's destiny or won recognition for an important discovery. Only historians of the Reformation know the name of the capital of that province, Kiejdany, where many Protestant books were printed and where the Princes Radziwiłł, powerful protectors of heresy, resided. If my country ever received the notice of educated men from various countries, it was only after German scholars discovered that its peasants speak the oldest Indo-European language, which is in many respects akin to Sanskrit. In the nineteenth century, several German universities introduced courses in Lithuanian as an auxiliary discipline for the study of Sanskrit.

My province shared the fate of not only the Commonwealth

but the whole of that part of Europe. The rhythm of development, at first similar to Western Europe's, showed ever-widening disparities. While the countries that bordered the Atlantic were acquiring colonies across the seas and setting up manufactures, no such foolhardy ventures interested the Eastern Europeans, who were engaged exclusively in agriculture; and their consciences today are not burdened with the sufferings of black slaves or the first proletarians.

As if to counterbalance this inequality, a phenomenon came into being that is sometimes defined as "recurrent feudalism"; in reality it was only a form of internal colonization. Bigger opportunities for exporting grain prompted landowners to adopt the system of intensive farming and do away with the practice of accepting tribute from their peasants either in coin or in kind. While the tribute was not very burdensome for the peasants, it was not profitable enough for the masters. Only plantations, which were a kind of agricultural factory, could respond to the new demand and assure the supply of money that enabled wines, fabrics, spices, and luxury articles to be imported from abroad. A working force was available on the spot; one had only to constrain it; that is, undo laws made sacred by custom, a proceeding carried on not without struggle and resistance. The process was gradual; it began with the requirement that a peasant work for one day, later for two days, and so on, in his master's fields. The end result was the virtual disappearance of the "free" peasant, and if his fate was a little less bitter than that of the black slave on American plantations, it was because the organic ties of the village remained intact, together with a kind of semiprivate property. The peasant's real refuge was in certain local patriarchal traditions rather than in any law. Except on estates that belonged directly to the monarch, his misery was proportional to the splendor with which his exploiters, cut off from their human chattels by a whole hierarchy of stewards and servants, surrounded themselves. The outcome of these economic developments was a much more firmly entrenched caste system than in the West.

Actually, only two castes existed: peasants and masters, the latter containing many gradations, from wealthy magnates to their numerous, often very poor "clients." The crippling of urban growth, and consequently of the rise of the "third estate" which follows from it, was both cause and effect of this whole process.

Interior colonization enveloped Poland, Bohemia, Hungary, the Baltic countries, the Ukraine, and Russia, but it did not take the same shape everywhere. The farther east one went, the worse the situation of the peasants was (at the farthest extreme, in Russia, they were bought and sold by the head like cattle). This is a clue, incidentally, to certain traits found later among the "intelligentsia," who issued from neither the peasant class nor the bourgeoisie, but from the impoverished lesser nobility. No single date can pinpoint the end of "recurrent feudalism" or the transition to a system of hired labor, which depended on many political as well as economic circumstances. In my region, the emancipation of the peasant coincided with the era of the American Civil War.

The River Neman, not far from its mouth on the Baltic Sea, is fed by several smaller tributaries flowing from the north, out of the very heart of the peninsula. It was on the banks of one of these tributaries, the Niewiaża, that all my adventures began. Contrary to what inhabitants of warmer lands might imagine, the countryside is neither sad nor monotonous. There are no mountains, but it is hilly. And probably it was these first visual impressions that taught me my abhorrence for completely flat terrain. The land is fertile and, in spite of the severe climate, it is possible to grow sugar beets and wheat. There is an abundance of lakes and forests, both coniferous and mixed. The latter contain a number of oak trees, whose role in pagan mythology was, and in my own personal mythology continues to be, so important. Because of such childhood memories I tend to classify the places I have lived as "better" or "worse": "better" means that there are lots of birds. The beauty of spring and summer in my region makes up for the long winters. Snow falls in November or December and melts in April.

The year was 1911. The parish had two churches. To the nearest, the wooden one, people drove or walked to Mass. The other, a baroque structure of stone (baroque was introduced by the Jesuits) and three miles away, housed the civil registry. The name of the parish is difficult to pronounce and I do not know enough about old Indo-European roots to decipher its exact meaning. There I was baptized and received into the bosom of the Roman Catholic Church. At the same time, the entry of my name in the civil registry confirmed the existence of one more subject of the Russian Empire.

In the country, Lithuanian and some Polish were spoken. The little town, where crops were brought to market, used Polish and Yiddish for everyday. But all the officials imported for administrative purposes—the military gendarme trailing his long, clumsy saber behind him, the tax collector, the train conductor—addressed the local population in Russian, on the ground that everyone had to understand the official language. On a higher level, there were Russian schools and universities, offices, ministries, the state religion (Orthodoxy), and at the very top of the pyramid—the throne of the Czar.

Every new child added to the several millions of subservient peoples was a child of defeat. Behind him or her stretched a past of bloody battles, desperate uprisings, gallows, deportations to Siberia, and, whether the child willed it or not, all this shaped his subsequent life. The past had not been annihilated, although it was irretrievable. The Commonwealth could not be restored nor could the Grand Duchy of Lithuania. This once vast state had disintegrated into nationalities who hated not only their sovereign, Imperial Russia, but each other, thus affording the Czar an opportunity to play sides for his own ends. All that remained was to reflect on the causes of the catastrophe, which many saw as merely the first stage in czardom's march westward. Little Moscow had once been an adversary, held in contempt by the Lithuanian princes who kept

her at bay by supporting her enemies, the Tartars, or by
making pacts with Novgorod and Tver. Later on, their successors, the Polish kings, looked upon Moscow as a dangerous
foe, though weaker than they and unable to stand up against
Commonwealth armies in a full-sized battle. Toward the middle
of the seventeenth century, the scales began to tip; Peter the
Great forced them down. In the end, nothing except shame
and a feeling of impotence was left of the Commonwealth's
former glory.

Was it destiny, or was it proof that absolutism is the only
safeguard of power and that democracy will always lose out in
the end? Whatever may be said about the organism that bore
the title of *Respublica* and boasted an elected king at its
head, the evils inherent in it should not be judged by our
standards, but rather by comparison with neighboring states of
the same epoch. A greater contrast is hard to imagine: on
the one hand, a chaotically ruled agglomerate, a sort of coral
reef formed from the adhesion of a myriad of tiny particles;
on the other, the centralized domain of the czars, where the
ruler was omnipotent, temporal and spiritual power were one,
conspiracy and palace murders were basic political tools. In the
former, a climate of relaxation prevailed: habeas corpus, tumul-
tuous sessions of the parliament, an absence of regicide, corrup-
tion and traffic in votes, anarchist leanings on the part of individuals and groups and even whole regions. The peasants
were exploited and politically they did not count (as they did
not count anywhere then), but class democracy was a fact.
A plurality of groups battling for their own interests con-
tended for power: magnates who flattered the hordes of petty
noblemen; a monarch whose powers were so limited that he
frequently had to humble himself to get credit for the army;
towns intent on preserving what was left of their medieval
privileges; and, finally, the Church and her religious orders,
which answered to no one but Rome. In the parliament, any
deputy who declared *"Liberum veto!"* could break off a session
irrevocably—a law, unique in Europe, which implied that to pass

laws a rarely attainable unanimity was necessary, and that freedom of opinion carried the seeds of its own destruction. Meanwhile, Russian diplomats looked on, stroking their beards, at
first from a distance; but later, when their moves were backed
up by a strong military force, they found the use of pressure
or money to buy off parties or individual deputies a simple
matter. Their success proved to be complete.

While trying to master the complicated art of walking on two
legs instead of on all fours, I knew nothing of these hereditary
encumbrances which endure, not in the blood but in words, in
gestures, in the unconscious reactions of the people among whom
we live. Nor did I know then that old resentments were already
taking a new form; that there were not enough jails to hold all
the Socialists who dreamed of an era when the domination of
one nation by another would cease; that military police escorting
transports of government funds were being mowed down by
bullets and that the stolen money was swelling the tills of conspiracy.

I had inherited not only a distant past but also a more recent
one, still hovering on the limits of the present: Blériot's flight
over the English Channel, the Fords in America, Cubism and the
first abstract paintings, the movies of Max Linder, and also the
Japanese War of 1905, which had demonstrated, against all probability, that the Russian Empire was not invincible.

Ancestry

◆

NOWADAYS, in order to delve into family history one has to overcome inner resistances; that is, habits ingrained by fear or snobbery must be got rid of. Theories that lay the burden of original sin at the doorstep of individuals who happen to come from the "wrong" class or race create various taboos. There are few of us who have not witnessed some grand masquerading on this account. But nowhere was the spectacle so grand as in countries whose political life was dominated by a single party. Jews took Slavic names, affected anti-Semitism, and sold out their several-thousand-year spiritual primacy for a mess of pottage. Leaders of egalitarian movements (who rarely came from the proletariat) padded their genealogies to fit the prevailing ideal. Aristocrats described their parents as peasants in order to obtain the job of office clerk. But since even a peasant background was liable to suspicion, the career-bent young man passed himself off as the son of a worker. The worker's son, in turn, tried to cover up the fact that at one time his father had been active in trade unions. The model citizen was one who appeared out of nowhere, with neither memory nor traditions. An ancestor—not a matter of choice, after all—be he rabbi, apartment-house owner or miller, was no asset; he inspired fear and could bring on death or misfortune.

Snobbery has been equally effective in spreading atomization and uprootedness. Not so very long ago, it was customary for an Eastern European, newly arrived in the West and desirous of building up an image, to flaunt a title and tell stories of mythical riches. A cliché type was born, and innumerable novels and films cast every Russian as a prince or every Pole as a count. Basically, this was a case of mistaken sociology. In no matter what Carpathia, where towns and industry began to develop late, a title of nobility, conferring the right to use *de* or *von*, was a perfectly common thing: streetcar conductors, workers, cobblers, or petty officials could own one. Today, the fear of looking ridiculous and plebeian influences from America have almost entirely wiped out that mania. What is not durable must be amputated, whether it involves lost privileges or generations of small artisans working in wood or metal.

Curiously enough, much is said these days about history. But unless we can relate it to ourselves personally, history will always be more or less of an abstraction, and its content the clash of impersonal forces and ideas. Although generalizations are necessary to order its vast, chaotic material, they kill the individual detail that tends to stray from the schema. Doubtless every family archive that perishes, every account book that is burned, every effacement of the past reinforces classifications and ideas at the expense of reality. Afterward, all that remains of entire centuries is a kind of popular digest. And not one of us today is immune to that contagion.

If I mention my ancestors, it is because they are a source of strength for me. Thanks to them, the clothing and the furniture of past epochs, the handwriting on yellowed documents, are not completely dead objects. The awareness of one's origins is like an anchor line plunged into the deep, keeping one within a certain range. Without it, historical intuition is virtually impossible. That is why a writer of our century, William Faulkner, placed his stories in the stream of time and confined them to the borders of a single county.

For me, generalizations are filled with almost tangible concreteness. For example, my own family history illustrates that constant, easterly migrating of European peoples known as the *Drang nach Osten*. Thus, I transfer myself in thought to Berlin and Frankfurt-on-the-Oder, there to search for my origins. It is

common knowledge that the Germanic elements pressing eastward found their path blocked by the Wends (also called the
Lusatian Sorbs), Slavic communities, a small number of whose
descendants still survive today. The pressure must have been
powerful, for the local population sank to the lowest rung of
the social ladder while the most resourceful individuals escaped.
All traces of their flight, however, have vanished; it is impossible
to reconstruct the stages of their journey or to picture its wagons, horses, or riders. By the time dates and events can be
seized upon, the wanderers have already settled into their new
homes.

The sparsely inhabited forests of Lithuania provided ample
room for colonizing and clearing. Poles, Germans, even Scotsmen were attracted to the virgin land, and it was natural enough
that the immigrants from Lusatia should seek refuge there. All
this, however, is no more than a misty legend; yet it is a per-
sistent one and not without some confirmation: on the hereditary
lands that belonged to my family, there was a place called the
"Serbian cemetery." Here, rumor had it, were buried the faithful servants who had accompanied their master from a distant
land.

The first individual to emerge from the shadows—if not
bodily, at least by the presence of his signature in the civil
registries—is Hrehory Miłoszewicz Miłosz. A deed of purchase
and sale drawn up between him and a certain Anusewicz dates
from the year 1580. Or rather, did date, because the house where
the document was kept was destroyed by several large-caliber
projectiles fired by the soldiers of a certain Hitler. But that
incident will be treated as if it had not happened. In those
days, good quality paper was produced; it changed color, but
did not become brittle and would have lasted a long time. The
handwriting is, or was, fine and well formed, although its legi-
bility is somewhat diminished by the fancy calligraphy of the
day. Worse still, the contract is written in two alphabets and two
languages. To understand this procedure, a completely normal
one for its time, we will have to plunge into the hair-raising

complications of periods when no one had ever heard of the concept of nation.

The language of juridical documents in the Grand Duchy of Lithuania was a dialect destined never to reach full maturity, although later the Byelorussians began calling it their tongue. Fated, somewhat like Provençal, to give way before mightier neighbors, the dialect languished under pressure from Polish and Latin (the language of the legal profession) on the west and from Russian on the east. But as long as people used the dialect with any kind of frequency, they wrote it down in an alphabet derived from Byzantium, similar to the Greek. Thus the deed (which started this whole discussion) opens with a sacramental formula in Cyrillic, then switches to Polish, only to return to Cyrillic at the end. It is finished off by the signatures of the two parties and their witnesses in Polish; that is, in the Latin alphabet.

We can conclude from this that Polish was already an everyday language not only for my ancestor, but also for other settlers or families of local stock. As to the place where the contract was drawn up, it is still the same microcosm on the Niewiaża River, where people married, spent their whole life, and died, unless, as soldiers, they were mustered out in wartime to some distant battlefield. Theirs must have been a vertical vision of the world: a small patch of the earth—still thought of as more flat than round—and the sky above.

The masters of Labunava were average squires, and there is no evidence to indicate that they ever enjoyed an exceptional position in their microcosm. They held office, of course, but nothing higher than a judgeship. Like everyone else, they probably took politics seriously, but this was unavoidable, owing to a system of government based on small, local assemblies that elected deputies to the main parliament in the capital. The nearness of a strong center of Protestantism in the next small town and the policy of the local Princes Radziwiłł, who favored alliance with the Swedes against Catholicism and the Polish kings, gave rise, it seems, to bitter religious quarrels. It is worth noting that the Calvinists in the same little town printed collections of the Psalms in the peasant idiom, i.e., Lithuanian; in other words, the peasants and common people were somehow kept in mind. But their complete dependence on the manor was taken for granted as being part of the natural order of things, so that the only assuaging effect of Christian morality was the master's sense of responsibility for the welfare of his serfs.

It is difficult for outsiders to understand the acute national hatreds in Eastern Europe. Wherever nationalism is late in appearing, passionate attempts are made to relate it to a half-legendary heroic past. The Lithuanians, who did not regain an awareness of their identity until the age of steam and electricity, were very touchy about any traditions that had managed to survive under the Slavic crust. This is why they attached so much importance to certain names whose sound called up a feeling of the past, for example my mother's name: Kunat. Perhaps that name really had belonged to a Lithuanian chieftain whose tribe was eradicated during the Middle Ages by the Poles and the Teutonic Knights. At any rate that was the legend. And possibly not only the name but also the racial type had endured in her family—a certain shape of the nose, a special line of the cheekbones, a particular setting of the eyes. But even if this were so, what bearing could it have, if the family had long ago been Polonized and accepted into the clan of The Axe? The discrepancy is even more visible in another line of descendants on my mother's side: the Syruć, or Syrutis, line. The recurrence of the Lithuanian peasant type was so regular in this branch of the family that one gets the impression of a series of duplicates struck from a single matrix. Yet the winning of the purple and of a title—Castellans of Vitebsk—confirmed the Syrutis in their new patriotism and their attachment to the Polish language.

It would be a mistake to consider such matters either ridiculous or devoid of interest. In the twentieth century, and especially after the First World War, when Lithuania was established as an independent state, it was often such issues that severed even the closest ties and set brother against brother. One was forced to make a choice, the more emotional for being based on unclear data, yet, like every decision, demanding proper motives. But what argument could force people to sit down with a grammar book and learn endless conjugations that were valuable, perhaps, for Sanskrit specialists but of little use outside that tiny country? Race? The mélange of Polish, Lithuanian, and German blood, of which I myself am an example, was so common that admirers of racial purity could find little to boast of. Besides, the whole set of cultural notions was tied up with the Commonwealth and, through it, with Poland.

So far, the dominant motif in my family chronicle continues to be the march eastward. When it became too crowded on the Baltic, there was always enough room on the Dnieper. At the end of the eighteenth century, one of the Miłoszes set off to seek a fortune there. What prompted his venture is unclear, but to imagine that territory as purely rural would be to ignore the various functions connected with estate administration, commercial transactions, and the furnishing of credit. In any case, as a "client" of and an administrator for the Sapieha princes, Miłosz the emigrant acquired a valuable patrimony in the form of six- or seven-hundred-thousand acres of virgin forest, which yielded a fantastic fortune thanks to the rising price of lumber. The fruit of these endeavors was, in a paradoxical way, to lend a highlight—as we shall see later—to the splendor of French literature.

Facts, anecdotes, or whole scenes, if they can be put in a single sentence, get recorded in the family chronicle. One sentence is enough to report that the officer in Napoleon's army failed to return from Spain—not because he had perished, but because he had married some local beauty. Another event, a much later one, which took place in Warsaw and involved a different person, has to be shown within its whole context: The stairs in the English Hotel were steep; a veteran of the 1831 uprising who had lost his leg in the battle of *Ostrołęka* was picking his way down, supported by a wooden peg. Coming up the staircase opposite him was an overweight Russian general, sufficiently sure of himself to bump into the cripple without so much as an apology. The injured man grabbed his pegleg and cracked it over the head of the general, who found himself tumbling down the stairs. This incident sheds light not only on the man's temperament but on Poland's attitude toward her conquerors; it also suggests how that pitiful moment was reached when my grandfather had to toss pistols and sword into his native river after another abortive insurrection in 1863. But the political disruptions left more than just war stories in their wake. Up until the Second World War, when the pages of old books served mainly as cigarette paper for soldiers, my mother's family cherished the library of Stanisław Kunat, economist and exile, who taught at the émigré school of Les Batignolles in Paris.

Eccentrics and visionaries deserve a special place. My cousins from the Dnieper excelled in this sphere. No doubt they were trying to vanquish the boredom that comes with prosperity. After one of them died, five rooms of his house were discovered to be filled to the ceiling with hats and galoshes—as good a collection as any other. The family was also sensitive to aristocratic splendor and could not, for example, bear the idea that someone would be capable of thinking them related to the then famous Serbian dynasty of Miłosz Obrenowicz. One of them even wrote to a high czarist official in Petersburg:

*Yego vielichestvo Leshek Piatyi pozhaloval gierb Liubich i my nichevo obshchego s etimi serbskimi pastukhami Miloshami nie imieyem.**

Leaving behind their dogs, grouse and wolf hunts, and six-foot-deep snow, they traveled abroad, spending long months in Venice and Florence. One of these trips ended in a marriage: the Italian songstress who was brought to the Dnieper from her country of vineyards gazed in amazement at the fog (we can assume that this took place in the spring), the swamps, the horizon walled in by the forest, at the long-haired peasants in their

---

* Russian for: "We were granted the coat of arms of Lubicz by His Highness Leshek V and we have nothing in common with those Serbian shepherds, the Miłoszes."

linen breeches and bast shoes laced halfway up their legs. Although she had been virtually changed into a sovereign princess by coming there, those empty spaces must have robbed her of all that had been hers; her voice was worthless, no more than a relic. If only records had existed, at least she could have listened to her old self! But there was only stillness, choirs of frogs, and the monotonous melody played by the cowherds on a birchwood horn. That picture lingered in my imagination for a long time, and it could have been accurate. The fact is, however, that when Natalia Tassistro married the Polish-Russian War invalid, she encountered the hostility of her in-laws and never left Italy. She is buried in Vercelli, near Milan.

In the year 1940, the window of my room in downtown Nazi-occupied Warsaw looked out on a small square overgrown with weeds. One day I received a visit from a brisk old man who, like everyone else, was engaged in black-market trading. This was, at the time, the only way to avoid starving to death. My own attempts in the field always proved to be incompetent, and the old man made a mistake in thinking I could be of help to him in his transactions. He specialized in bluing, a product sought after by all laundresses. At one point he went to the window, glanced at the square below, and suddenly blurted out: "The track was here. In 1889 I won first prize in the bicycle races right here!" And our conversation strayed from bluing to the city's past, which in spite of everything interested me more. "Aren't you perhaps related to Mr. Władysław Miłosz? I remember him as if it were yesterday. What a handsome man! What a lion! When he strolled through the Saxon Gardens with that black beard of his, swinging his ivory-handled cane, women just fainted away. That was a personality! An eccentric, a Don Juan!"

Son of the Italian songstress and the seigneur of the Dnieper forests. Restrained by nothing and no one in the satisfaction of his caprices. He hunted lions in Africa. Flew in a balloon. As a rabid atheist, he was hostile to all churches; an anarchist by nature, he ridiculed all governments. During the Paris Commune, it was not politics that elated him but his own passions: at the head of his band of scapegraces he stormed a convent in order to kidnap a novice with whom he had fallen in love; for this incident he spent several weeks locked up in Châtelet. At home, he tamed bears; they served as his bodyguards and ran after his horse like dogs. His marriage was accomplished in keeping with his personal style. While crossing a street in Warsaw, he happened to observe the portrait of a beautiful girl in a shop-window. He stopped in front, just long enough to say, "That's the one," and went inside. His intentions were in no way altered by the news that the girl—Miriam Rozenthal—was the daughter of a Jewish schoolteacher. The old bluing expert knew all about this event, but he could not have known its consequences because the scene of action shifted far beyond that city, which he never left.

The only son to issue from that union between a globetrotting sportsman and a Jewish beauty became a great French poet who was also to play an important role in my life. Oscar Miłosz spent his childhood on his father's wooded estate in Czereia, and its landscape stayed with him forever as the memory of a mythical land, a true spiritual home. *"Une vaste étendue de lacs obscurs, verdâtres et pourrissants, envahis par une folie des tristes nymphéas jaunes, s'ouvrit tout à coup à ma vue,"* he wrote. *"O Maison, Maison! pourquoi m'avez-vous laissé partir?"** But when he reached the age of eleven, he was sent to a boarding school, the Lycée Janson-de-Sailly in Paris. After finishing there, he studied at the Ecole du Louvre and the Ecole des Langues Orientales.

Many mortifying events in that man's life explain his hostility toward the Poles. As a child he spoke only Polish, and achieved perfect mastery of the language. But a painful conflict arose, owing to the anti-Semitism of his milieu. He belonged to a caste for whom marriage with a Jewess was an unpardonable *mésal-*

---

* "A vast stretch of dark lakes, greenish and decaying, overgrown with an extravagance of sad, yellow water lilies, suddenly opened out before me. O my home! my home! Why did you let me go?" (Tr.)

liance and the violation of a taboo. Returning home for vacations, he realized that the caste would never "forgive" him. Besides, he had less and less in common with it; France had formed his mind and he looked upon his Eastern contemporaries from a safe distance. Summing up his recollections of that period of uncertainty about where he belonged, he admonished me: "Remember, in Europe there is nothing more stupid or more brutal in its petty hatreds than the Polish gentry." How true that was I was able to verify later, on my own account.

The Polish gentry liked to bring in the idea of treason at every step. Treason meant not only an improper marriage but also the act Oscar committed when he came of age—selling his immense, hereditary forest lands. The code of patriotism in those provinces by the Dnieper was oddly bound up with the code of ownership. Whoever sold his family estate diminished, thereby, the "possessions" of his national group and facilitated Russian penetration. Oscar Miłosz sold his—to Russian merchants. The break with his caste was complete.

Faithful to family tradition, he carried his spleen and melancholy around the whole continent during the years before World War I. There was probably not a country in Europe he failed to visit. Passionately interested in literature, he read, with equal facility, German, English, French, and the Bible in Hebrew. In Paris the poets' café then was the Closerie des Lilas, on the Boulevard Montparnasse. Oscar Miłosz's first books of verse, his drama *Miguel Mañara*, and a novel, *L'Amoureuse Initiation*, put him on an equal footing with its habitués. At the Closerie des Lilas he was usually seen in the company of old Oscar Wilde. There, too, he probably made the acquaintance of Guillaume Apollinaire, another "Frenchman" with a similar background: Wilhelm Kostrowicki was also a descendant of the soldiers and adventurers of the Grand Duchy of Lithuania.

The slim young man with the romantic air possessed an incredible amount of money. He wasted it on extravagances such as huge banquets given for his "court" of young friends, both men and women. Those orgies remained vivid for a long time in the memories of their participants. When I lived in Paris as a student, and the Clemenceau era seemed as remote to me as the Stone Age, I ran into some of the survivors—poets and actors. Their hair had turned gray, their faces were furrowed, they raised cats. In speaking of their former host, they displayed a great deal of affection. He himself lost his entire fortune. The capital he got from the sale of his forests had been invested in czarist stocks, and the Revolution turned them into worthless pieces of paper.

Yet that cosmopolitan longed with intense nostalgia for a native land. It is visible in everything he wrote. The contours of his landscapes are not French; his sensibility is foreign and captivatingly exotic. But what was his native country? A piece of earth defined by geographic parallels? That territory was no longer inhabited by people who said simply, "We come from here"; now they looked upon their neighbors from the village, who spoke in a different tongue, as if they were enemies. Oscar Miłosz's real tie was to a certain tradition. So he turned his gaze toward the one point to which his family chronicle was anchored: the small county on the Baltic peninsula. But even here one had to decide between Lithuania or Poland—a similar controversy in Finland set Swedes against Finns, only there it was resolved better.

Inspired by slogans of autonomy, various delegations from Eastern European nations in Paris began to step up their activities during the First World War. Oscar Miłosz, then a press official at the Quai d'Orsay, made his choice. The Polish-Lithuanian conflict was in large part a class conflict between landowners and peasants, or, rather, between gentry traditions (regardless of how much property was owned) and peasant traditions. Miłosz's aristocratic instincts and the old resentments left over from his youth inclined him to the side of the slow-moving, systematic, stubborn peasants, who were the true founders of the Grand Duchy, before being victimized by various colonizations. If historical continuity existed anywhere, it was in them. His love for them was real; and, for their virtues lost elsewhere, he dubbed them the redskins of Europe. Miłosz became a member of the first Lithuanian mission to the League of Nations. Afterward, he represented independent Lithuania in Paris. He was offered the position of Foreign Minister and rejected it. His gravestone in Fontainebleau, where unknown admirers of his poetry often place flowers, bears his name in Lithuanian (with the ending *ius*).

Like many others who were Lithuanians by choice, he learned the language rummaging through dictionaries. In 1919, when an international commission under the chairmanship of the Swede, Branting, met in Brussels to seek a solution to the thorny problem of Wilno, Miłosz headed the Lithuanian delegation, but it was in Polish that he quarreled with Professor Ashkenazy, the spokesman for Poland's delegation. All his works, however, are written in French, and he was deeply attached to France.

My closer acquaintance with him can be explained by the vehemence with which he decided his likes and dislikes. Having severed all contact with his nearest relations, he turned his whole attention to the other branch of the family, which, for various complicated reasons, had never subscribed to a strictly national outlook. Happy to have found in me a poet, he considered me his nephew, a designation not altogether accurate, as the degree of our kinship was more distant. He wrote me letters of advice, sometimes in French, sometimes in Polish. During one of his trips to Lithuania, he described my maternal grandfather (Kunat) as "*un gentilhomme du XVIIIe siècle*," and the characterization captures rather well the graciousness, mildness, and humor of that gentleman-farmer, a citizen of the Lithuanian Republic, who held on to his Polishness but repudiated chauvinism. It was only with hindsight that I could appreciate how ironic nationalistic Europe seems to those who, thanks to just such an ancestor, had been exposed to an old-fashioned way of thinking far more humane than the new way, with its fanatical discrimination. The respect Oscar Miłosz felt for Sigismund Kunat also showed that within the social strata for which he felt such distaste he recognized two different mentalities: one attached to the principles of classical European education—and the closer the attachment, the better; the other guided by wounded pride and an appeal to some vague national values (which had never required justification before)—and the more these emotions dictated behavior, the worse.

The process that was taking place in Eastern Europe, more or less simultaneous with the building of railroads, was not paralleled in other parts of the continent; it is closer to what happened in the American South after the Civil War. It was not accidental that I mentioned Faulkner earlier. Poles find the atmosphere of his novels considerably more familiar than that of Balzac's or Zola's. In Poland as in the American South, the equilibrium of a whole community was disrupted by a sudden shock. The impoverished gentry fled to the cities, but their former customs and habits did not altogether disappear. Far from it. They left their stamp on all classes; thus, the Polish proletariat, not to speak of the intelligentsia, which maintained close ties with the surviving members of the nobility, inherited many of the gentry's characteristics. My own family provides an example. My father did not have a single acre of ground, but he was sent to a Russian high school and the Polytechnical Institute in Riga (Department of Roads and Bridges). The old Hanseatic city of Riga, which later became the capital of Latvia, was the chief center of learning in the Baltic region, and attracted students from both Poland and Russia. The townspeople spoke mainly German, and the students led much the same sort of life as their colleagues in Leipzig or Heidelberg.

Born without the security that comes with inherited money, I had to make my own way in the world. The pressure was somewhat mitigated by the care that my parents, who belonged to the intelligentsia, took to prepare me for a profession. Private industry and trade had only just begun to develop. Thus education amounted, with very few exceptions, to a ticket of admission to the bureaucracy, which, thanks to the revolutionary upheavals, was to have an astonishing career. While I was throwing stones into the water and climbing trees I was doubtless acting as a free human being. Only occasionally, during vacations at grandfather Kunat's (where I was born), I was troubled by the difference between the country boys and myself. Yet even then, like it or not, I was already "classed."

My "place" did not correspond in the least to what is generally known as the "bourgeois way of life." Along with my feeling that one should know who one is went a pinched pocketbook and an enforced curtailment of my personal needs. My material existence was so primitive that it would have startled proletarians in Western countries. The impoverishment of rural property holders (the way my uncles and aunts lived never made me envious, and they were still landowners), a certain incompetence in practical affairs, a contempt for "elbowing one's way up" (because social standing clearly did not depend on wealth), and, finally, the widespread economic difficulties after the First World War, all spelled one thing. As a schoolboy I wore shirts and suits of coarse homespun because it was cheaper. Every day for weeks on end, I pressed my nose against the windows of bookstores or shops selling scientific instruments, well aware that I could not purchase the objects of my dreams; and I learned, not how to save, but how to stifle temptation. If the urge to earn and spend money testifies to the acquisitive spirit, it was the opposite attitude that took root in me—a passive vitality. When I was down to my last penny, I preferred to go to bed. That way the organism consumes less, and one can go without dinner and supper. This may have been largely a question of personal pride, but it was surely not unrelated to the scale of values considered proper for my social group, which had inherited, if not privileges, at least the strong persuasion that wage-earning was somehow below a man's dignity.

Later on, when I was working for the "People's Democracy," my origins caused me no trouble at all. On the contrary, my superiors viewed them very favorably, and in this showed great acumen. The real demons for them were the defenders of private initiative, the entrepreneurs, whether in trade, industry, or agriculture. By exterminating the acquisitive instinct, they believed that mankind could be raised to a higher level. On this point, they and I were in perfect accord—an accord that went deeper than any rationale, growing as it did out of an inborn aversion to counting, measuring, and weighing, activities that symbolized the unclean. There is really nothing more antibourgeois than certain segments of the intelligentsia who are defenseless when it comes to money. They retain a medieval disgust for usury because private capitalism never rubbed off on them. My superiors, not necessarily realizing it, professed an ideology strongly marked by the atavistic resentments of impoverished noblemen, those begetters of revolution in literature and politics. One of these was Dostoevsky—when, in the person of his hero Raskolnikov, he killed the pawnbrokeress, he was anticipating, in a sense, the expropriation of private capital (this was observed, I believe, by Alberto Moravia) and the nationalization of private property. Another was Lenin. Still another was my fellow-countryman from the Grand Duchy of Lithuania, Felix Dzierżyński, the organizer of the most powerful police force on the globe, the Cheka. So a well-trodden path lay open, making it easy for the intelligentsia to become a partner of the "apparatus." Emotionally I did not condemn the destruction of private shops and farms (this does not mean that I always approved of it intellectually); it even gave me a sadistic pleasure—which was certainly noted down in my dossier as a positive indicator.

Besides, I was a poet; that is, a so-called intellectual. Although such a profession depends on strictly personal factors, my choice was not made, or so I think, without some social motivation. A society that clearly distinguishes an individual's social status from the amount of money he is worth—i.e., when the one does not determine the other—is applying a scale of values that is, in one sense or another, aristocratic. Thus, for the Eastern European the drive to gain recognition in the sphere of literature, science, or art has all the earmarks of a search for identity formerly conferred by a coat of arms. Nowhere outside of this

part of Europe does the artist, writer, or scholar enjoy such
exceptional privileges, and this is not the result of transformations brought about by the Communist Party, which understood
just enough to make use of such a setup. Exceptional privileges
and a high income do not always have to go together, because
money can be replaced by fame; nor must they necessarily go
with freedom, for the state, even as it tames and subjugates
an artist or scientist, by this very effort pays homage to his role
and his importance. It is interesting that only in France is
there a similar respect for the intellectual—but, as has often
been remarked, the ways of the cultural milieu in Paris resemble
the behavior at a royal court. In the bourgeois world one islet
has survived where poverty is not a disgrace: when it is decorated with a title; that is, with publicity.

If such an intellectual's loyalty to an all-powerful state coin-
cides with his own interest, there will be no reason to doubt
him. The difficulty arises when the motive of self-interest is
complicated by the presence of other tendencies. Sometimes the
fondness for state prizes and medals conflicts with the pride
that drives the intellectual toward moral leadership and winning
favor with the nation. Obviously I do not want to reduce moral
impulses to social determinants. Yet the struggle, often going
on within the same man, between the artist (or scholar) and the
bureaucrat reflects to a great degree the structure of a hierarchi-
cal society that has never lived under the reign of money and
never fully accepted it as a gauge of worth. It is as if such a
society had some permanent formula of crystallization, and its
new crystals always tend to form in the same pattern.

The offspring of any family ruined soon enough—that is, before the Revolution—frequently possesses the advantage of a
dialectical flexibility. The dimension of time is not strange to
him, he juggles it easily. Since his imagination is capable of re-
creating past centuries from photographs, a scrap of cloth, or a
manuscript, he observes a period of several decades with a shrug
of the shoulders. This makes his decision easier should he ever
intend to become a partner to terror. In the eyes of the authori-

ties, however, this virtue sometimes changes into its opposite, for a mind that is too flexible is powerless to restrain its own dialectical movement. Who knows if it is not this very quality that makes the Jews dangerous for totalitarian states? Unlike the uprooted masses, prone to see the past as it is drawn for them, the Jews at least have a memory.

At many a reception in Washington or in Paris, where enthusiastic ladies would approach a Red with a delicious shiver, I felt that I was only half-present. Too many shadows enveloped me: the clanking of sabers, the rustling of Renaissance gowns, the fragrance of old houses full of animal hides, hunting arms, coaches, rusted armor; and this robbed what was going on around me of some of its reality. Generations of men tormented by the devil, fingering their rosary beads, wavering between Catholicism and heresy, winked at me with humor. No doubt my colleague, also a Communist official, was protected from those ladies (one of whom gravely asked us how we intended to solve the Negro problem in our country) by a similar crowd of phantoms. Except that his ghosts were pious women in hennaed wigs, rabbis sitting all day long over their books in a muddy small town, merchants bargaining with peasants over wool and calves but in their souls seeking the absolute. One should appreciate, after all, the advantages of one's origin. Its worth lies in the power it gives one to detach oneself from the present moment.

Journey into Asia

———◆———

MANY OF MY CONTEMPORARIES hold the opinion that industrialism in Russia dates from the Revolution. This is a gross exaggeration. Throughout the entire nineteenth century, Europe had due respect for the Russian Army, a fact that is all too willingly forgotten. The maintenance of the world's largest army required munitions factories, and the weapons these produced were, by all the standards of the time, good ones. But the same government that was so mindful of the country's military strength seemed not to care about the material or cultural betterment of its population. First-rate artillery divisions rode through village streets whose inhabitants knew nothing of modern technology. This state of affairs (just as I was getting acquainted with things around me in the neighborhood of the floor) had, for some ten years or so, been undergoing a change. It was a violent one, recalling America's sudden leap forward. New railroads, highways, and factories sprang up. Agricultural machines appeared in the fields—usually with the trademark "McCormick, Chicago." In addition, Russia became the greatest book market in the world. French, American, and English authors reaped more profits from Russian translations of their books than from any other editions. The success of literature that celebrated energy and accomplishment—Whitman, English adventure novels for boys, Kipling, and, later, Jack London—is significant. The cult of America in Russia dates from this epoch.

It is not at all certain that Russia would have been less powerful industrially than she is today if the Revolution had not taken place. But since in such cases all "ifs" are meaningless, it is pure speculation to suggest that her strength might have been more equally distributed and that extreme primitivism might not have existed side by side with atomic arms and tanks, just as in the days of the czars it had gone hand in hand with modern artillery.

In any case, great opportunities opened up for technicians and industrialists in czarist Russia. Those who knew how to take advantage of them were mainly from the more advanced territories in the West—the Baltic Germans and the Poles. It was my father's government contract that occasioned my first journey—by no means a short junket—to the city of Krasnoyarsk in Siberia, not very far from the Chinese border.

In Petersburg I saw my first automobile, and I know, from hearing stories about it, that it made me wild with excitement. Clinging to the door handle, my foot on the running board, I yelled and screamed; they could not tear me away, and the uniformed chauffeur laughed. It seems improbable that something that happened so early in one's life can be remembered, yet I would swear that I can see the curb, the shiny black paint, or, rather, that I carry the aura of that experience within myself.

We made the trip to the Urals on the Trans-Siberian line. From the many days and nights spent on the train and from our year's stay in Krasnoyarsk (all this took place just before the outbreak of the First World War), only one memory has stuck with me: the little chamber pot on the train wobbled while the compartment wall swayed in the background. Later, however, I often came upon traces of our Siberian episode. Over the table where I did my lessons, for example, hung a photograph showing my father on the deck of a ship captained by the Arctic Ocean explorer Fridtjof Nansen: the tall, thin man next to him was Nansen; the fat ones in the fur caps with the earflaps were Russian merchants.

My father had no talent for "getting ahead" or for making money. He lacked the necessary weapons for fighting people;

any intrigue or tactic employed to gain one's own personal ends seemed ignoble to him. If he came up against cunning and deceit, he simply bowed out of the game and sought work elsewhere. On the other hand, the struggle with nature excited and intoxicated him, because it was an adventure. He had been raised on the books of Maine-Reid and Marryat, which were extraordinarily popular in the Empire. Untamed Siberia was no poor second to Alaska and Northern Canada; for him it was arrayed in romantic mystery. He did not care about earning a living but about enjoying life—which meant his bridge-construction projects and his long wanderings. He would take a boat down the Yenisei River, for example, then travel overland, using teams of reindeers and dogs, up to the mouth of the huge river on the Arctic Ocean. There was also his passion for hunting. A good shot, he could not complain about lack of game in Siberia. He chased deer in the Sayan Mountains, wild geese in the tundra beyond the Arctic Circle. He lived his dream of exploration. For him Siberia, which had engulfed so many of our compatriots, was not a land of exile. Having certain literary interests, he filled thick black notebooks, bound in cerated cloth, with hymns in honor of the wild north.

The wilderness is not always romantic. One of my father's stories engraved itself in my imagination, and I have often meditated over it: after trudging many miles in the frozen taiga, he and his traveling companions at last spied chimney smoke. They entered the hut, which was as hot as a bathhouse inside, and found a peasant in a white shirt sitting down. When my father went up to him, he noticed that the shirt was heavily stained with red blotches. "*Eto nichevo, khlopy,*"* said the peasant, pressing his shirt with a finger and squishing another bedbug. The same calm was applied to killing people. If a row broke out in the market place, a professional would appear and, taking one of the parties aside, discreetly propose a deal: "*Daj piat' rublej, ya yevo zariezhu.*"†

* Russian for: "It's nothing, just bedbugs."
† Russian for: "For five rubles I'll slit his throat."

But Russia was open space where a man did not run into his fellow-man at every step, and whoever grew to like her was bound to feel unhappy in other, more civilized countries. This is what happened to my father. When he lived in Poland later on, he constantly complained of the lack of breadth, of the smallness of everything, of stagnation—the Czarist government, of course, had not stinted on money for engineering projects. The stifling atmosphere of petty worries at last drove my father to emigrate—to Brazil, a country that seemed to offer possibilities similar to those he had found in Asian Russia. This rather chimerical escapade ended in failure. My father returned, it seems, mainly for psychological reasons; he never recovered the same kind of room to breathe in that he had had in the East.

What the Russian Empire was like in its last phase I cannot know; I can only piece together a picture from the spoken accounts of various persons, daubing in here and there my own impressions from childhood (mustaches, uniforms) and interpreting them anew. Revolutionary propaganda condemned that era to nonexistence because its industrial upswing did not fit the thesis that everything began in 1917 as if it were the first year of creation. But Europe's *belle époque*, with its frenzy of initiative, riotous living, colonial exploitation, cosmopolitanism, and the fever of its port cities also defined the tempo of the Russian Empire, and one cannot help wondering how things would look today if the same economic system extended from the Atlantic to Kamchatka.

War

MANY YEARS AFTER WORLD WAR II, when Hitler and Mussolini
were no more than specters, I found myself on the beach at
the Ile d'Oléron, off the French coast north of Bordeaux. Low
tide had uncovered the iron hulk of a shipwreck half sunk in the
sand. The water's constant swirling had made hollows around
the rusty beams, and the pools of water formed a convenient
place for my son to practice his swimming. We guessed that the
derelict had probably been lying there since the Anglo-Ameri-
can landing. It turned out to be of considerably older date.
A ship flying a Uruguayan flag had run ashore there, carrying
copper for the French troops who were at war with the army
of Wilhelm II. The permanence of things and the impermanence
of people is always surprising. I touched the bulwarks overgrown with barnacles and sea moss, still not quite able to accept
the thought that two great world conflicts were already as unreal as the Punic Wars.

My first awareness came with war. Peeping out from under
my grandmother's cloak, I discovered horror: the bellow of
cattle being driven off, the panic, the dust-laden air, the rum-
bling and flashing on a darkened horizon. The Germans were
arriving in Lithuania and the Czarist army was retreating, accompanied by hordes of refugees.

A scene from that summer of 1914 is still very clear in my
memory: bright sunshine, a lawn, myself sitting on a bench
with a young Cossack whom I like a lot. He is slim-waisted
and black-haired. On strips, crisscrossed over his chest, there

are cartridges. He twists a bullet out and empties the powder grains onto the bench. Then a tragedy occurs. I was very attached to a little white lamb. Now the Cossacks are running him into the green grass, heading him off. To slaughter him. My Cossack tears off to help them. My desperate cry, the inability to bear irrevocable unhappiness, was my first protest against necessity. From the same period come the cemeteries, which later on all my friends and I used for our favorite playground—stone crosses above carefully kept flowers, or wooden ones half-hidden in thickets of blackberries and raspberries; they bore the names Schultz, Müller, Hildebrand. Someone's hand will tend the graves of the German dead. No one will give a thought to the Czar's soldiers.

Throughout all my early childhood, rivers, towns and landscapes followed one another at great speed. My father was mobilized to build roads and bridges for the Russian Army, and we accompanied him, traveling just back of the battle zone, leading a nomadic life, never halting longer than a few months. Our home was often a covered wagon, sometimes an army railroad car with a samovar on the floor, which used to tip over when the train started up suddenly. Such a lack of stability, the unconscious feeling that everything is temporary, cannot but affect, it seems to me, our mature judgments, and it can be the reason for taking governments and political systems lightly. History becomes fluid because it is equated with ceaseless wandering.

A chaos of fascinating and colorful images streamed over me: guns of various caliber, rifles, tents, locomotives (one looked like a gigantic green wasp and for a long time inhabited my drowsy fantasies), sailors wearing daggers, which bounced on their hips as they walked, Kirghiz in smocks that reached to the ground, Chinese with their pigtails. Near some depot, I gaped at a maze of cloth surfaces and ropes that was supposed to be an airplane. The presents I received were always games about battleships and war. All my scribblings and drawings were of soldiers running to attack and shells bursting.

Since I heard Russian around me all the time, I spoke it too, completely unaware that I was bilingual and that I altered the position of my lips depending upon whether I addressed a member of the family or a stranger. What I acquired of Russian has stayed with me and I have never had to relearn it. Whenever it was needed, the accent, the meaning of words have suddenly popped out of the locked storehouse of memory.

My vocation came to light in one of the places where our stopover was more prolonged. It was completely in the spirit of the bureaucratic caste for which I was destined. With my friend Pavlushka (he was the son of a bearded Old Believer, and after knowing his father, Abram, I could never imagine the Biblical Abraham any other way) I sneaked into the rooms where uniformed men were writing and calculating on abacuses. We made ourselves comfortable at an empty table, and I called out in a severe voice: "*Pavlushka, davay bumagu!*"* Brow furrowed, I scrawled something illegible that was supposed to be a signature—the movement of the pencil filled me with a feeling of power—and handed it to Pavlushka for further processing.

Shortly after these visits to the military office, a red band was placed on my sleeve. The winter of 1916–17; the abdication of the Czar. I boasted that my armband was a prettier color than those the local children wore. I found out that this color, amaranthine, was Polish and patriotic. If the Czar had been driven out, that was very good; he deserved it. But we were one thing and the Russians another.

. . . The tide had washed over the Uruguayan wreck on the sands of Oléron not only while mustard gas was disabling human bodies on Flanders' field, and thrones and empires were toppling, but also while I was living my personal life of hopes and disappointments, and while the gas chambers and watchtowers of the concentration camps were being built. There is always a taste of nothingness in the roar of the ocean. It is better to try to seize the small drops of time that are man's.

* Russian for: "Pavlushka, hand over the papers!"

Ten Days That Shook the World

———◆———

IN A PARK THAT DESCENDED to the Volga stood an imposing mansion. Its birch-lined drive led to the town of Rjev, a mile away. In the basement of the mansion, an army kitchen had been installed; the middle part was occupied by the owner and his family; and we—that is, the "fugitives"—lived in the attic rooms. The Russian soldiers were my best friends. Their reddish beards tickled softly like the little monkey that had been sewn for me out of rags. I assisted at all their meals downstairs in the kitchen, perched on one of the bearded men's laps. They would thrust a spoon into my hand and order me to eat. I treated that activity as a boring duty, which, for some unknown reason, had to be fulfilled in order to win the privilege of their company. Then I would go upstairs and submit to the ritual of a second dinner, cleaning the plate my mother set before me, not because I was a glutton, but out of obedience. As a result, I became a martyr to an asceticism in reverse, like those women who take up vice for pious ends. But my stomach finally revolted, and I fell seriously ill from overeating—which, as I see today, was not the most appropriate thing in view of the coming, grave events.

I made no friends among the noble proprietors of the mansion and never penetrated to their rooms, which remained a secret and inaccessible domain, except for a good old woman who used to take me to her quarters through a long hall stacked with trunks. It smelled of incense there; the gilding on the icons gleamed, and a red glow came from the vigil lamps.

Besides this, I was in love with Lena, I guess. I could admire
her only from a distance. This important person was twelve
years old, but proud and haughty. Every morning a carriage
with a coachman on the box drove up to the porch. It took her
to school in Rjev. I stood off on one side, swallowing hard and
contemplating her neck, which showed above a sailor collar.
"Thy neck is like the tower of David wherein a thousand
shields hang and all the arms of potentates," I could have said,
but did not. That my idol had freckles and pockmarks did not
bother me. But then everything was mixed up. All around me I
heard the word "Lenin, Lenin." The sound, repeated incessantly,
meant nothing to me, but I associated it with that neck and
thus, in my imagination, Lena and Lenin became curiously entangled.

The "Ten Days" appeared to me as follows: I was lying in
bed. Opening my eyes, I saw one of my bearded friends in
front of me. His army shirt was spattered all over with blood,
and he was behaving differently than usual. He asked me in a
sort of husky whisper, as if he were in a hurry, where my
parents were. Then he vanished. Immediately afterward my
parents rushed in, thinking that I might have taken fright.
"Seryozha's slaughtered a rooster," I said in answer, then rolled
over and fell asleep.

There are many definitions of freedom. One of them pro-
claims that freedom is the ability to drink an unlimited quantity
of vodka. In Rjev, the soldiers let go with an attack on the
building that housed the spirits monopoly. Alcohol flowed in
the streets, and the townspeople, unable to bear the sight of
such wastefulness, lay down and drank out of the gutters.
Seryozha had taken part in this drunken uproar and had diligently slain not a rooster but his own buddy; the others were
now out for his blood. He burst into our attic looking for cover.
I think my parents hid him somewhere, which was tactful of
them.

We are always putting people into categories. Were we to
distinguish those who know Russia from those who do not, our

division would not be the least meaningful one. For the secret, often indefinable attitudes of these two groups of persons to the various phenomena of life are not the same. Knowledge does not have to be conscious. It is incredible how much of the aura of a country can penetrate to a child. Stronger than thought is an image—of dry leaves on a path, of twilight, of a heavy sky. In the park, revolutionary patrols whistled back and forth to each other. The Volga was the color of black lead. I carried away forever the impression of concealed terror, of inexpressible dialogues confided in a whisper or a wink of the eye. The mansion waited resignedly for the promised murder of all its inhabitants, a murder that, presumably, would not have spared the fugitives. And among those refugees, who were there by chance, fear was rampant. I also carried away the image of Orthodox church cupolas seen against a bluish-red sky with flocks of circling jackdaws, the paving of Rjev's streets, on which a passing cart would leave a fine trail of seeds from a torn sack, and the shrieks of fur-capped children as they launched their kites.

For some reason, probably the usual roving of my father's office, or perhaps for safety, we were soon on the road again. This time we settled in the western borderlands of the ex-Empire in the town of Dorpat. Our flat had shabby wooden stairs; the courtyard was dreary. Talk about hunger never ceased. One could get bread that contained more sawdust than flour, saccharin and potatoes, but no sugar or meat. At night I would be awakened by battering at the door, stamping of feet and loud voices. Men in leather jackets and high boots would come in and, by the light of a smoking kerosene lamp, dump the contents of cupboards and drawers onto the floor. My father did not figure on the list of suspects. He was a specialist, endorsed by the workers' council of his company. But house searches were no doubt a matter of routine. The terror-stricken faces of the women, my brother's screams from his cradle, the whole miserable family sanctuary, or rather den, turned topsy-turvy—all this was not healthy for the heart of a child.

More Wars

———◆———

NEXT, IT WAS THE YEAR 1918. The Germans came, and I got a taste of change. I was curious about the leather-jacketed men who had been shot and whose corpses were stacked in the town squares, but no one would take me to see them. There were enough interesting things without that, though. Army bands played in the streets, but the soldiers did not look at all like the Russians; they were more like mechanical toys. The color of their uniforms was delightful, and they blew into trumpets painted almost the same shade, only grayer. Each of them had a little music stand in front of him to hold the notes.

The city reverted swiftly to German, the language most widely spoken by its older residents; and every time I went to the store with my grandmother I was amazed at the cooing that came from her throat. I had never suspected she was capable of making sounds like *eine kleine*. But my grandmother was a native of one of the Baltic cities, and she was simply using her second language.

For the first time in my life, I found myself inside a movie theater. Helmets and guns flickered across a taut piece of linen. Soldiers were shooting from a trench, their guns propped against the sandbags protecting the rim. From behind the screen came the strains of a lilting waltz.

How to picture the chaos of newly emerging forms? There, where the Russian Empire had held sway for over a century, new countries were taking shape. The town where we lived already belonged to independent Estonia. To the north, Finland was consolidating; to the south, Latvia, Lithuania, and Poland. A state of affairs prevailed that was neither war nor peace—two-day battles, two-day truces, chessboard patches of land occupied *manu militari* by whoever had the forces.

. . . Once again on the move. The trains were remarkable in that they could be boarded only through the windows. Most of the inveterate travelers hung from the buffers, or lay on the roofs of the cars, holding on. Shrieking masses of people pushing and pulling one another were nothing new to me, but in such a brutal jungle, a small, defenseless creature is prone to panic. At one station, which belonged to the Bolsheviks, I got lost. But at the last moment, just before the train left, some commissar brought me back to my parents.

In reward for all this, when I arrived at the end of the journey I found an earthly paradise. The contrast between the life I had known until then and the life I was to lead in the home of my birth was as great as, say, the contrast between the various circles of European hell and a farm in the American Middle West. Four years of German occupation had not changed anything in Lithuania. The days unfolded, just as they had for centuries, to the rhythm of work in the fields, Catholic feasts, solemn processions, and the rites of Christian-pagan magic. Except for relatively light shocks—one of these was the agricultural reform, which affected the majority of landowners—the same rhythm persisted up to the Second World War. I entered into a stunning greenness, into choruses of birds, into orchards bent low with the weight of fruit, into the enchantment of my native river, so unlike the boundless, dreary rivers of the Eastern plains. Even today I feel grateful to the girls who took so much care twining garlands of leaves and flowers to decorate the church. It was, I think, these flaxen-haired Lithuanian maids and not Lena who influenced my erotic predilections.

A child's time is not the same as an adult's: one day brings him as many impressions as a month to a grown person; one month as many as a year. How little the dates 1918–1920 mean in this perspective! I was living a regular epic then, or rather an odyssey. To enumerate all the complicated circumstances would be impossible. They were tied up with war again, this time with the Polish-Russian War, out of which newly organized Lithuania tried to draw some gain for herself by guarding a friendly neutrality toward Trotsky's army. While Oscar Miłosz was pleading the Lithuanian cause in Paris, my father was carrying out a different decision: he already wore the uniform of a Polish combat-engineer officer. As for me, this meant I had to abandon the orchards beside the quiet river and all my happiness.

It is probably impossible to determine to just what extent a basic instability, if endured at the age when habits are formed, affects the way a certain generation pursues its destiny. Later on, when I read about the pioneers who struck out for the Far West in covered wagons and faced Indian raids, I did not connect it with what I myself had gone through. One was colorful and exotic, the other drab and everyday. But after all we, too, traveled in a covered wagon. I remember the sight of my mother's back as she sat in the opening of that cloth tunnel. We, too, forded rivers, stopped in the middle and whistled at the horses to get them to drink. Like a continuous roll of pictures, new landscapes ceaselessly unfolded in front of us. Nights were spent in barns on the hay or around bonfires in the forest. The flash of hatchets chopping up kindling, a teapot hanging on a stick over the fire, wind blowing in the pines.

One night I remember very clearly. We were passing rather cautiously through a deep wood. The spot was dangerous, not so much because of possible interference from the regular armies, but because of the bandit gangs that operated unchecked in this no man's land. Whispered conversations, the crunch of sand as the wheels sank up to their axles, the silence ringing in our ears, a full moon over the black, jagged wall of trees, and sometimes, between the trunks, the glimmer of a small lake. Next, the sky became transparent, outlines of branches with dewdrops appeared, but still no sign of a human settlement. The sky was already pink when we heard the barking of a dog. It was as extraordinary as if we had stumbled onto a lost tribe.

The sound of shattering shrapnel is hollow and flat. That morning, after getting up on a farm, which stuck out nakedly on the empty prairie, I put on my pants hurriedly and ran to look out the window. The view was a strange one. A stone's throw away, a piece of turf, which had been there when I first looked, was there no longer. It was spurting into the air and falling back in clods of dirt; in its place were uneven lumps of torn-up ground. Their tawniness stood out sharply against the surrounding green. A wail went up behind me. So fascinated was I by what I saw, I had no time to understand that artillery fire had been turned on the building. This seemed well advised on my part because the artillerists missed their target.

The feverish retreat has remained graven as cleanly in my mind as on a photographic plate, but it is hard to put into words. The highway was a swarm of interlocking wagonshafts, eyes of terrified horses, manes, mouths open in a scream, whips raised. Along the ditch by the side of the road, a soldier without cap or gun was slipping past, bareback astride a colt and lashing it with a switch. Further ahead, the outskirts of a town opened out. July heat, wooden houses in the sun, and not a trace of life. In the middle of the street stood a huge tank, and my remembrance of this sight is so intense that I feel as if I could reach out and touch every rivet. A paralysis and a helplessness hovered over it. Soldiers smeared with oil (drops of it visible on the sand) poked in the motor with trembling hands.

Our duel with the armored train was funny, although the laugh was probably not on us. An armored train is a big contraption, and if its machine guns keep spitting bullets onto an empty highway where nothing is moving but a wagon with women and children, there is something unfair about it. I am incorrect: in the wagon, upright, stood a she-goat surveying the scene with her yellow eyes. This personage was very important to our family—for my little brother she was a live dairy. It may be that she was behaving provocatively. At any rate, she noticed the danger first, pricking up her ears at the whiz of bullets, which sounded like bees' lightning-fast maneuvers during honey gathering. I observed that bullets can make another sound too—something like a click of the tongue—and then little puffs of dirt fly up. I was two people at once: along with the rest of the living contents of our wagon, I spilled into the ditch and crouched there in the sticky mud, praying and sobbing; but at the same time, I did not stop being curious, nor did my senses cease to collect impressions as keenly as ever. To make matters worse, it was raining torrents; my feet were soaked and water poured down the inside of my collar. A slight rise in the terrain protected the horses. On the bank leading down into the ditch was a tree with protruding roots. I grabbed on to them, wanting to see what was going on. To this day I do not know why an empty highway should have had strategic importance. It ran through the territory where the Polish-Russian front touched the Lithuanian border. After half an hour of crawling through the ditch, a Lithuanian noncom arrived in our midst. From him we learned that the armored train was Polish. Reloading his rifle and steadying it against the tree where pieces of ground were still bursting into the air, he took aim and fired, which was impressive; I saw his back and leather belt just above me. Soon a second soldier crawled through, and they both ordered us to flee because it was going to "get hot." Our wagon rolled off with a clatter and a clanging of the bucket tied onto the back; the whip drew dark lines on the horses' withers: the "bees" buzzed furiously, and mingled with the noise were fragments of the litany to the Blessed Virgin.

This war of constant advances and retreats where the principal weapons were the rifle and the sword was played for high stakes. In it, a remarkable, even the main, role fell to the Polish leader Joseph Piłsudski. A great deal can be said about his personality, I think, if a parallel is drawn with a spiritual cousin of his, Felix Dzierżyński. Both men came from gentry families of modest means; they were born not too far from each other in historical Lithuania; both became professional revolutionaries, varying their militant activities and sojourns in Czarist prisons with readings in Polish Romantic poetry. Who knows, perhaps both had in them more of the poet than the politician, but if so, they were poets who wrote with blood instead of ink. At first the differences in their socialist orientations were only slight, but the vortex of events forced them further and further apart: sometimes one pebble is enough to determine the direction in which the avalanche of a man's destiny is to roll. While the one strove above all for liberation from Russia—Czarist or non-Czarist—the other staked his future on nothing less than global revolution, and, as Lenin's right-hand man, was to win unlimited power over the bodies and souls in an immense state.

Piłsudski's armed struggle against revolutionary Russia cannot be interpreted as a crusade against Communism. Equally distrustful of "Whites" and "Reds," he foresaw still worse complications if a victory of "Edinaya i Nedelimaya"* were to become a reality. Only his territorial origin can explain his decision. For him, a Poland confined within ethnic boundaries was an alien concept, and as such he had no real love for it. He cherished a different vision, inherited from many generations, of the *Respublica* such as it had been during the last phase of its existence in the eighteenth century. His was, therefore, a vision of a non-national state embracing both the Polish kingdom and the Grand Duchy of Lithuania. A dream that was either an anachronism or too modern—depending upon how it would have been realized in practice. At an hour of awakening nationalisms, such a conception was both too late and too early. Piłsudski's biggest enemies were Polish nationalists—and because of his opposition to the right, he was viewed by liberal and leftist opinion as an ally.

In trying to restore the Commonwealth as far as the Dnieper, Piłsudski did not have in mind an attack on Russian lands, but simply an expedition to regain the property of his ancestors, which had been seized by the Czars. The failure of this attempt shifted the front line of battle to the environs of Warsaw. What was now at stake was Poland's survival (defeat would mean

* "One and Indivisible." Party slogan for Russian nationalists opposed to autonomy for non-Russian populations. (Tr.)

annexation to the Soviet Union). At the rear of the victorious Red Army, a preconstituted government stood ready to assume power in Poland. Its most distinguished member was Felix Dzierżyński. One can make a safe guess that he would have become the real ruler of the country.

Humanity's progressive wing addressed its sympathies not to the Poles but to the Russian dawn of freedom; in Western European ports, strikes broke out protesting the supplies of ammunition sent to Poland by the terrified governments of the Entente. What would have happened if Piłsudski's army had not won in August, 1920, outside of Warsaw? One can only make conjectures. How would the Germans, seething over their defeat, have reacted to a triumph of the Revolution at their doorstep? Had not Trotsky already lost his gamble? The Baltic countries would not, of course, have been able to hold out. The Lithuanian soldiers had had to fire at the Polish armored train to preserve appearances, but perhaps they did not really wish to inflict damage. One thing is certain: I myself would have become, like several million children of my own age, someone else. I would have worn the red tie of the Komsomol, and instead of catechism lessons I would have been spoon-fed a vulgarized Marxism. I did not suspect at the time this link between my fate and the trembling hands that repaired the engine in the tank. If the Germans had won the First World War, no radical changes would have disturbed a French child's environment. But in 1920, what hung in the balance was completely different.

Piłsudski resisted successfully, however, and like Mannerheim in Finland, he was given the title Father of the Fatherland. The peace treaty was a compromise. For many Europeans, the division of Germany after Hitler's defeat was something unprecedented; but for the inhabitants of the eastern marches of Europe, displacement of borders was a well-known fact of life. By splitting the Ukraine and Byelorussia in two (these territories, ethnically neither Polish nor Russian, had constituted, along with Lithuania, the former Grand Duchy), the peace of 1921 created a trouble zone, and Moscow did not hesitate to exploit the slogan of reunification, based on the premise that whoever has a part of something should have the whole of it too. The traditional pretexts of "reasons of state" were at work here: Russia, had it not been for her acquisition of the Ukraine and Byelorussia at the end of the eighteenth century, would have turned into an almost exclusively Asian power.

Poland, ethnically heterogeneous and incapable of realizing Piłsudski's dream of federation, found itself embroiled in unending domestic conflicts arising out of the absurd problem of national minorities. Such a fragile equilibrium cannot be durable; and I must always have felt this, growing up as I did just beside the border of the Soviet Union. Yet it was only much later, as a university student, that I came to a more or less clear understanding of the really provisional nature of this state of affairs.

When I started to go to school, the year the peace treaty was signed, everything in my world seemed to be just as it should be. The thought that it might be strange to someone on the outside never entered my mind.

City of My Youth

I SEE AN INJUSTICE: a Parisian does not have to bring his city out of nothingness every time he wants to describe it. A wealth of allusions lies at his disposal, for his city exists in works of word, brush, and chisel; even if it were to vanish from the face of the earth, one would still be able to recreate it in the imagination. But I, returning in thought to the streets where the most important part of my life unfolded, am obliged to invent the most utilitarian sort of symbols and am forced to condense my material, as is usual when everything, from geography and architecture to the color of the air, has to be squeezed into a few sentences. A certain number of engravings, photographs, and memoirs do exist, of course, but these are generally little known beyond the narrow confines of the region itself. Moreover, the natives lacked perspective and most of the time paid no attention to what now seems to me worth thinking about.

The foreigners who ventured into these marchlands of the West were rare. One of them was G. K. Chesterton, and our city gave him a solemn welcome. Apparently he was enchanted by that miracle of continental exotica. As a Catholic, he felt at home with the several dozen churches and the sound of bells, which continually hung in the air. Narrow cobblestone streets and an orgy of baroque: almost like a Jesuit city somewhere in the middle of Latin America. The comparison is not farfetched because at one time Wilno was among the most powerful Jesuit centers in this part of Europe.

Are there many cities whose names people disagree about?

Poles say Wilno; Lithuanians, Vilnius; Germans and Byelo-russians, Wilna. Even the river running through it has two names: Wilia is one; the other is more musical and seems to be invoking the spirit of some Nereid: Neris. Another, smaller river flows into it near a cone-shaped mountain. Here stands the ruined castle of the Lithuanian grand dukes—the former capital of the Grand Duchy. Whenever the city changed hands, the first thing the conquerors did was to plant their flag on what was left of the castle's dungeon walls. A third and mysterious river flows underground. Its undefined course, with its various passageways and corridors—which, people used to say, would take you out-side the city walls in case of a siege—provided a subject for legends and fairy tales. There was an aura of legend about the large, circular cathedral tower too—it was very old and had been built on the spot where pagan priests had kept a perpetual fire burning—not to speak of occasional discoveries such as the heap of corpses that was found under the church of the Dominican Fathers. Because of the unusually arid atmosphere in the cellars, the bodies had remained intact and still showed traces of violent blows. These dolls, dressed in the clothes of many centuries ago, represented the civilian population, victims, it would ap-pear, of one of the Russian invasions.

Wilno: around two hundred thousand inhabitants plus tons of memoranda, notes, and stenographs in the League of Nations archives. Oscar Miłosz was largely responsible for the accumula-tion of those documents. Few nowadays remember that an at-tempt at federation was tried here in the year 1921: the Wilno district was set up somewhat like an independent canton or state. I used to paste the postage stamps from "Central Lithuania" into my album. Today they are a philatelic rarity. The little state was, however, soon incorporated into Poland. In protest, the Lithuanian Republic invoked history. The Poles invoked the will of the people. It is hard to say who was right in this quarrel. Probably no one. If a problem is stated in the wrong terms, it cannot be solved. The residents of Wilno spoke either Polish or Yiddish; a very small percentage spoke other languages:

Lithuanian, Byelorussian, Russian. If, however, language were taken as the basis, there would have been enough territory to carve out a Canton of Geneva. Nothing more. Let us draw a vertical line and describe a circle on it; this will stand for Wilno and its environs. The vertical line above and below the circle will represent the ethnic frontier between the Lithuanians and the Byelorussians. What we have then is an enclave, of which Europe has a great many. But the concept of nation-state holds good only where, as in France, the Bretons and the Provençals look upon themselves as Frenchmen, which certainly does not follow from the nature of things because it might have been different. The mosaic of contending nationalities is a characteristic of the European scene that exasperates, say, an American. The question here is not only one of language, but of cultural belonging. And this is often connected with the question of religion.

Roman Catholicism predominated in the Wilno area; Judaism held second place. Other groups were few in number and merely added a dash of color. In school I used to have some Karaite* friends. The Karaites claim to have sprung from the sect of the Essenes, whose two-thousand-year-old manuscripts have been found near the Dead Sea. In our region these very Arabic-looking southerners, with their steel-black hair, were mainly farmers and gardeners; their place of worship was called the Kenessa. There were a few Protestants left over from the once-powerful Calvinist movement, and I also had Moslem schoolmates. They were descendants of Tartar prisoners of war (quite well treated by the Lithuanians) or of Tartars who had enlisted in the service of the grand dukes; I was always intrigued by what one did in a mosque, though I could never find out. The long Russian dominion, too, had left its traces: bad paving, the incredible difficulty citizens had conforming to hygienic regulations, and two huge Orthodox churches with onion-

* The origins of the Karaites, a Jewish sect, are controversial; they reject the rabbinical tradition of the Talmud in favor of a strict adherence to the Bible. (Tr.)

shaped cupolas—a sign of Czarist governmental solicitude for the
spiritual well-being of its imported functionaries.

The Catholic population was conspicuous for its fanaticism,
a trait common to most frontier areas. It was aware, after all, of
being one of the Vatican's easternmost strongholds. To a great
extent, its passionate attachment to Catholic Poland can be explained by its search for protection and security. Lithuania had
her smallness and weakness against her. But another factor—
which would require a whole separate treatise—was involved,
and that was contempt for a nation ninety-nine per cent of
which was peasant. On the other hand, Poles and Lithuanians
were united by their common hostility to Orthodoxy and its
followers. The odium fell on the Byelorussians, who were known
for their passivity, shiftlessness, and defeatism in the face of
destiny.

I must admit that the Byelorussians are still a puzzle to me—a
mass of people, spread over a large expanse of land, who have
been constantly oppressed, who speak a language that could be
described as a cross between Polish and Russian with a grammar
systematized only in the twentieth century, and whose feeling of
national identity was the latest product of Europe's nationalist
movements. But their case brings us up against the fluidity of all
definitions; such a mass can easily be transformed from subject
into object in foreign hands. Moscow encouraged schools and
opened the first Byelorussian university, but at the same time
suppressed all separatist tendencies by arresting and deporting
patriots and even removing words from Byelorussian dictionaries that sounded too unlike Russian. Warsaw conducted an
absurd policy. With a couple of exceptions, Byelorussians were
forbidden to have their own schools and the threat of jail was
used to discourage any attempts to organize from the grass
roots. One has to admit, however, that Polish officials faced an
extremely difficult dilemma. Nothing had prepared them for
their task because up to that time the notion of a Byelorussian
nation had never existed. The language had always been considered a local dialect, like *langue d'oc* in France. Even if,

overcoming their psychological resistance, they did permit the establishment of separate schools, the results, from their point of view, were disastrous. The peasant's son, once he had justified his well-founded resentments through knowledge, almost always initiated himself into civilization's first degree by becoming a Communist and working for the cause of "reunification"; i.e., of depriving Poland of her eastern provinces.

This formless rural society lacked those elements of crystallization that were so manifest among the Balts. Hence, perhaps, their readiness to accept such elements from the outside. One thing is clear: the Byelorussians never fared very well. They were simply given the choice of jumping into the frying pan or the fire, Polonization or Russianization.

In Wilno, very few people were interested in their problems. The peasants in their long sheepskin coats who brought the fruits of their harvest to market had a way of speaking that, as a rule, was not easy to classify as either Polish or Byelorussian. To the despair of their more advanced brothers, the Byelorussians understood nothing of nationality (unlike the Lithuanians, who sharply set themselves off from the Slavs) and when asked about theirs usually replied "Orthodox" or "Catholic."

The countryside around Wilno is wooded and hilly. In winter the town acquired a polar look. Small sleighs, presided over by drivers in fur caps, who resembled centaurs, served as a means of transportation. City buses also plowed their way assiduously through the snowdrifts. Children used the middle of the sloping streets for sledding—they usually lay on their stomachs and steered with their feet—or for skiing. When spring came, the sleigh drivers harnessed up their old-fashioned droshkies. But sometime in 1930, not to be left behind by progress, they introduced an innovation: they put automobile tires over the wheels.

Provincial quaintness should not be exaggerated, however. The Jewish commercial districts looked like their counterparts all over the world and used the same kind of advertising. Façades were decorated with all sorts of colored signboards on which artists had drawn lions and tigers seemingly taken straight from the paintings of Rousseau Le Douanier, gloves, stockings, and brassières. Movies were publicized by rows of electric lights and lurid billboards of love scenes placed at the entrances to the theaters. Shortly before the outbreak of World War Two neons made their appearance. Later on, while I was walking on New York's Third Avenue, I stopped short with the feeling of having seen something before: here, too, the dreary walls had been covered with a front of colors and lights to attract customers. Whatever one may say, we belonged to that same economic circuit, although it was only by experiencing the contrast of completely different systems that I was able to understand the fact. We also belonged to the same cultural circuit. I grew up, after all, in an era that was unlike any other; and what made it basically different was the motion picture. Thanks to movies, I existed parallel in time to people my own age in France, Holland, or America. For me and for them, Lillian Gish, Mary Pickford, Chaplin, Buster Keaton, Greta Garbo meant pretty much the same. Strictly speaking, though, if it is true that movies create their own fantasy world, then this fantastic quality was even more accentuated where I lived. Details that elsewhere were part of daily life I tended to take as tacit fiction simply because in my city they happened only on the screen. Yet at the same time movies did influence the shape of women's hats, the hairdos and smiles of local vamps, and this lessened the gap between the "dream factory" and our environment.

Movies were divided into films for adults and films for teen-agers. In order to divert the latter from the adult pictures and to make things easier to control, the city fathers founded the Municipal Movie Theater in a huge auditorium. The ad-mission fee was nominal, and the battle for seats was carried on with great savagery. First-row balcony was the most desirable. From the seats by the railing one could look down on the bald pate of the piano player behind the screen and tease him with nasty remarks. One could also spit on the heads of those sitting

downstairs. Many a time in a moment of silence, dialogues such
as this could be heard: "Tony!" "Yeah?" "Spit." "Nah, I'm not
gonna spit." The projector was faulty and the picture constantly
broke off, but at least these authorized amusements did not
expose anyone to the danger of being caught by his teachers.

Poland, as I look at it in retrospect, had better organized
theaters than many "Western" countries. Instead of casts created
to perform in one play, the principle of repertory theater was
universally recognized, and the work of director and actor was
regarded as a kind of service to society. Hence Wilno's large
theater (the small one put on mainly operettas) co-operated
closely with the schools and the university. The avant-garde
quality of its stage direction and set design, its use of anti-
naturalistic devices, introduced us early to the concept of magic
as the essence of the stage. Classical dramas were performed
(the actor whom I first saw as the Cid I was never able, later on,
to separate from that role), as well as Polish Romantic dramas
(which can be ranked with some of the most bizarre works of
theatrical literature) and even the brutal documentary plays of
Weimar Germany's writers. Since my childhood, I have taken
for granted an institution such as the Théâtre National Populaire,
which many Parisians, after the Second World War, discovered
to be an instrument of progress and social awareness.

Besides movies and the theater, books kept us parallel in
time with the rest of the world. International best-sellers were
translated and published immediately, although it was not quality
that guided this effort, but rather snobbery and an uncritical
admiration for anything that came from abroad. I went from
Jack London and Kipling to Joseph Conrad, then stumbled upon
a chaos of book jackets where Emil Ludwig, Stefan Zweig,
Ilya Ehrenburg (then an émigré), Upton Sinclair, Thomas
Mann, and Soviet authors such as Boris Pilnyak, Babel, or
Katayev were all neighbors on equal footing. Bustling little
Warsaw publishing enterprises also flooded the market with dime
novels in the most slovenly translations.

The city changed gradually. The wooden sidewalks with

their rickety boards under which the mud spurted out were replaced by concrete slabs; smooth paving blocks slowly dislodged the cobblestones on the roadways; large, modern buses were introduced; in winter the streets were more effectively cleared of snowdrifts; the number of taxis increased. Nonetheless the city and the surrounding area were condemned to economic stagnation. As a rule, Western governments let their generosity show only when it is a question of reducing some danger to themselves at the cost of shedding the blood of natives somewhere or other, but not often in peacetime. While she opposed the Russian Revolution, Poland received military equipment, but it was not so easy to obtain credit later on. Poland, a conglomeration of three unequally developed areas, whose structures had come down from Austria, Germany, and Russia, had to strive first and foremost toward a unified administration and a unified school system. The punctuality of her trains was no slight accomplishment. About a third of the budget went for the Army. The industrial centers were in the hands of foreign capital intent on making the quickest profits through the use of cheap labor. The overcrowded countryside, owing to the great disparity between the prices of agricultural and industrial products, could not buy farm machinery or tools. This almost permanent state of crisis was even more aggravated in Wilno by the specific plight of that narrow corridor wedged in between Lithuania—whose border was closed because of the cold war with Poland—and the Soviet Union, with whom there were practically no exchanges. The length of the communication routes to the West increased the cost of export goods, and one may well ask oneself if local sawmills, tanneries, or glove manufacturers did a good business. Handicrafts and cottage industries prevailed throughout the whole country, but here this type of economy was even more in evidence.

In a word, Wilno was Europe's "other side of the tracks" and, within that area, one of the poorest of her borderlands. One should be cautious, however, about equating economic inferiority with weakness in all spheres. The school I attended was a good one, and the organizing abilities of the teaching profession, forced to improvise as a result of the war, which had lasted here six years, can only be admired.

School was, of course, a great turning point for me because until then I had not known the bitter taste of social conventions. Learning had been a strictly individual activity. My mother had taught me reading, writing, and figuring during our journeys. In the spring, a few months of daily going through the little gate into the verdant garden where my tutor lived sufficed to prepare me for my entrance examination.

. . . An eight-year high school for boys. Besides this one, there were many other schools in town, both public and private, where the teaching was in either Polish or Yiddish, Lithuanian, Russian, or Byelorussian. Our school had chosen King Sigismund August for its patron, a very local figure, as he was a Jagiellon; that is, of the Lithuanian dynasty. A few years after I entered the school, a portrait of the monarch painted by our drawing instructor was hung in the "hall of records" where ceremonies were held. The instructor was a happy giant of a man and a favorite with his pupils because he would shout obscenities while correcting their work. He had drawn Sigismund, King of Poland, Grand Duke of Lithuania, *Rus'*, Prussia, Samogitia, Mazovia, and Livonia, etc., etc., with very broad shoulders, Renaissance-style, and trim legs hugged by tight-fitting, hip-length hose. His eyes gazed down at us from his triangular face, and in his hand he held a scroll of laws—in keeping with his vocation, since he was less a warrior than a diplomat, lawgiver, and arbiter between Catholics and Protestants. Our drawing instructor, who was a rather well-known artist, achieved more than just a realistic likeness, it seems to me, for his ordering of masses and somber colors comprised a whole that was full of power.

While I was adapting to life in a crowd, I learned to handle new problems; for example, oppression. As one of the youngest in the class, I stood at the very bottom of the tribal hierarchy, which was based on respect for the fist. At the top reigned the fifteen-year-old bullies. They had been held back in their studies because of the war; but they were very efficient whenever they had to bloody a few noses in order to uphold their power. What was worse, being shy and oversensitive I saw that I could revenge myself during class for my humiliation and fight my way to a position above the tribe's by quickly becoming the best student and the teacher's favorite. It was only in the upper grades that I gave up my first place for a pose of arrogance and recklessness. The gym, however, never ceased to be a torture chamber for me, with its icy bars and ladders, the whistle-commands and the armylike drills. No gunshots ever brought on such teeth-chattering as the thought that it was nearing the time to change my clothes for gym practice. It took me a while to learn how to escape those unpleasant hours.

My unclear attitude toward my superiors and colleagues in the Boy Scout troop also revealed asocial propensities. Scouting had its appeal—hiking, bonfires, camping out, following animal tracks, pocketknives, and rope knots. But it had its dreary side, too, with all the "form up into two ranks," "count off to the right," "stand at ease," and the clubroom—a big hall set aside by the school for the use of the Scout troop. It was hung with paper festoons and the emblems of "Wolves," "Foxes," and "Eagles." The dominant mood in there was: "We should be doing something, but what?"—in other words, boredom. The talks and speeches, which consisted mostly of slogans, made no sense to me, and I felt that neither speakers nor listeners took them seriously. Many years later I understood that Baden-Powell had been a remarkable prophet of social centralization: Communism then seemed like scouting raised to the nth power.

Our large school building had places that were famous for various reasons. For me, the teachers' room, where our grades hung in the balance and which we could only glimpse now and then through a half-opened door, has remained the epitome of secrecy. Around the washroom, where the older boys smoked cigarettes and told dirty jokes in artificially deep voices, there are always an air of pleasantly exciting scandal. The laboratory

lured us with its retorts and the smell of chemicals. This was the
domain of old Mr. John, the janitor, who had been inherited
from the school's Czarist days. His nose reddened at the same
rate that our supply of laboratory alcohol dwindled.

We wore regulation hats: navy-blue, high, round, and flat-
topped, just like the kepi worn by French policemen. It was
considered chic to rip out the stiff cardboard lining and change
them into soft caps. For a couple of years, we had uniforms
too; steel-gray with maroon trim on the collar, and trousers
buttoning below the knee. They were designed by our other
drawing instructor. We often made fun of him because he wore
an artist's cape and plumed hat, which made him look like a
rooster. He passed as the protector of the city's Scout troops
and was a terrible pederast. My brief love for him (every
Thursday he held tea parties at his home, giving lessons in
fencing and conversing with a chosen few about art) ended one
afternoon when he sat down next to me on the sofa, put his
hand on my genitals and started trembling. From then on he
treated me with hatred.

School, a rather shabby flat in an apartment building, and
my chaotic reading, in which I was engrossed to the point of
absent-mindedness, were not the sole events of my life. The
lakes and forests that surrounded the town gave one a sense
of being constantly in touch with nature. And many times my
father, whose passion for hunting provided an outlet for his
excess energy, took me with him. So I was initiated early into
the habits of animals and birds, into the species of trees and
plants, and as a supplement I had my textbooks on ornithology
and botany.

My war adventures, or at least what resembled war adventures, were not over either. My mother was responsible for
this. The tangle of contradictions I see in myself becomes clearer
when I try to understand the inner principle that guided her
up to her calmly accepted death in the typhus epidemic during
the mass migrations of 1945. Seemingly weak and frivolous, she
used superficiality as a mask and delighted in playing a role

because it led people off the track. Her relationships were formed at the least cost to herself, and showed her not as she really was but as others expected her to be. Doubtless this mimicry was the result of a disbelief in her own worth and a complete inability to take command, or, possibly, of pride: "What I know is not for others." Under the surface there was stubbornness, gravity, and the strong conviction that suffering is sent by God and that it should be borne cheerfully. Still another trait of hers was patriotism, but not toward the nation or the state— she responded rather coolly to that brand. Instead, she taught me a patriotism of "home"; i.e., of my native province. I had an obvious penchant for my mother's family, for grandfather Kunat and for my grandmother (née Syruć). As I ranged over the past, for some obscure reason it was my mother's family, when I recognized its importance, that stimulated my imagination the most. Its women were made of tougher fiber and my great-grandmother Syruć held a special place of honor in the temple of my ancestors. Her husband perished in one of the first railroad accidents in Europe, around 1850, near Baden-Baden. Left alone with her children, she displayed great administrative talent and tenacity in clearing the estate she inherited of all its debts. The women of the family stood out for their complete disregard of their own personal needs and for their gift of self-control.

But this home with its miracles of family intimacy was "abroad." Though it was no further from Wilno than Dijon from Paris, it belonged to another country: Lithuania. Because diplomatic relations between Poland and Lithuania had been broken off, it was impossible, legally, to get there. But such obstacles, like other political stupidities, seemed to my mother quite unimportant. The two of us, therefore, set out. The first task was to reach the settlement where the proper smugglers lived, usually deep in the forest. In their hut we decided on a plan of action: either to bribe the frontier guards or to avoid their posts entirely. For a certain period of time, the two countries shared a so-called neutral zone, which meant that everyone shot at everyone else. Those who accompanied us, specialists in border crossings, carried a gun for doing away, if need be, with any inconvenient figures. Once the peasant who was leading us dropped down suddenly on one knee and raked through the bushes with his rifle. Our moment of fear ended after he muttered, "A doe." I had many another scare, though. When you are ten years old, it is especially unpleasant to be caught by Lithuanian guards and made to sit in a pigsty all day as a lone prisoner. Nonetheless, our expeditions were rich in the joys of victory, and my mother infected me with her love of risk. I learned to value the forest even more; one is safe there and invisible.

Gradually it became more and more difficult to cross the border. We found other ways. My mother, like all her clan, was a Lithuanian citizen. This did not hinder her from using a second passport—a Polish one. After all, documents were thought up by bureaucrats to poison people's lives, and one should not have to stick too closely to regulations. With a Polish passport one could get an entrance visa for Latvia, and, once there, all one had to do was change passports in order to ride into Lithuania. This brilliant though simple discovery was in practice applied by many.

Wilno was not, therefore, the center of my world. Spending the summer months in a different country gave me the opportunity to make comparisons. Lithuania was much more old-fashioned in its habits, but it was a peasant civilization, which, in order not to disappear, always requires what we would call today a "kulak" structure and a minimum of prosperity. Nationalist and class fanaticism might be regrettable, but it demonstrated that the countryside knew how to read and write and thus was open to ideas. Disinclined toward great flights of the spirit, it preserved its rather Flemish heaviness. Curiously enough, that same fondness for matter may be observed wherever, in the course of history, the ethnic Lithuanian element —a steadily diminishing one—has maintained its integrity. Unlike the aristocracy, who accepted the culture of Poland's gentry, the Lithuanian peasant never became Polonized. He did, however, undergo a kind of second-degree denationalization: on the east and south the Byelorussians gnawed at Lithuanian territory, like water slowly eating away land. Only then, after the villagers had assimilated the Slavic language, did they experience Polish influences. The misunderstandings over Wilno came about because it had once been surrounded by Lithuanian settlements—as local names attest. My own encounter with these embroilments was not theoretical but real. Even if I was unable to define them at the time, the differences between particular national groups gave rise to at least some thoughts during my travels. On the other hand, Poland, the country to which Wilno belonged, was thoroughly unfamiliar to me.

In a certain sense I can consider myself a typical Eastern European. It seems to be true that his *differentia specifica* can be boiled down to a lack of form—both inner and outer. His good qualities—intellectual avidity, fervor in discussion, a sense of irony, freshness of feeling, spatial (or geographical) fantasy—derive from a basic weakness: he always remains an adolescent, governed by a sudden ebb or flow of inner chaos. Form is achieved in stable societies. My own case is enough to verify how much of an effort it takes to absorb contradictory traditions, norms, and an overabundance of impressions, and to put them into some kind of order. The things that surround us in childhood need no justification, they are self-evident. If, however, they whirl about like particles in a kaleidoscope, ceaselessly changing position, it takes no small amount of energy simply to plant one's feet on solid ground without falling.

What then is ordinary? Films and books or some other reality entirely? War or peace? The past or the present? An old-time custom or a parade with red banners? This chauvinist point of view or that? Doubtless, in order to construct a form one needs a certain number of widely accepted certainties, some kind of background of conformity to rebel against, which nonetheless generates a framework that is stronger than consciousness. Where I grew up, there was no uniform gesture, no social code, no clear rules for behavior at table. Practically every person I met was different, not because of his own special self, but as a representative of some group, class, or nation. One lived in the twentieth century, another in the nineteenth, a third in the fourteenth. When I reached adolescence, I carried inside me a museum of mobile and grimacing images: blood-smeared Seryozha, a sailor with a dagger, commissars in leather jackets, Lena, a German sergeant directing an orchestra, Lithuanian riflemen from paramilitary units, and these were mingled with a throng of peasants—smugglers and hunters, Mary Pickford, Alaskan fur trappers, and my drawing instructor. Modern civilization, it is said, creates uniform boredom and destroys individuality. If so, then this is one sickness I had been spared.

Catholic Education

＊

THROUGHOUT OUR EIGHT YEARS OF HIGH SCHOOL, every day began with a prayer and the song "When the Morning Lights Arise." For this event, all classes and their instructors gathered in the long, wide corridor. Only the non-Catholics were exempt from prayers, and they were very few: Jews, Karaites, Moslems, Orthodox Christians, and Protestants. Doubtless they felt a little awkward in being thus set apart from the community.

Beeswax candles and a white suit for First Communion, the fragrance and blue haze of incense, flashes of gold from the chasuble and monstrance, the suction in the pit of your stomach from fasting as you returned from church, the good feeling of virtue regained. . . . The check list of sins to confess frequently gave rise to misunderstandings, especially the heading "impurity." I once owned up to breaking wind in a loud and indiscreet fashion, and as I peered through the lattice of the confessional I saw the priest strangely doubled up, biting his lips. That whole area of duties and rituals eluded reason; it existed in its own right as if it were part of nature. It acts on us most powerfully that way, of course, and leaves the most durable traces.

Nonetheless, the study of religion in our school, limited at first to Bible stories, before long changed into a serious affair. The mark given by the Father Prefect had a decisive influence on our certificate of promotion at the end of the year. His demands were higher for those students he suspected of anarchical or rebellious leanings. On the other hand, the subjects

he taught—Dogma, History of the Church, Apologetics—rarely
fell below the level of early seminary training. I was faced
with this intellectual complexity at a time when my head was
already swarming with syllogisms.

Catholic doctrine is very difficult because it contains, as it
were, several geological strata. One would not immediately guess
that the catechism's naïve questions and answers have about
as much connection with what underlies them as plant life
has with the seething core of the planet. Yet hardly do you
peel off the first casing when you stumble into the snares that
brilliant minds have set for one another. Many a youthful explorer thrashes around in these snares like a trapped rabbit. His
ordeal is made no easier by the collision of two closed systems
which, to all appearances at least, have not contaminated each
other: the religious and the scientific (which dates only from
the Renaissance).

I was drawn to the science laboratory, with its modern
microscopes, as to a workshop of learning that was the least
abstract because it related to my experiences of hunting and
walking in the forest. In the laboratory, we cut up blood-
suckers, observed the beating heart of a dissected frog, and,
holding our breath as we turned the micrometer screw, focused
the microscope on sections of plant or animal tissue. Zoology,
botany and then biology were taught by a docent from the
university's medical school. He specialized in cytology, the
science of cells. Thin and sallow-faced, he had the caustic disposition of someone who suffers from a liver ailment, but he
liked his subject and knew how to communicate it. He founded
a circle of nature lovers of which I was one of the leading
enthusiasts. Not content with manuals and workbooks, I sought
out the professional texts. Halfway through high school, in the
fourth class, I delivered my first talk: on Darwin and natural
selection. It was at just this time that my crisis began. It had
been delayed by the flood of additional chores that my kingdom of aquariums, glass jars, and cages of birds or white
mice imposed. But I had no doubts about one thing: my future

profession of naturalist was settled. I would have listened with dread had anyone predicted that I would betray my calling.

Here I must take a moment to discuss the human background behind the play of our likes and dislikes. For the teachers, only some faces must have stood out from that unkempt and shrieking mass of boys, thanks to some quirk of individuality. Similarly for us students, the Olympus of instructors was divided into a few protagonists and a choir. Lesser authorities merited attention on account of their eccentricities. So, for example, the geographer whom we called Gorilla was somehow to us an incarnation of the past. He must have taught in a Czarist school. A huge, dark-complexioned fellow, he had a black mustache and wore striped trousers and a cutaway. He sprawled in his chair and yawned terribly, showing a palate that seemed to be black, too—in dogs this is usually a sign of a mean character. It certainly was in his case. His boredom spread immediately to everyone, and it released pandemonium. Too lazy to use words, he would aim a finger at the benches and trace a kind of semicircle in the air. The boy who had been singled out walked to the front of the classroom and stood in the corner. By the end of class, practically all the benches were deserted. But teachers like this man, or the historian, old Kałaszeuski, with his heavy Byelorussian accent, were secondary figures, and besides they were frequently replaced.

The center of the stage was dominated by two personalities, powerful because of their respective influences, who battled against each other for our minds and were destined, regardless of the passage of time, to remain with us forever. When I read Thomas Mann's *The Magic Mountain* at the university, I saw that it was really a book about these two—that is, if we regard the quarrel between the Jesuit, Naphta, and the humanist, Settembrini, as more important than the story of Hans Castorp. It is not my fault that these portraits are so literary; reality now and then delights in such seemingly "bookish" contrasts. Our Naphta had a round, boyish, though somewhat faded face, close-cropped straight hair, and all the movements, including the averted eyes, of a humble servant of God. Nothing in him betrayed how or where he had lived before becoming a priest, whether in the country or in town, whether in an aristocratic or a plebeian family. He resembled none of the other priests we knew, some of whom had retained under their cassocks the impetuosity of former soldiers and adventurers, others their peasant slowness or clumsiness. Our prefect must have grown up in the shade of a church porch. If he had been the son of a sacristan, gliding around the gilded altars with hands folded, it would have suited his looks entirely.

His unprepossessing body housed a rabid and afflicted soul. One could tell by the bitter furrows around his mouth, as well as the hard blue gaze when he lifted his eyelids, and the deep flushes of repressed fury. By preference, he was an inquisitor. He was able to detect a guilty thought from the twitch of a facial muscle or the tilt of the head. He dwelt in a dimension where constant watchfulness and tension were obligatory, where one must be ready at any second to resist the devil's attacks. For him, sin was not simply the breach of a regulation; it spread its tentacles everywhere, taking on the appearance of innocent diversions. Our ball-playing in the school yard was looked upon with disfavor by Hamster (our perversion of the prefect's name), who saw in it a portent of our approaching manhood—when the devil *must* triumph. The huskiness in a boy's changing voice brought forth a grimace of disgust from the priest, and he treated the smell of cigarette smoke as the material sign of an evil presence: sex. With children he was very gentle, but when we had become adolescents he made it obvious from his behavior in class that he was dealing with fallen creatures. Once, during the break, one of us made a diagram of an electric battery and its wiring on the blackboard to explain some problem in physics. Hamster happened to be passing by in the hall and he opened the door unexpectedly, as he liked to do. One glance at the chalked circles and ellipses was enough to bring one of his darkest blushes to his face and send him running to the principal's office, where he reported that the boys had made a drawing on the blackboard of the sexual organs.

According to his gloomy vision, no spiritual remedy could cure the evil in human nature. One may conclude that he did not believe in the efficacy of grace, since it evaded human control, and that he did not look on mistakes as sometimes needful on the road to salvation. At the same time he clung to the idea of light shining in the darkness: the saved can be recognized by outer proofs of virtue—by their obedience to rules, their innocent tone of voice, their humble movements; in other words, after training. But who belonged to this elect? Probably only the Children of Mary with a blue sash across their chests and a taper in their hands. In any case, since goodness is out of reach, one should at least impose discipline on oneself and on others, because if some hope does remain, a change of nature can be accomplished only from the outside in, and not vice versa.

Hamster was actually an extreme proponent of an old thesis in the Catholic Church: that man can approach God only through the intermediary of the senses; and that individual faith and virtue are a function of group behavior. By going to Mass and receiving the sacraments, we absorb, in spite of ourselves, a certain *style*, which, just as copper is a good conductor of electricity, serves to guide us to the supernatural. Since men are weak, it would be madness to give them free rein, counting on their ability to find union with God on their own regardless of the style of their environment. Rather, one should make that union possible, if only for a few, by mass conditioning. While forcing us to take part in rituals, Hamster doubtless had no illusions. But neither did his predecessors, who converted heretics with the sword.

His position in the school enabled him to see that his own will was fully carried out. His authority was not so different from that acquired later on in Central and Eastern European high schools by the lecturer in Marxism-Stalinism. Hamster worked constantly at tightening the loops in his net. Presence at Sunday Mass was obligatory, but the churches in town could not guarantee supervision. So he set up a chapel in our school building, and his trusted deputies marked off on an attendance list the names of those who were absent. The deputies were recruited from his auxiliary guard: the Marian Sodality. Every quarter we went to Confession and received Communion. At Easter time there was a big retreat. In order to prevent lies and excuses, our theocrat introduced a sure means of checking up on the cleanliness of our souls: written proof. After making your confession, you received a stamped strip of paper, which was then handed over to the prefect. To be fair, it must be said in his favor that he did not organize a system of informing. If such a thing did occur, it was the result of bootlicking or the overzealous piety of Sodality members.

His lectures were sprinkled with rather coarse gibes at other religions, at fashions, or at human reason. He did not hesitate to shower abuse on the Socialists, trying to create in us an automatic reflex of hostility to the very sound of the word. The skillfulness of his arguments suddenly broke down whenever he passed over into contemporary affairs. The simple outrage to good taste alone would have sufficed to drive some of us to resist.

His adversary, the Latin teacher Adolf Rożek, was his complete antithesis, if for no other reason than his elegant, scarcely perceptible irony, the limits of which he never overstepped in battle. Otherwise he treated the priest with courtesy. His smooth-shaven face made one think of a Roman sculpture, modeled as if by his acceptance of the rules of classical restraint. Impeccably groomed, he sometimes had a red flower in his buttonhole, but he should really have worn a toga. Without ever raising his voice, he kept us in hand merely by his slightly sardonic gravity. The son of a Galician laborer, he belonged to perhaps the last generation that, as pupils during the Hapsburg monarchy, had from their earliest years absorbed large doses of Latin and Greek and commentaries on the classics. In the classroom he was not only concerned with vocabulary and grammar; after we had left behind Julius Caesar and Cicero, with their gymnastics of subordinate clauses, and tackled Ovid and Horace, Rożek's sessions turned into a Renaissance art of the beautiful arrangement of words. First the text was read, and if the student scanned a hexameter or an Alcaic strophe faultily, a hissing came from the teacher's lips as if he had been stuck with a pin. The real work began after the grammatical analysis. Then we searched together for words that most nearly expressed the original shade of meaning. "Yes"—he frowned—"that's not bad, but it sounds harsh. Who has something better to propose?" Polish syntax allows for a great deal of freedom in sentence order. Rożek was careful to stay within the bounds that kept us from falling into artificiality, although sometimes his sensitivity to Latin carried him away, as it had many Polish writers in the past. "The golden honey seeped . . ."—we were just finishing up a translation of the passage from Ovid describing eternal spring. He stopped us with a movement of his hand. Once again we pivoted between subject, predicate, and modifiers until at last, after many tries, we read off the collective achievement: "And golden from the green oak seeped the honey. . . ."

Frequently we would spend the whole hour on one such line, and we could not have totaled more than a few lines of verse for the entire school year. But today I see that the effect those exercises had on me cannot be measured by the sparsity of the material. The time we devoted to them, although I did not suspect it then, was to have far greater weight than whole days of storing up useless facts from different fields. And it was not a matter of nostalgia for the Golden Age, or for the Castle of the Sun, which stood on glistening columns, or for Phaëthon falling from the sky, or for the snowy peak of Mount Soracte, or for the shepherds from the *Bucolics*. Nor was it a matter of those fragments of verse that came back to me with such insistence later in various circumstances, although their sonorities did awaken a love for rhythm and a dislike for poetry that is too slick: *"Trahuntque siccas machinae carinas"* (with a very long "i" in *carinas*). Most important was the ability I acquired, once and for all, to concentrate not only on the meaning but on the art of connecting words, the certainty I gained that what one says changes, depending upon how one says it. Rożek's stubbornness taught us that perfection is worth the effort and it cannot be measured by the clock; in other words, he showed us how to respect literature as the fruit of arduous labor.

Rożek told us about Roman institutions and laced his biographies of poets with anecdotes; for example, the one about Ovid, who, when his mother whipped him for being too fond of poetry, promised tearfully (but in verse): *"Iam, iam non faciam/Versus carissima mater!"* Sometimes he ventured into discussions on art and the contemporary theater. His collaboration with the theater in town was very lively—his children (a little boy and a girl) took part in some of the presentations. We were also indebted to Rożek for our own school theater, and he proved to be a good director of a Fredro comedy.* As our adviser, he helped us set up a class government, and as one of the speakers and firebrands, I discovered through this experience some of the difficulties of directed democracy. Political pronouncements he avoided, although it was known he was a Socialist. He radiated optimistic faith in human reason, in teamwork, and in progress.

The mere presence of such a Naphta and such a Settembrini gave us an option. My rebellion against the priest weighted the scale in favor of the Latinist. But my religious crisis was not a final thing; it did not end in a clear "yes" or "no," so that when I entered the university it was not at all something I had behind me. Which does not mean it was any less acute. I was striving to build intellectual bridges between two dissociated entities. Such an endeavor was, in general, alien to my schoolmates, who considered religion a separate sphere, subject to the rules of convention. My intensity won me the position among them of a Jew among *goyim.*

* Alexander Fredro (1793–1876), Polish author of sparkling comedies in verse. (Tr.)

If nature's law is murder, if the strong survive and the weak perish, and it has been this way for millions and millions of years, where is there room for God's goodness? Why must man, suspended on a tiny star in the void, no more significant than the microbes under a microscope, isolate his own suffering as though it were different from that of a bird with a wounded wing or a rabbit devoured by a fox? Why must human suffering alone be worthy of notice and redemption? If man is an exception, then why the cruelty of death, disease, and torture inflicted by men upon each other, the proof that nature's law extends to this species, too? How does a crowd in the street differ from a collection of amoebas except that elementary human reflexes are more complicated? Such questions plunged me, sometimes for weeks, into a state bordering on physical illness. Time in the natural sciences is spatial; it cannot be imagined except as a line extending backward and forward into infinity. The theory of evolution is purely spatial: either eternity can be thought of as a line, or it eludes the mind entirely. It is not easy to arrive at the notion that eternity is beyond time and that therefore, from some sort of divine perspective, the destruction of Nineveh, the birth of Christ, the date written on one's school notebook are simultaneous and that ultimately in this perspective spatiality perishes, too, so that the "magnitude" of a galaxy may be equal to that of an atom.

I searched for answers in a textbook to which I owe a large part of my education: our manual of Church history. The chopped-up, chronicle-like bits of information that were stuffed into our heads as the history of Poland and other countries I got very little out of. The manual, on the other hand, contained the history of Europe in its entirety. This is why I now think that going through a Catholic school is very helpful for the person who wishes to keep alive in himself a "European consciousness."

Several chapters of the book included, for variety, sections in small print that gave rather accurate descriptions of various heresies. My favorites were the Gnostics, the Manichaeans, and the Albigensians. They at least did not take refuge behind some vague will of God in order to justify cruelty. They called necessity, which rules everything that exists in time, the work of an evil Demiurge opposed to God. God, separated in this way from the temporal order, subsisted in a sphere proper to himself, free from responsibility, as the object of our desires. Those desires grew purer the more they turned against the flesh; i.e., creation. I did not yet know the Manichaean phrase: "A soul torn asunder, divided into fragments, crucified in space"— with its clear attack against our temporal-spatial world. Nevertheless, the information I found in the small print was food enough for thought.

The bitterness of dualism, the Absolute saved at this price, intoxicated me like the feel of a harsh surface after a smooth one that is impossible to grasp. The authors of the manual sharply condemned the debauchery practiced by certain Manichaeans as a means of "combatting the flesh," but their arguments never seemed convincing to me. I understood that psychic leap: if we are in the power of Evil, we should sin out of spite, immerse ourselves in it as deeply as possible in order to despise ourselves the more. Later on I realized that dualistic elements are strong among Catholics—those girls, for instance, who spend the night with someone for a lark, knowing that they must wake up in time for Mass next morning; there is something more in this than ordinary hypocrisy. Similarly, to call a priest who lives in concubinage a hypocrite is insufficient. While Catholicism treats the coexistence of corporal wretchedness and spiritual aspirations with a certain tranquillity, that calm goes against a young soul's extremism. Youth longs to decide finally: let it be either/or. Hence my propensity for Manichaeanism.

My heresy, which had been fertilized by my interest in biology, did not, strangely enough, incline me toward the humanist but, because of my revolt, toward the prefect. My feelings about him were no less complicated and no less perverse than my attitude toward the masters of Gnosis. If nature is an abode of evil, then the prefect came out as a supporter of anti-nature.

He proclaimed another law, battled with the enemy, the Prince of This World. Like the rest of our class, I snickered at Hamster's sometimes foolish performances and at his suspiciousness. Yet his old cassock, his tormented face, and his inner tension aroused my pity and created something like a feeling of kinship. What could Rożek oppose to that? What was his basis for encouraging faith in *natural* reason, subject as it is to necessity and to falling into any traps that we, physiologically, as members of the animal species, may set for ourselves? On what did he base his conviction that "here the animal ends and here man begins"? The Church's teaching was clearer. Thus my relationship to Rożek could be described as sympathy corroded by mockery, and my relationship to the prefect as mockery corroded by sympathy.

I also uncovered one more reason to distrust human nature. Every now and then I experienced intense religious feeling; at the same time the other half of me reflected on the sensation. I did not reach very pleasant conclusions. Take good deeds or the forgiveness of sins in Confession. At the moment of doing a good deed, resisting temptation, or coming from Confession, we think we are good. In other words, we commit a sin of pride, putting ourselves above others because we cannot forgo the comparison. We pity the sinners who are worse than we are. Of what value then is virtue? Unaware that I was treading the path of St. Augustine, I had hit upon one of Christianity's key problems. I could relate to the prefect because of the stress he placed on wounded human nature. At the same time, he repelled me by forcing us to take part in rituals. While avidly reading in my textbook about the quarrel between those who made everything depend on grace and those who left some leeway for human will, I was cultivating in myself Protestant leanings.

Hamster, who winced in disgust at the sound of a boy's changing voice, who smelled sin in tobacco smoke, was, one must admit, not so far wrong. Innocence ends as soon as the "I" appears, the old pride of the Fall: "You shall be as gods, knowing good and evil." Never was this brought home to me so clearly as on Sunday mornings. Owing to various circumstances, pupils of the higher classes did not go to Sunday Mass at the school chapel. Instead we went to St. George's Church in town. St. George's was attended by "good society" who, after Mass was over, would parade down the front walk: officers saluted, lawyers and doctors dispensed bows, women displayed their smiles, furs, and hats. As I moved out with this crowd or watched them from the nearby square, I was nearly bursting with hatred. A man, in my opinion, was only worth his passion for nature, hunting, literature, or whatever, so long as he put into it everything he had. But these people were apes. What meaning had they? What did they exist for? I was soaring at some sort of divine height, poised over them as if they were specimens under a microscope, which are born, last a second, and die without leaving a trace. Just look at their coquetting, their little intrigues, their showing-off, their mutual favors, their bustling for money: they have nothing more to them. I remained wrapped up in myself, believing that I was called to great tasks. I treated these people, in other words, as *things*.

It seemed to me that my feeling was incommunicable because it was mine alone. I would have been surprised if someone had explained that it was not as personal as I thought and that it was called "hatred of the bourgeoisie." That type of contempt, although intellectually useful, led me into many errors later on, which is why I react rather suspiciously today to intellectuals who declaim about revolution. Love for the oppressed supplies them with a pretext, but they play their own games. Broader understanding (e.g., of "historical processes") is also, ultimately, a pretext. What they are really after is to push others into the position of objects in order to look upon themselves as subjects. Already during my early childhood I had drawn a feeling of superiority from my meditations on the universality of death: those around me did not think about this, I thought about it, and this alone gave me the upper hand. Is it not the same with a man who, in his mind, undresses a woman walking down the street? What interests him more than sex is power.

I was, it could be feared, a potential executioner. Every man is whose "I" is grounded in a scientific way of thinking. The temptation to apply the laws of evolution to society soon becomes almost irresistible. All other men flow together into a "mass" subordinated to the "great lines of evolution," while he, with his reason, dominates those "great lines." He is a free man; they are slaves.

If I should have confessed a sin, this was it. But, as usual, things were too complicated. My sadistic fifteen-year-old imagination heightened the natural pride that inclines every man to fence himself off from others. Was I myself guilty or the old Adam within me? In any case, I was brimming over with the spirit of protest, and I set out openly on the warpath.

Taking part in rituals along with apes humiliated me. Religion was a sacred thing; how could their God be mine at the same time? What right had they to adore him? "But when thou prayest, go into thy room and, closing thy door, pray to thy Father in secret."

In the face of clearly inferior creatures, it would be better to proclaim oneself an atheist in order to remove oneself from the circles of the unworthy. Religion, insofar as it was a social convention and a constraint, ought to be destroyed. In my battle with Hamster, it is apparent that the best and the worst motives converged. A taste for independence, a loathing for all hypocrisy, a defense of freedom of conscience joined with intellectual arrogance, an obsession with purity, and the conviction that I understood more than anybody else. Hostilities opened with minor skirmishes: in class I would ask the prefect loaded questions concerning subtleties of dogma. My struggle took on the intensity of full-scale war when I publicly refused to go to Confession any more because of the system of stamped slips of paper. Hamster must have shivered interiorly as he began his lectures to us. To be sure, the class behaved passively enough, merely snorting occasionally to show its wild satisfaction with the spectacle of one hothead's clashes with the school authority. The black sheep, however, contaminated the rest with his insolence. Hamster soon became so touchy that even if I was sitting quietly, he would interrupt himself in the middle of a word to shout at me: "You have an unseemly look on your face, leave the room!" If it had depended on him alone, he would probably have expelled me from the school, but a group of teachers, who might be called "Rożek's party," protected me as a "capable student."

A remarkable part of this conflict had to do with the peculiar features of Polish Catholicism, which had been shaped by Poland's historical situation as a country on the peripheries of Roman Catholic Europe. This meant, especially in the nineteenth century, resistance to Protestant Prussia and Orthodox Russia. Polish culture developed entirely within the orbit of the Vatican. Even the short-lived ferment of the Reformation was no exception, since the great quarrel, far from permanently alienating anyone from the Papacy, awakened interest in it. After Poland had disintegrated as a country and a wounded nationalism had made its appearance, the notions of "Pole" and "Catholic" came to be equated. Under Czarist rule, a convert to Orthodoxy was excluded from the community; such a man incurred distrust as a potential or real collaborator. Thus religion was turned into an institution for preserving national identity; in this respect, the Poles were like the Jews in the Roman Empire. To make the analogy more complete, messianic currents were as popular with the Poles as they had been with Israel. So solid a coalition drove Russia to despair, for she was unable to digest the Poles. The latter, however, paid a high price for their tenacity in the face of outside pressures: when the line between national and religious behavior is erased, religion changes into a social power; it becomes conservative and conformist. By the same token, any attempt to sever the bonds imposed upon us by our milieu must necessarily be an attack on our religion. In the light of this distinction, my protest against a sentimental mythology and a national morality, against an older generation devoid of any misgivings—in other words, against those elegant parishioners strutting down the front walk—becomes intelligible. But where had the impetus come from? One might talk about my sensitivity to the fluids of the *Zeitgeist*, but that does not explain much.

Polish Catholicism, despite its having profoundly penetrated the Polish mind and provoked a morbid hatred of the Vatican among the Russians, has remained above all an attachment to the liturgy. Its Biblical traditions are weak; the details of Revelation's journey in time are scarcely mentioned, which discourages any evolutionary view of external forms. Hamster never opened the Old Testament with us. He considered it unsuitable reading. However, if he had devoted even a fraction of the time that the humanist spent on one verse from Horace to reading and commenting on the Book of Job, for example, it would have profited us much more than his short accounts of the prophets, whom he treated only insofar as they prefigured Christ. He could have taught us the value of a respect for mystery, which forbids utterance of the highest name. He could also have shown us that Judaism, contrary to its rival beliefs in antiquity, with their cyclical vision of the world, conceived of Creation in a dynamic way, as a dialogue, a perpetual upsurging of constantly modified questions and constantly modified answers, and that Christianity has inherited this trait. Had he proceeded in this manner, he would have vaccinated us against the reality that things human not only are but become. To put it another way: he would have accustomed us to history. But the priest lacked imagination, and he warded off the impingements of the modern world with the shield of a rigid outlook.

Polish Catholicism also has a strong tendency to regard sin almost as if it were an offense against Roman law, and Hamster was no exception. This did not exactly fit with his deeper conviction that human nature was basically depraved and thus could not hope for salvation in any precepts. But he multiplied one casuistic distinction after another as if applying a principle of

the criminal code: *nullum crimen sine lege.** Is it or is it not
a sin to eat something at the stroke of midnight when you plan
to go to Communion the next morning? When is the breaking
of one's fast a mortal sin, and when is it a venial sin? What are
you allowed to do on Sunday? What happens to unbaptized
children when they die, since they cannot enter Purgatory or
Heaven? The hairsplitting could have gone on forever. In this
respect, Hamster belonged to the priestly clan of the Old Testament. Because of my overscrupulous conscience, I lived with a
constant feeling of guilt. And this feeling, as one might guess,
extended especially to matters of sex. Catholicism treats such
matters rather indulgently, but I doubt whether many of the
prefect's pupils were ever able to liberate themselves from the
guilt he induced. Every sexual act, even one sanctified by the
Church, was evil. They could have found a way out only
in Manichaeanism: triumph over oneself through deliberate debauchery, since the ideal of behavior is inaccessible.

Hamster was unable to show us that our real moral duty
is toward the person of another human being. His system of rewards and punishments, like paragraphs of a legal code provided
with sanctions, was geared to the salvation of the individual soul.
In "giving others their due" one was fulfilling only a negative
condition; the real work of perfecting oneself began when one
had, as it were, closed the window after having driven away
bothersome insects. It was not contemplation he was encouraging, but the ritual purification of our own person. I see this, too,
as a trait of Polish Catholicism, which, in putting the accent on
responsibility to collective organisms (i.e., to Church and Fatherland, which are largely identified with each other), thereby
lightens the responsibility to concrete, living people. It fosters
idealism of various kinds and makes an absolute out of action,
which should always aim at high goals. Perhaps this is the source
of the Pole's capacity for heroic élan and of his casual or careless
way of relating to another person, his indifference even to

* There is no crime without law. (Tr.)

another's suffering. He wears a corset—a Roman corset. After a certain amount of alcohol, it bursts open, revealing a chaos that is not often met with in Western European countries. Religion is rarely an inner experience for him; most often it is a collection of taboos grounded in habit and tribal prejudices, so that he remains a slave to Plato's Social Beast. His literature is filled with the problem of duty toward the collective (the Church, the Nation, the Society, the Class) and the conflicts it engenders. Little wonder that in some Poles the strength of their negation was directly proportional to the strength of that tradition.

The priest took me for an atheist, but he was mistaken. I had, it is true, led him into error from jealousy: what we keep hidden is dearer to us than if we were to talk about it publicly. I noticed a similar tendency later in crypto-Catholics who had become part of the political apparatus of a Communist country. They were more ardently religious than those who practiced their faith openly.

I did not have the makings of an atheist, because I lived in a state of constant wonder, as if before a curtain which I knew had to rise someday. My temperament was contemplative, little suited for active life. And my naturalist's notes, the moments I spent over a microscope or, later, on literature were all functions of the same inner law that kept my attention fixed upon a single point.

Moreover, nothing at home could have induced a religious revolt. My father's attitude was indifferent but this did not give rise, as it often does, to devotional fervor in my mother. She was a practicing Catholic without making a big issue of it. On the other hand, in her eyes all things were interconnected and predestined. Her cult of the mystery hidden beneath events indicated the persistence of that slightly pagan mysticism so frequently met in Lithuania. For her the world was a sacred place, although the key to its puzzles was to be found only beyond the grave. Her tolerance expressed itself in the phrase "Everyone praises God in his own way," and it would have been difficult, I think, for her to have accepted it as certain that Catholicism is the only true religion. The stern categories of Heaven and Hell were dismissed with a shrug of the shoulders: "What do we know?" My bickering with the school authorities did not upset her at all.

How is one to cope with beauty and at the same time with the mathematical cruelty of the universe? What is the illusory appearance here and what the real content? I used to step on a caterpillar in my path as if I were committing a sexual offense: one would rather not, but we do it because we live on earth, caught up in its relentless round. What difference does it make, I asked myself, whether I step on the caterpillar accidentally, or whether, after I see that my shoe is already touching it, I then put my foot down to spite my nature? If God is evil, what is there to justify my prayers? When Hamster threw me out of class, I, Protestant-like, was groping for my own private answers. For help, I went to two books: *The Confessions* of St. Augustine and William James' *Varieties of Religious Experience*.

How these books have been interpreted or what they are in themselves is not of great importance. I took from them what I needed. If one rejects the idea of punishments and rewards after death as indecent (what sort of shallow transaction is that?) and if the history of Christianity raises doubts not only because it has often served as a mask for oppression but also because the first Christians deluded themselves, anticipating the end of the world; if dogma is out of harmony with scientific thought—then one must uncover a different dimension where the contradictions can change key and find new validity. This dimension exists parallel to biology or physics; it does not inhibit them. The intricacy and richness of St. Augustine's experiences were a fact, just as the religious ecstasy of many average men and women, as described by James, was a fact.

The conclusion I drew, it seems to me now, was not the pragmatic one: as long as a thing assures happiness and energy, the true-false criterion is useless. I had wanted, rather, to make sure that my needs were not exceptional, and I came away convinced that such a universal hunger could not go unsatisfied. In other words, I recognized that reality is a good deal more profound than what I might happen to think about it and that it allows for various types of cognition. In this I was loyal to my mother and loyal to Lithuania—a Lithuania haunted by the ghost of Swedenborg. Nothing could stifle my inner certainty that a shining point exists where all lines intersect. If I negated it I would lose my ability to concentrate, and things as well as aspirations would turn to dust. This certainty also involved my relationship to that point. I felt very strongly that nothing depended on my will, that anything I might accomplish in life would not be won by my own efforts but given as a gift. Time opened out before me like a fog. If I was worthy enough I would penetrate it, and then I would understand.

The clowning, the hysteria, and the stupidity of young men often go hand in glove with a seriousness of mind. For girls of the same age these dirty, boisterous creatures, who hide their timidity under a mask of insolence, must be perplexing. It is probably no easier for teachers to differentiate the traits that portend future defeat from those that might carry a boy through to a useful role in some field or other. Coolheaded Rożek felt his way about this psychological maze with greater assurance than the priest. He was also more successful in the battle against dirty jokes or fits of collective laughter at the slightest allusion to certain details of human anatomy. When confronted with Rożek's cold irony, the culprit blushed, squirmed, and had to admit the unmistakable truth: that he was an ass. Hamster, on the other hand, by staking out forbidden preserves and by failing to perceive that the elements of this complicated chemical process function not separately but together, in constantly changing combinations, hindered our growth in any kind of self-knowledge.

Yet I felt that somehow I had to fit him into the picture. Besides, the constant warfare began to bore me. By distrusting mechanistic views of the universe (very nice accomplishments but nothing comes of them) I was permitting myself the luxury of superstitions. Had I offered sacrifices to little forest divinities, it would have been fully in keeping with my nature. I would have been aware that my behavior was absurd but, even more, that it was right because a sense of oneness with those forces we know exist but are unable to name demands symbolic gestures. Perhaps I am exaggerating, but all those dawns and twilights spent watching for birds, and all my childhood memories of the dangers of war, did not dispose me to a belief in chance.

With my feeling of being immersed in a great whole, I was, as they say, religious to the core. The Catholic Church was awesome in her immensity, and she was addressing herself to me with no more than a plea to submit to her discipline while suspending my judgment. As a diligent reader of Church history, I agreed, in spite of everything, that discipline was necessary, since by myself I would have been unable to invent one. Was this resignation? I still hoped to dismantle that puzzle in order to put the pieces together again in a new way. Hamster no longer loomed so large; his figure retreated from the foreground. He was a sorry creature, but the Church, after all, was a human institution, a hive of generations of men; could it have avoided relying on people like Hamster? In my last year before graduation, a sort of cool politeness grew up between us. He realized, no doubt, that force would never break me. When he stopped pressuring me, I went to Confession. But because the act of humbling oneself before Existence ought to be a strictly voluntary, personal thing, beyond social convention, I swore never to form an alliance with Polish Catholicism—I did not necessarily use those terms. In other words, I would not submit to apes.

I see the two of them before me now. Rożek's hazel eyes sweep over us quickly as we sit on the benches in front of him. Sometimes the alert face of a peasant boy, of a mountaineer from a village in the Tatra mountains, looks out from under that mask of a Roman senator. Hands folded behind his back, he paces back and forth, weighing his words as he lectures us on the court of Augustus. Hamster digs into the folds of his cassock and pulls out a handkerchief. Since it is none too clean, he uses it discreetly, hiding it in the hollow of his hand. There are dark circles under his eyes, and signs of a sleepless night show up in the tired lines of his face. In my life, both men were a bit like bombshells that go off later than expected. It was Rożek I could thank for the distaste that plagued my first literary attempts. Romantic torments or the automatism of inspiration merely covered up my need for a transparent, logical structure; they could not supplant it. To Hamster I owe my sensitivity to the odor of brimstone, my basic dualism, the difficulties I have in being a friend to the "other" in us, over whom we have no control and for whom we must swallow our shame.

The war with Hamster increased my inborn secretiveness, my rebelliousness, and my propensity for false poses, assumed either to deceive myself or to make the game more complicated. Doubtless such pedagogical results merit little praise. Yet I never severed the tie of unfriendly brotherhood that had been established between us. When I learned that Hamster had refused to leave our city during the Second World War after it had been taken over by the Soviet Union, I felt very close to him. Terrible and inflexible, he had preferred to remain with his parish.

One never stops being a member of the Catholic Church. This is what her doctrine teaches and what the two attitudes of acceptance and opposition confirm. Extenuated or acute, the central problem persists, and I would say that for all who have been raised in Catholicism, philosophy, whether they like it or not, will always be *ancilla theologiae*. And maybe no other exists. If so, one must admit that those who oppose religion are right when they denounce all philosophy as suspect.

Catholicism's force lies in its manysidedness, which is revealed not only in the course of history but also in the successive phases of an individual life. Despite crises of faith among the masses, the centuries-old tension between the Catholic and the "scientific" outlooks has been rather favorable for both antagonists. After all, modern science is a Judeo-Christian creation, and doubtless that is why it was able to reach a conception of the universe that cannot be translated into any clear or obvious image, that can be expressed only with the help of signs. Whoever has had the occasion to experience that controversy in his own soul will agree that contradictions can be fruitful.

Nationalities

◆

THE CHILDREN'S GAMES that we played in the courtyard, where
you could see the wooded residential district across the river
and where, in the summer, the stench from a tannery made you
feel sick to your stomach, always included Sashka and Sonka.
They had full rights of citizenship in our group, except it was
understood that you did not visit them at home. Playing tag
or climbing trees they were just like everybody else. But when
their mother leaned over the balcony railing and called them in
for supper, the similarity ended because she addressed them in
Russian. They were Jewish, and they did not speak the same
language at home that the rest of the children did.

European Jews used to call Wilno the Northern Jerusalem,
and rightly considered it their cultural capital. Here were institutions of learning (subsequently transferred to New York);
here the Zionist movement developed a strong center; and here
the pupils of the local Hebrew schools contributed, perhaps more
than anyone else, to the rebirth of the Biblical language in
Israel. In the tiny stores where I used to buy stamps, there was
always a collection box with a Star of David on it for Zionist
causes. A whole community with multiple currents, orientations,
and strivings had grown up within this city, famous for its
exegetes of the Talmud and its vehement disputes between
rabbis and Hasidim—in other words, it was an old abode for
the Jews, whom it would have been difficult to call newcomers.

But what about Sashka and Sonka? Why did they speak Russian? Russia, before it absorbed the Ukraine, Lithuania, and

Poland, had no Jews. They were forbidden to settle on Russian territory, and for a long time the restriction was enforced. So the term "Russian Jew" means (with very few exceptions) a descendant of those inhabitants of the Commonwealth who had become subjects of the Czar. For the Wilno rabbinate, Russia's annexation of the Grand Duchy of Lithuania was a tragedy, and they expressed as much in their proclamations to the faithful. Gradually, however, in the course of the nineteenth century adjustment to this new statehood made some headway.

There was no bridge between these two groups in our city. The Catholic and Jewish communities (some districts were almost entirely Jewish) lived within the same walls, yet as if on separate planets. Contact was limited to everyday business matters; at home different customs were observed, different newspapers were read, different words were used to communicate —the vast majority of Jews spoke Yiddish, an emancipated minority spoke Russian, and a very small percentage used Polish. For this reason our school had, out of Judaism's two branches, more Karaites than Jews. A greater impediment to common experience than the discrimination to which some teachers were prone was the mutual impenetrability of each milieu. Everyone in Wilno went to his "own" school. Only at the university did we all gather in the same lecture halls, and even there student organizations were divided into Polish, Jewish, Lithuanian, and Byelorussian. Thus the barriers were still kept up in accordance with an unwritten law.

The isolation of the Jews in this area was an old story. The reasons for it must be sought in differences of occupation (the Jews were merchants amid a rural population) and of religion (the rhythms of Catholic and Jewish customs did not coincide). Political anti-Semitism, however, appeared very late. It was devised by Czarist officials, when the monarchy was already deteriorating, as an instrument of *divide et impera*. Before that, there were rare cases of crowds getting out of hand in a context of religious fanaticism, but the quarrels among Christians—for example the battles with stones and clubs between Catholics and

Calvinists, which filled the seventeenth century in our city—attracted more attention. There were, of course, the "Judaizers" —radical Anti-Trinitarians who carried on cordial discussions with rabbis and put the Old Testament before the New. But these breakthroughs were limited to such a narrow élite that they failed to arouse the Christians' anger.

Politics changed that. The Catholic population, in its furious resistance to Russia, gradually began to look upon the Jews as a separate nationality that was not even an ally, because the game they were playing with the authorities was not the Polish game. Thus the old image of the Jews as the enemies of Christ was replaced by a new one: young men in high-necked Russian shirts, rallying to a foreign civilization. The Socialist movement, which was becoming stronger and stronger, split into two currents: anti-Russian (independence for those countries seized by the Empire) and pro-Russian (one revolutionary state formed from all the lands of the monarchy). Russian-speaking Jews (called Litvaks) were the mainstay of the second current, only to become, in revolutionary Russia, fomenters of all kinds of heresies.

The emotional attitude of Christians in that part of the world bore traces of various stratifications. From the old *Respublica*, with its rural and patriarchal customs, there had remained the idea of "our Jews" without whom life was unimaginable, who comprised an integral part of the human landscape, and whom it would never have entered anyone's head to disturb in the exercise of their age-old commercial functions or in the ordering of their internal affairs. A relatively recent acquisition was the idea of a Jew as a man who dresses, eats, and lives like everyone else but who uses a different language. The hostility toward him doubtless involved a resentment at the breaking of caste barriers: he violated the code that everyone ought to "know his place." But mainly it involved a conflict the past had not known, which after the First World War gave impetus to racial or economic arguments imparted mostly from Warsaw, where the situation was different. Poles of Jewish extraction were fairly numerous in ethnic Poland, but in Wilno such individuals were still treated as exceptions. For such a weak bourgeoisie as our town had, the slogans usually cherished by shopkeepers and petty manufacturers were a little outsized and not quite applicable to actual conditions.

The psychological portraits of anti-Semites that writers are fond of drawing rarely get to the heart of the matter because they overlook those peculiar traits that belong to geography and history rather than to psychology. The Age of Enlightenment made itself felt among the Jewish masses inhabiting the Polish-Lithuanian *Respublica* in a movement to oppose religious taboos and the ghetto. This drive appeared just at the time the *Respublica* was losing its independence. Three capitals became the new centers of attraction: St. Petersburg, Vienna, and Berlin. The history of the Freud family illustrates how those centers absorbed energies, talents, and skills: Sigmund Freud's father emigrated to Vienna from Galicia. But the flight from the medieval community also took another direction, provided by Polish schools and universities, which gave Polish literature and science many eminent representatives. This split among the enlightened was as wide as the distance that separated them both from the little closed cells of the diaspora. The Zionist movement stirred up a new ferment, and perhaps it is not accidental that its leader came from the eastern part of the former *Respublica*, where ethnic diversity inhibited fusion with any one collectivity.

It would be a mistake to draw analogies with France or Germany; it would also be hard to count any group whose numbers in the cities varied from thirty to seventy per cent a minority. The complex distinctions within each community and the existence of an ill-defined middle stratum (where exactly did the professor, the doctor, the actor, the writer of Jewish extraction belong?) were reflected in the many types of relationships between people, which also changed, of course, according to the region. In general, Poles were unusually aware of Jews and anti-Semitic. Yet if ever the object of their oddly ambivalent feelings were somehow missing, they would be overcome by melancholy: "Without the Jews it's *boring*." Many political movements and periodicals found their reason for existence in anti-Semitism because they appreciated the blessing of such a convenient theme—without which life would be empty—for demagoguery. No cabaret could get by without Jewish jokes, and the pungent gallows humor peculiar to cities like Warsaw bears the clear stamp of Jewish popular humor. This symbiosis prevented indifference. At the opposite pole it produced specimens of philo-Semites for whom even non-Jewish women had no appeal because they were regarded as intellectually inferior.

The Jews helped to form a complex in me thanks to which, at an early age, I was already lost for the Right. The nationalist party—the party of the "right-thinking people"; that is, of the newly arrived petty bourgeoisie—came into being at the end of the last century and was active mainly in the Vistula River basin, where it combated the Socialists. Its principal appeal was the vague but positive aura that surrounds the word *nation*. This was to be a linguistic, cultural, religious (meaning Catholic), and soon racial unity, although more than one descendant of a rabbi could be found among its most energetic propagandists. The press and slogans of this party entered my field of vision early. My allergy to everything that smacks of the "national" and an almost physical disgust for people who transmit such signals have weighed heavily upon my destiny. It is possible that a certain incident which seemed to foreshadow precisely the opposite tastes occasioned the breakthrough.

In our city, people called May 1st the "Jewish holiday." There was a big parade with banners and flags. And indeed in the crowd, which represented various species of the Left, young Jewish people were predominant. This was doubtless because the Christian working classes were composed chiefly of artisans who belonged to guilds under the patronship of saints or of laborers who still retained their peasant mentality.

I have the scene before me now: spring sun shining into our classroom windows, sparrows chirping, the first of May. Our French teacher (we called him Sock because he once pulled a dirty sock out of his pocket instead of a handkerchief) looks at me suspiciously. He beckons me to him with his finger. I go up to his table, my hair is unkempt, I am twelve years old. "What do you have there?" Sticking out of my pocket are the forks of a slingshot. "What are you going to do with that?" I try to give my voice a hard, masculine ring, "Beat Jews." He narrows his eyes in a cold reflex as if he were looking at an animal. I feel hot, I feel as if I had turned beet-red. He confiscates the weapon.

Had I really meant to use that slingshot against Sashka and Sonka? Not at all. No concrete man was my adversary. I carried within myself an abstraction, a creature without a face, a fusion of concepts bearing a minus sign. What is more, I was aware of it not as my own, not something inborn, but as alien. And during my run-in with the teacher, the shame I felt was made all the more painful by a sudden illumination that revealed the real instigator. It was one of my relatives, whom I despised. I suddenly saw the connection between my attitude and his political harangues at the dinner table, when I seemed not to be but was in fact listening. From that moment on, every nationalist slogan was to remind me of his pitiful person.

I was immunized by that relatively light bout of fever, which gave way shortly afterward to an almost obsessive hatred for the apostles of nation. But it seems that there were other, more complicated factors. My nonconformism rested on foggy Socialist impulses, but above all on something that I could not have named then, so submerged was it in my subconscious. My roots were nurtured by a soil that was inhospitable to new plantings; a great many precepts advocating tolerance had penetrated me, and they were out of step with my century. But what finally tipped the scales was my distrust of "trueborn" Poles. My family practiced a cult of separatism—much as the Scots, the Welsh, or the Bretons did. Our Grand Duchy of Lithuania was "better" and Poland was "worse," for what would she have accomplished without our kings, poets, and politicians? In that local pride which was very widespread in our corner, the memories of a fame long past persisted. Poles "from over there" (that is, from the ethnic center) had a reputation for being shallow, irresponsible, and, what is more, impostors. My anti-Semitic relative from Warsaw paid the price of that opinion by becoming in my eyes the symbol of a "Pole." My family defined virtue as stubbornness and perseverance, the reverse of "their" short-lived enthusiasm. The more or less unfavorable tone in which Poles were spoken of could hardly have awakened in me any response to the Polish ideology of the divine nation.

Although I outgrew family principles like a tight suit of clothes, something did remain with me that counteracted the influences from school. Several of our history or literature teachers would have been surprised to learn that their textbooks were one-sided because they had been put together by nationalists. They were for the most part good people who severely condemned chauvinistic excesses. But they imbued us involuntarily with a special way of seeing: the past of the Commonwealth was transformed into the past of Poland. For example, Prince Jagiełło, who initiated the union of the two states, was presented as a noble personality, while his brother, Prince Witold, who tried to maintain Lithuania's autonomy, was treated as a malicious troublemaker. In the nearby Lithuanian school the pupils were taught completely opposite truths; for them Prince Witold emerged as the noble personality and his brother as a tool in the hands of the Poles. Both versions were equally far from the truth.

A similar thing happened with the history of literature. The only writing worthy of attention was in Polish. Nothing was said about the rich and beautiful Lithuanian folklore, although the pagan past survived in it; or about the eighteenth-century Protestant pastor named Donelaïtis, who composed a poem in Lithuanian hexameters, *The Four Seasons of the Year*, which is interesting to compare with *The Seasons*, by his contemporary James Thomson. Not a single textbook included samples of the dialect that was once used for juridical writings in the Grand Duchy, although we would have understood it perfectly.

Such a school, by replacing a many-cultured heritage with national attitudes cut according to the latest fashion, must also have laid the foundations for anti-Semitism among its pupils. The Jewish religious literature that sprang from this part of Europe was translated into many languages and won recognition all over the world. One has only to pick up the first good anthology of religious thought that comes to hand to run across Hasidic proverbs and to start thinking with respect about the wise men in out-of-the-way small towns—the Baal-Shem Tov, Rabbi Nahman from Braclaw, Rabbi Jitzik from Lublin, and Rabbi Pinkas from Koretz, men who had obviously reached the summits of evangelical love. Here too, later on, Yiddish secular prose and poetry were born, with their unique combination of tragedy and inimitable humor. But we, in the very city where those books were printed, knew literally nothing about them. Several fell into my hands many years later when I brought them in New York—I had had to learn English in order to make contact with something that had been only an arm's reach away.

If familiarity with Jewish literature, which would have removed many prejudices, was practically nonexistent, the progressive and Leftist intellectuals of Jewish origin must share a serious part of the blame. From general ideas about the equality of men they drew the conclusion that the past does not count. Avid for all that was new, they played up to cultural snobbery in Poland, a force that is obviously at once useful and destructive. Both publishers and the most ardent readers of such authors as H. G. Wells, Freud, and Aldous Huxley were recruited from the Jewish intelligentsia. Their journals carried on campaigns for "conscious motherhood" and sexual freedom. But they were unwilling to take an interest in Yiddish literature or to translate it into Polish because they saw it as provincial and inferior, a leftover from the ghetto, the very mention of which was a tactless blunder. Only if a book became a best-seller abroad would they import it, certain that they could praise it safely since it had the approval of Paris or Weimar Germany. If anyone mentioned the Jews in their presence they took offense, at once reading racism into the remark. They tried at all costs to forget who they were, betraying a completely unjustified sense of inferiority.

The whole country was in any case permeated by an unhealthy atmosphere. Christians, when they said that someone was a Jew, lowered their voices as if a shameful disease were being mentioned, or added, "He's a Jew, but he's decent." Worse still, the same scale of values was more or less adopted by "assimilated" Jews who were diligently erasing their traces. In such conditions every personal contact evaded the laws of friendship and brotherhood, only to fall captive to a situation. One: "He thinks that I am a Jew." The other: "He thinks that I think he is a Jew." Or the pyramid grows. One: "He thinks that I suspect him of thinking that I am a Jew." The other: "He thinks that I think that he suspects me of thinking that he is a Jew." There is simply no way out of such a situation.

These ambiguities, however, were rare in Wilno, a city with practically no middle stratum. At high school everyone in our class was Christian (some Moslems spent a short time with us). There was no racial discrimination. I thought of the Jews as something on the outside, and as an adolescent I had absolutely no interest in them. When I finished high school my hazy political opinions were completely clear on only one point: I could not bear Polish nationalists. And it was this feeling that usually provided an outlet for all my rebellion against the Boy Scouts and later against the prefect and other authorities.

After entering the university I began to realize that the division into Left and Right in Poland was closely connected with the "Jewish question." I observed that my colleagues, depending on their origins, chose completely different paths. Jewish boys and girls were possessed very early by the spirit of progress, and their protest against the mentality of their fathers and their religion was incomparably stronger than that of the Christians. They ridiculed superstitions, read Lenin, and usually proclaimed themselves Marxists. They took a rather dim view of the country whose citizens they were, and rightly so, since they saw little opportunity in it for themselves. The road to government positions was, with very few exceptions, closed to them; a career in the Army was almost an impossibility; commerce and the professions remained, but because of the massive influx of Jewish candidates in medicine, for example, the universities were more severe toward their applications. No wonder they yearned for large state structures that provided freedom of movement, or sometimes confessed that Poland seemed to them a trivial creation compared with Germany or Russia. Ebullient intellectually, more capable of human warmth than the Catholics, they were also socially more aware. Their associations were Zionist- or Socialist-oriented (often both, although in different proportions) —Poaley-Zion, Poaley-Zion-Left, the Bund, and the Communists. The Communist movement, which was weak and combatted by the police, recruited its militants and sympathizers mainly from among Jewish young people, and those in our city were particularly receptive, owing to their penchant for Russia.

As for the pupils trained by various Hamsters, they were usually fanatical patriots, conservatives, and fond of ceremonies copied from German universities in the Baltic countries. The fraternity men wore special caps and ribbons across their chests, carried rapiers on holiday appearances, and spent their evenings drinking beer and fencing. Their organizations catered to social snobbery or to Rightist politics, and their style was a combination of cocky pride and military honor. In all this they resembled the officer caste. Intellectually they developed more slowly. Their emancipation and progress to radical positions were accompanied by great suffering and inner turmoil.

Our university provided a stage where the clash of two world views was acted out, but it appears to me now that it was more like a puppet theater. It is as if a malicious magician had pressed a button and the embattled heroes of the spectacle had all dropped through a trapdoor. The interpretations offered since then to explain their differences seem to me superficial. Class distinctions were the usual refuge. It is true that a very small percentage of Christian students came from peasant or worker families, while a greater number of their Jewish rivals had proletarian parents who placed a high value on learning. Yet to weigh each side on the basis of money is to ignore greater differences. The son of a Gentile doctor, lawyer, or shopowner inclined to the Right, while his Jewish professional counterpart was a liberal or a Leftist. The exceptions only proved the rule. Historians studying the evolution of the Polish intelligentsia commonly sidestep this riddle, if only to avoid slippery ground. To elucidate the situation, one should probably apply a cultural model rather than categories borrowed from countries whose urban civilization took shape sooner. The manor-village model, transplanted to the cities, developed autonomously, and I will not dwell here on the question of why this model evolved from liberalism and Socialism in the last century toward Rightist, totalitarian slogans in the next. The urban model, which was almost exclusively transmitted by the Jews, functioned according to completely different laws. For this or for other reasons, the Right fought the Leftist minority at our university with a cry of protest against "Jewish lackeys."

The Left posed a real threat to "right-thinking people" because it was taking strides to smash the barriers. It organized, for example, an "Evening of Revolutionary Poetry" at which Polish, Lithuanian, and Byelorussian verse were recited; a small tailor literally magnetized the whole hall, packed as never before, by turning one Yiddish poem of Ernst Toller's into a rhythmic dance. What drove me toward the Left, which was rather fluid and heterogeneous, was not Marxism but my resistance to nationalist obscurantists, or perhaps destiny hidden within the cells of my body: those individuals who are cut off one way or another from a milieu (heredity in this case means more than one might suppose) have to universalize their conflict, because when the problem is not only theirs but a general one it ceases to be degrading. Similarly, the choices made by my friends stemmed from a background of resentments and personal circumstances that diverged from the accepted norms of behavior, so that our Left was something like a league of sufferers.

At the outset of my life at the university I began publishing my poems and articles, and through this I penetrated to a new milieu, becoming a member of that special literary-artistic free-masonry that is the same in every country—nonconformist. Our constant scrutiny of one another's merits absorbed too much of our attention for us to be distracted by the shape of someone's nose. It was perfection that counted, or at least what passed for it. Besides, I communicated more easily somehow with Polish writers of Jewish origin. They were not from Wilno, of course, given the city's linguistic structure, but our freemasonry covered central Poland and Galicia. We exchanged volumes of poetry and periodicals (whose lack of funds usually augured a quick demise). At least half of the names we valued could not have produced an "Aryan grandmother," that favorite target of ridicule in all the humor magazines. But my entrance into new literary alliances was far from frictionless.

Actor's movements when seen through a soundproof window look odd and nonsensical. Access to that inner circle where the racial and national mystery played itself out was closed to me. But perhaps that was because of my sensitivity to *these* and not *those* shapes and colors and because of that deepest stratum of myself, which was formed, thanks to my mother, in the countryside of Lithuania. This position of an outsider permitted me to enter the mentality of writers of Jewish extraction who also stood in front of closed gates. We had a common fatherland: the Polish language. But they struggled to force the gates, giving their works an ultra-Slavic flavor. Almost none of them bared their dichotomy; they wore stiff masks, and those masks crushed them. They dragged me with them; I forced myself to mimic them, but what I really wanted was to have them stand up and oppose, and allow me, too, to stand up and oppose in my own way. In the name of what? I did not know. Somewhere in the depths glimmered the thought that my Leftism and theirs was a disguise for our otherness. As they repudiated the ghetto, so I hid away the Grand Duchy of Lithuania among dusty souvenirs. But I was more proud than they, if only of my ear—I considered the trueborn Polish ear insensitive to complex rhythms hidden beneath a deceptive simplicity, and it was only proper that a great poet like Mickiewicz had found his medium in our region.

I present the period between the two wars in condensed form. Perhaps this is unfair, since everything was in motion. At first, the Right stressed democratic legality, but gradually, under the influence of a hopeless economic depression and notions borrowed from Germany, it acquired a totalitarian hue. People shouted about a "national revolution," and the political scene swarmed with petty tyrants whose ambitions, it must be admitted, resembled those of the later Arabian dictators more than they did those of Hitler or Mussolini. Demagoguery turned its sharp edge against foreign capital and "Judeo-plutocrats," which students as well as the small-town *Lumpenproletariat* took as a signal for assaults on peddlers' stands. Wretches battled against wretches.

In Wilno during the spring of 1934, disorders of this sort lasted for three days. They were touched off by a quarrel over cadavers. The "Radical-Nationalist" cell at the university had scored an important victory because the students who worked in the anatomical laboratory declared a strike, demanding that the supply of Jewish cadavers for dissection be proportional to the number of Jews in the Department of Medicine. The strike became a street demonstration which headed toward the former ghetto district, breaking windows along the way and beating up pedestrians. However, it ran up against the resistance of strong Jewish butchers and freight loaders. A cobblestone torn from the paving struck one of the students on the head, and he died several hours later. The city found itself at the mercy of mob fury. Shops were bolted up, and people went into hiding, keeping an eye on the danger through cracks in their shutters, while the rabble surged down the middle of the street in search of victims. The police were indecisive. They tried to break into the student dormitory where the leaders lived, but the besieged used fire hoses to pour water on the police from upstairs, and finally they dispersed. Their hesistancy was the result of inner frictions within the government of "the Colonels," where elements in favor of flattering not the Leftist but the Rightist opposition were steadily gaining prominence. To these elements, "Radical-Nationalism" appeared as the wave of the future, which should not be obstructed.

In defense of the Poles it must be said that despite the hooliganism in that part of Europe, they betrayed less of an urge to strike at the life or health of their neighbors than one might have expected. Anti-Semitic incidents usually stopped at material damages. Though excitable and anarchic, the people of this nationality seem not to lose moral restraints, even in a crowd, and an impulse of hatred rather quickly gives way to shame. They submit to discipline with difficulty, and only discipline can justify cruelties committed in cold blood. Thus the foreigner who tries to understand Polish politics constantly runs into the unexpected. Party divisions are not very clear; they are held together more by spiritual kinship between individuals than by an agreement on platforms. Assassination of one's adversaries, that most acceptable of twentieth-century tactics, is applied unwillingly because it compromises the perpetrators in the eyes of public opinion. Almost every Polish system eludes outside definitions. Under the dictatorship of "the Colonels," the parliament was a fiction and one concentration camp was opened (so that Poland would not lag behind its neighbors), yet outright Fascists, though the government wooed them, were an opposition force. The Communist Party was illegal, yet a number of journals propounded its ideas, and dignitaries of the regime hobnobbed with revolutionary poets who were protected from jail by a telephone call from above. These same curbs, which were relative of course, operated later on in the Resistance movement, whose various splinter groups exterminated each other with considerably less fervor than, say, in Yugoslavia. Finally the Communists, most of whom were dissatisfied with the role of headhunters, which had been assigned to them by the Russians, engaged in some artful dodging to avoid a giant show trial of Gomułka on the order of Rajk's trial. Some sort of filter mitigates extremes in Poland. Perhaps it comes from habits formed during the age of the *Respublica*, when adversaries were crushed by speeches laced with Latin quotations and when lawsuits and intrigues were preferred to other, more drastic political methods.

It is hard for me to write about the Jews, because no small effort is demanded if one is to distinguish these prewar tensions from one of the greatest tragedies of history: the slaughter of some three million "non-Aryan" Polish citizens by the Nazis. As an eyewitness to the crime of genocide, and therefore deprived of the luxury of innocence, I am prone to agree with the accusations brought against myself and others. In reality, however, it is not so easy to judge, because the price of aiding the victims of terror was the death penalty. Individual behavior depended upon too many circumstances and motives to be able to establish for certain the connection with prewar anti-Semitic tendencies. Religious motives (convents particularly distinguished themselves in rescue operations), personal courage, neighborly ties, or greed for money clashed with physical impossibility, fear, or apathy. Blackmailers, recruited from the scum of the citizenry, constituted a grave danger for refugees from the ghetto, who presented an opportunity for easy plunder. If some political organizations in Poland had openly collaborated, as they did in other countries Hitler conquered, the picture would be clearer. But Polish collaborationists were simply killed. So any Nazi sympathizers (and there were some) had at least to keep up the appearances of noncollaboration. The extreme Right had not, of course, disappeared; it fed the ranks of the underground Home Army and the National Armed Forces (a not very numerous Fascist group). If the Home Army permitted more than one furtive slaying of Jews who had taken cover in the forests, it was a decision made by individual officers or soldiers, and it depended on personal attitudes. The National

Armed Forces, on the other hand, officially planned many of their raids. As for the Left, both Socialist and Communist parties entered the war either weak or divided, and it was not they who set the tone for the Resistance movement.

The responsibility for the Jews being regarded as a *different nationality* by most of the population lay, above all, with nationalist writers and journalists. At a hypothetical court trial, however, they could appeal to the schools, the textbooks, and historical conditions, since it was, after all, historical conditions that had prevented the two "nations" in Polish cities from merging into a single whole. Nevertheless one must still charge these writers with irresponsibility in submitting to irrational impulses and with stupidity. Similarly, the Home Army leaders acted like Molière's Monsieur Jourdain, who did not know that he was speaking prose. They condemned the whole ideology of Nazism, but at the same time refused to admit Jews into their forest units; this seemed to them quite natural. If any of them are alive today, they would doubtless be astonished to hear themselves accused of racial discrimination.

A country or a state should endure longer than an individual. At least this seems to be in keeping with the order of things. Today, however, one is constantly running across survivors of various Atlantises. Their lands in the course of time are transformed in memory and take on outlines that are no longer verifiable. Similarly, between-the-wars Poland has sunk beneath the surface. In her place a new organism has appeared on the map, with the same name but within different borders, an ironic fulfillment of the nationalist dream, now clear of its minorities, or at least with a very negligible number. Flames consumed the old synagogues; the foot of some passerby in the city suburbs trips over the remains of a gravestone with Hebrew letters—all that is left of the old cemeteries.

Although I witnessed a great deal of what Europe prefers to forget, because it fears the vengeance of specters, I had already left my city when the Germans murdered its Jews. For that purpose they chose Ponary, a forest of oaks in the hills, the place where we went on school and university excursions. They used up large quantities of paper on the circulars that spelled out the details of the massacre, many working hours of their personnel—who supervised the transport of tens of thousands of men, women, and children to the secluded clearings hidden from the eyes of the uninvited—and much ammunition for machine guns. An organization of Jewish fighters in the ghetto resisted. I knew a man who had never imagined he would be one of the leaders in that battle, but who fought only so that he might die without begging for mercy. He was a lawyer with an athletic build who liked to recite Mayakovsky's poems while drinking vodka. Although he was not a Communist, he adored this poet of revolution and knew perhaps half of his works by heart. To this day, I can see his hairy wrist with the gold watchband, gesturing in measured movements to the rhythm of the lines.

Marxism

◆

OUT OF SEVERAL TOPICS presented to us on our baccalaureate examination, I chose a poem by a poet of the last century and used it as a pretext to write an essay on the "river of time," for which my paper received the highest mark. I was stirred by the mystery of universal movement, where all things are linked together, are interdependent, create one another, transcend one another, where nothing conforms to rigid definitions. It would be hard for me to say now whether my exposition revealed me as an unwitting pupil of Bergson or whether it showed a glimmer of what is called dialectical reasoning.

In school I had almost no contact with Marxism. I did read Kropotkin's book about the French Revolution, which did not exactly agree with the textbooks, since it treated the great upheaval as a series of betrayals perpetrated against the people by their bourgeois leaders. What is more pertinent is that shortly before my final examination I was drawn into a conspiratorial group.

Conspiratorial does not mean revolutionary. Liberals, dismayed by the extent of nationalist influence in the schools, were searching for ways to counteract it, and the societies approved by the school authorities hardly lent themselves to this purpose. The anxious concern of enlightened circles (mainly university professors) was the maintenance of a liberal élite, so they took steps to set up at least a small nursery. Our cell, therefore, had nothing subversive about it; the secrecy added to its charm, but it concealed no more than free discussions and ties of friendship.

It was certainly no conduit for Marxism. Marxists were Russia's spokesmen, and no Polish liberals who were patriots, whether they supported or opposed Piłsudski, would have trusted them. Our elders kept an eye on us from a discreet distance without becoming involved in our affairs. Their only wish was to prepare a nucleus that would be hostile to their enemies, the nationalists. Both boys and girls from the upper grades of several Polish high schools belonged to the circle, as well as beginning university students. My initiation was held to the sound of footsteps along the creaking parquet floors of the school corridor during a break. I was proud of belonging to a chosen few, a brotherhood, and of the oath of secrecy.

Our activities were confined to gatherings at the home of one of the members and to writing in "The Book." "The Book" was a thick black binder which each of us in turn kept for a few days. Everyone was entitled to read what those who came before had written and to put down whatever he wanted—personal confessions, a critique of works or theories that interested him, or a polemic on something he found in "The Book." A dialogue of friends was thus created, and I, who had been completely deprived of the company of girls my own age, because of both my own timidity and my upbringing, made an extraordinary discovery—that girls also feel and think. The idea was hard to get used to.

It must be acknowledged, however, that it was the male side of the group whose adventures bore witness to more clearly etched individualities. Johnny, who had a rosy, boyish face, was six feet tall and a star basketball player, studied mathematical logic in Wilno and later at Cambridge on a scholarship, showing great promise in his field. He died in unspecified circumstances as an infantry officer in 1939, on the territory surrendered to the Soviet Union under the Molotov-Ribbentrop pact; he probably refused to be disarmed. Little Stanislas, a lawyer and a theologian, became a journalist and a Catholic politician, faithful to the Vatican but not to the Right. Joseph also became a lawyer and a journalist; we called him Plumbum—no doubt because of his portly build. The mosses of the Soviet north now cover his anonymous grave of a labor-camp prisoner. A different fate awaited that bundle of laughter, vitality, and humor, the poet Theodor. He put his pen to work for the Soviet authorities when they took over our city, and for that he was shot by the members of an underground organization. Dark-haired Tonio, with his Mephistophelean eyebrows, survived the war and emigrated to People's Poland, where he became famous for his huge novels. Censorship could find little to reproach him with, since he had prudently chosen as his subject the medieval epoch.

It is obvious from this lineup that we were a group of fledgling intellectuals united by a common awareness that we both opposed our environment and dominated it with our minds. Our inevitable sense of clannishness, which I found again and again later on in every group, coterie, or editor's board with which I happened to be associated, was far more important than our rather foggy ideas.

Soon after entering the university, I acquired a wide black beret with a red tassel—the mark of my membership in the Student Vagabonds Club. One of the reasons for the club's existence, and its members' greatest source of pride, was contempt for the sword-carrying snobs, drunkards, and fools in the fraternities. The club was democratic and scorned social formalities. It supported anarchy and thumbed its nose at undue solemnity. In university processions, while the fraternities carried their banners we marched with our own symbol—a huge pilgrim's staff. A brotherhood of fanatics espousing action and youth, we opted for kayak trips, skiing, long hikes, and overnight stops in barns or in the forest. Our excursions took us all over the region of lakes and forest rivers near Wilno (how well I know the weight of a Canadian canoe carried from river to river). But that was not all: there was a journey of almost six hundred miles through Poland, and a kayak trip down the northern tributaries of the Danube and then down the Danube itself, all the way to the Black Sea and Constantinople. The Vagabonds took an especially active part in university spectacles, adding gaiety to the city. For example, they dragged a huge dragon built by students of the Art Department through the streets, and were the main promoters of the annual *szopka*, a satirical marionette show put on by the Student Puppet Theater. They imposed no restrictions on themselves, did not avoid alcohol, but usually drank milk, and waged a constant war of wits with the fraternities, whose members were powerless against colleagues who recognized neither duels nor matters of honor.

Internal quarrels over leadership sometimes intruded on our idyll when the sheer *élan vital* of some members, their sense of risk and their lightheartedness, collided with the intellectual or even political passions of others. The principal representative of the first tendency was tall Kilometer (all of us had nicknames), who was, incidentally, always to retain the dash and nonchalance of a boy. The outbreak of the war caught him in Brazil, where he had gone as a ship's doctor. He remained there and joined an expedition to collect rare birds in the jungles of the Mato Grosso for the Zoological Museum in Rio de Janeiro. Later he practiced medicine in central Africa. It would be hard to find a greater contrast than existed between him and the leader of the intellectual wing, Robespierre, who was destined to become a member of the Central Committee of the Communist Party and one of the economic dictators in People's Poland.

Actually, we began quite soon to break out of the ideological framework of the club, which amounted to nothing more than a cult of adventure in defiance of the boring world of solid citizenry. Thanks mainly to the brilliant and sarcastic mind of Robespierre, our group turned out to be the germ of a Leftist movement that was to cause a stir far beyond the university campus.

The subsequent history of several other Vagabonds would not have been so easy to predict. I never suspected that chubby, quiet Bacchus would emerge as a talented writer. The career of another member outstrips the imagination of societies less exposed to historical upheavals. He was a professional student and a faithful servant of the Church who spent more time on propaganda for Catholic Action than he did preparing for his exams. After the Second World War he showed up in Warsaw as a high official of the Security Police. Reportedly he still attended early Mass before beginning his daily work. I have no idea whether he used his cigarette on the bodies of the delinquents he questioned or whether he had anything to do with the fabrication of confessions. No doubt he left that to his less squeamish colleagues.

Trying to reconstruct the development of our own opinions brings us up against a difficulty very familiar to modern physics: the instrument—which in this case is we ourselves, along with whatever accretions have grown up within us—transforms the object under investigation. Though we are close to ourselves, able to feel our old selves from the inside, we have already become inaccessible to ourselves. And so, as I trace the steps toward my encounter with Marxism, I must allow for a margin of error.

Despite my literary intentions, I studied law. If I rightly understand the motives for my choice, I was guided by an exaggerated fear that if I revealed what I wanted to become too early I would bring down defeat upon myself. There was also the precaution of a bureaucrat-to-be and the need for mortification, since nothing could be more deadly than Roman statutes, and we began with them, of course. At the same time, some instinct whispered that literature should not feed on itself but should be supported by a knowledge of society. The four-year course of studies at our university was incredibly eclectic. Roman law, the history of political institutions in Poland and in the Grand Duchy of Lithuania, canon law and economics were matched by subjects that, in practice, provided the professors with an occasion for lectures that were not altogether juridical. Thus criminal law changed into anthropology and sociology, the history of the philosophy of law into philosophy, statistics into higher mathematics torturing my antimathematical brain. Some of these fields really interested me, but I became convinced (and I still am) that whoever enrolled in the Law Department was wasting his time. I got through my final exams only on the strength of endurance and great quantities of black coffee. Afterward I put away my beautifully printed diploma with the title *magister iuris* and got no further use from it. I had shown, however, a capacity, or perhaps even an attraction, for swallowing unpleasant things just because they are unpleasant. That difficult training, which inculcated respect for order and precision of thought, was to come in handy after all.

People of my generation absorbed Marxism through osmosis, and the Marxists not without reason valued the doctrine as the inevitable outcome of a nineteenth-century scientific world view carried to its logical conclusion. The situation was like a natural slope: any ball placed on it would roll down, picking up speed as it went, and regardless of where it started from it would always end up in the same gorge. Marxists therefore regarded progressives as immature Marxists still awaiting their real initiation, while conservatives warned against trusting democrats or liberals, as if any breaking away from mindless obedience to God and Country must be due to unconscious Marxism. In this context the hostility of the fraternity set, who were unaccustomed to intellectual effort, to our friendly sessions on the sandy riverbanks where we pulled up our boats and gathered to air our views was quite understandable.

The vitality or sterility of certain ideas—their accord or disaccord with the *Zeitgeist*—shows in the expressions on people's faces. I have often wondered why an audience quietly dozes when a speaker expounds eloquently on democratic institutions, but immediately springs to life when the economy is brought up, or the need for removing injustice by violent means. Our little faction, which had grown out of the Vagabonds under Robespierre's leadership, scored a hit at the university. Our success came from the trenchancy of the questions we asked to shatter lofty phraseology. Marxism was still beyond our reach, but we were already using its gibes as a method.

While I was turning into a Red, I doubt if I understood

what makes revolutionary theories so appealing. I did, of course, have moments of intuition. Today, I would say that all the young people in Europe who had similar illuminations were seeking, above all, an instrument that would allow them to come to terms with the phenomenon of movement; that is, with time. Nature's time, thought of as linear, was more or less encompassed by the formula of evolution: the passage from inanimate matter to the first vertebrates, to fish, birds, animals, and at last to man, was progressive. As the natural sciences developed, the line was extended even further to the history of human societies. Here, too, there was to be constant progress, but until Marx there were no guarantees beyond a rather vague faith. The immensity of a past, made up of one event after another stored in chronicles, overwhelmed the mind and produced the boredom I so often observed in university lecture halls; it also produced anxiety, the feeling of powerlessness in the face of chaos. The connections between one event and another were unclear. They are not all that clear in the transition from fish to ichthyosaurs, but at least one gets some picture or more precisely a mnemonic abbreviation of the theory. Here, then, was a dialectic of development that operated with the same necessity in society and in nature, and it supplied a key that would explain everything. From then on, separate facts did not exist; each was seen against a "background," the soil from which it sprang, while at the same time, as if someone had pressed a button, a signal flashed across the consciousness: "Feudalism," "Capitalism," and so on.

Much has been written about the need for faith in our century. Perhaps it would be more correct to remember that a need for a simplified outlook on life, which could be contained in a catechism or a brochure, has always existed. Marxism probably had such great drawing power because it appeared at a time when the world had become too difficult to grasp either scientifically or humanistically; and the more primitive the mind, the greater the pleasure in reducing unruly, disparate quantities to a common denominator. One often heard the re-

mark, "If Marxism is rejected, then history has no meaning."
In trying to give it meaning, one had to make unjustifiable
leaps: the leap from nature to history (but history's "laws"
cannot be established as nature's are, in a laboratory, because
it is impossible to experiment, and human desires color even
the choice of the data to be examined); the leap from a more
or less scholarly investigation of the past to prophecies in
scholarly garb.

But even in a vulgarized Marxism there is "something" that
eludes the grasp of both those who profess it and those who
disparage it. It is as if a considerably greater phenomenon were
imprisoned in imperfect symbols, which distort its contents,
or as if an elephant had been reduced to the shape of its trunk.
I suppose one cannot call oneself a Marxist or an anti-Marxist
with impunity because that "something" perceived by Marx
will take its revenge by turning each of these positions into
its opposite.

While I was at the university, I did not call myself a Marxist
out of modesty, because I had not read *Das Kapital*. I was
governed less by reason than by a sense of smell (but I cannot
say whether it was my own or that of my era) and this, in
turn, put me on guard against any ism as a temporary construction bearing the imprint of the nineteenth century. My
high-school study of Darwin both made my entrance into the
labyrinth easier and, once inside, protected me like Ariadne's
thread, because it had accustomed my mind to isolating a certain totality (e.g. nature) and allowing it to coexist with others
without disturbing them. I condemned the capitalistic system
but was suspicious of becoming enmeshed in philosophical in-
tricacies. Sacred texts, such as Feuerbach's *Essence of Christianity*, Engels' *Anti-Dühring*, Lenin's *Materialism and Empirio-
Criticism*, I read as literature, unable to prevent humorous
images of beards, mustaches, and frockcoats from creeping into
my thoughts. Nevertheless, my "Marxist experience"—a very
complicated one in fact—was necessary for me, and I am seldom
able to find a common language with people who have not

gone through it themselves. There are no accurate definitions of a reactionary and a progressive, but the division is not a fictitious one. And one might say that during the first half of our century the test was whether one's ear was attuned to Marxism or not.

The dates are important. The years 1930–1935. Mass unemployment. The destruction of wheat and coffee. Hitler's seizure of power. All those aroused a violent protest from everyone who was not ready to accept the absurd. The poems I wrote then did not call for revolutionary action, but there was terror in them and a foreboding of what was to come. The gloomy visions of our so-called "catastrophists' school" (I was to be considered one of its leaders by the historians of the era) set us sharply apart from the poets of the older generation. Our visions had a historical dimension in which all phenomena and all laws were part of Heraclitus's river. If the Communists who reproached us for apocalyptic fears and pessimism did not see much importance in our discovery of this new dimension, they at least appreciated our bitter tone of negation, which coincided with their belief in the impermanence of the existing order of things. That my works carried no promise of a bright, happy society in the future showed, however, that I took from Marxism only its criticism of changeable and fluid institutions, but stopped at the threshold beyond which one must approve the millennium as the fulfillment of all time.

Our university politics underwent the same polarization as the politics of all countries: the Right became more and more Fascist, and the Left more and more Stalinist. Gradually we abandoned the Vagabonds Club for the I.C.—the Intellectuals Club—which resembled a Jacobin organization planning strategic moves in the war against the extreme Right. Even though the latter was weaker at our university than at any other in Poland, it usually won the elections to the student union over the leftist and liberal bloc (Jewish students had a separate union). The principal supporters of "the bloc" were Marxist-oriented Catholics. Their leader, a man of great personal charm and an excellent speaker, shortly afterward became a Communist. Considering his exceptional abilities and his dynamism, he would probably have played an important role later on in Poland (or would have landed in jail) had he not been executed by the Germans in 1941.

There is an extensive literature on the subject of the individual's road to Communism or, to call it by its right name, Stalinism. I, on the other hand, am trying to answer the question of how I was able to resist that creed. The completely baseless belief that only people with proletarian blood in their veins are capable of throwing themselves enthusiastically into the class struggle must be rejected from the start. Nor do I think my property status influenced me, since I lived off scholarships and occasional literary earnings during most of my stay at the university.

My mind worked, I think, like the mind of an artist, with all the virtues and the faults that implies. It advanced from negation to negation and actually delighted in the contradictions it attempted to resolve. One of my literary games was to lead the reader in a certain direction for a while, then throw him off the track so he lost his way, which, of course, caused many misunderstandings. I suspect, too, that my mind was more complicated and more prone to hidden irony than the minds of my colleagues. Long years of theological skirmishes with the Father Prefect had left me with a fondness for fencing with myself. Had I passively accepted my Catholic training and then shed it like a useless veneer, I would have been a clean slate on which the words of another faith could have been graven. But I did not. Through my heretical tendencies I remained at bottom a Catholic, in the sense that I carried in my memory the whole history of the Church. To me, for example, the Nicene Council of 325, which condemned Gnosis and Arianism, was not an abstract date. My imperviousness to the usually rather shallow progressive-atheist arguments was like the chess-player's contempt for cards. Besides, thanks to my family memories the past spoke to me vividly, and it hardly disposed me toward submitting to Russia. Obviously I did not then know how to sieve out these traits of mind, and I was often agitated by the desire to jump out of my skin.

Timidity, a feeling of inferiority, and, joined with that, a wild ambition led me to meditate on the gaps in my character. To this day I am not sure that all intellectual talents are not like orchids, which nourish themselves on the rotten wood of decaying trees. Quite early I learned to treat my literary triumphs as a compensation both deserved and somewhat discomfiting, because to me it was proof of my inferiority in other areas. Completely incapable of action, unfit for organizing or leadership or even blind obedience, I compared myself to my colleagues: they were drawing conclusions from their reading of Lenin; they were courageous and purehearted. The somnolence and passivity of a country of thatched roofs called out for a revolution and a *Dneprostroï*. As our group moved further to the left, my own feeling toward it became tacitly more and more disaffected. But I did not want to cut myself off from it because that would have totally isolated me and left me defenseless before the Fascist-inclined Right. Despite my very exclusive taste for French poetry, I felt the guilty conscience of a citizen who turns away from urgent tasks. I could not shield myself with ignorance, if only because I had studied law and economics and had taken part in countless political discussions. Caught between the devil and the deep, I reacted emotionally, and out of habits of friendship sought a place among those whom I looked upon as my intimates—only they were becoming less and less so.

I remember the shore of the lake. On one side were postglacial hills covered with fields and villages; on the other, forests. In these swampy woods a small river had its source. It was so well hidden that once I paddled around in my kayak among the trees, which stand in the water, for an hour before I found it. Our camp was on the high ground. When we went swimming I saw the red kerchief a friend had tied around his head, pirate-style, in front of me. Swimming races, campfires—

everything seemed to be just as it had been in the carefree days of the Vagabonds Club; but only a few years had been enough to dampen those spirits. In the bushes they read and commented on the so-called classics of Marxism; knowing smirks appeared on their faces; a hierarchy was established which could be felt in a wink, a sudden lowering of the eyes, a sentence broken off in the middle. They sang revolutionary songs, and an atmosphere of sweetness and demonism, which I came to know well later on, was created. I felt desperately left out, sad, betrayed—but I think that the others, too, though they put on a good face and would not have admitted it to themselves, mourned in some corner of their hearts over the premature end of real friendship, or even of youth. What was I, with my liking for St. Augustine, doing here? What could I talk about when the uninhibited exchange of thoughts and impressions had been replaced by the certainties of Progress and Revolution? But stronger than anything I could articulate was a vague disgust, complicated by what is known as a bad conscience. Thus the agonies and subterfuges of Parisian writers after the Second World War were already familiar to me, and I later observed them with the malice of one who looks back on a phase long outlived.

An article that I published in 1936 in a journal put out by my friends (our earlier magazines, full of youthful stammerings and verve, had been laid to rest) still astonishes me, not so much because of my intelligence as because of my ability to make distinctions (an ability I owed to my high-school training). Various "actions" in defense of culture were being organized, and, as part of a move to cement the Popular Front, young writers were asked to declare themselves. I announced my adherence, but at the same time expressed the fear that many of the alleged defenders of culture also intended to disembowel it. Such a clear attack on the light from the East was received with a wry smile of indulgence.

If one is right only because one's whole "I" refuses to jump in head first, to surrender completely to some cause, what then?

Should one force oneself, impose a discipline of self-renunciation to prove one's worth? Happy are they who can avoid radical choices. My imagination, playing in an historical dimension, knew no restraints—what prodded it will come out in the rest of the book. I felt the future very keenly. On one side were the Germans—Hitler and the Four Horses of the Apocalypse. On the other was Russia. In the middle was the nauseating Polish Right, which, in the perspective of time, was doomed to failure. The groupings of the Center—Populists and Socialists undermined by Communist sympathies—were difficult to take seriously. Parliamentary methods were discredited in the eyes of my generation. I do not claim that I foresaw clearly the dilemma that part of Europe would have to face: either Hitler's victory or Stalin's. This would suggest that I was freer from various emotional taboos than was actually the case. But somehow, in the year 1939, I did manage to utter such a pronouncement aloud. My state of mind in those days could be described as the same dream over and over: we want to run but cannot because our legs are made of lead. I had come up against the powerlessness of the individual involved in a mechanism that works independently of his will.

I was right in rejecting the light from the East, but the Communists were also right. Thanks to the Red Army, they soon seized power and then I had to serve them. Whoever claims that force cannot suffice as an argument overlooks the character of politics, where the winner takes all. If it were possible to withdraw from politics, then the values of truth and ethics would hold. But it is not possible to withdraw, so all one can do is try to save these values or embody them in politics.

I touch here on a basic question so difficult that my contemporaries tried in vain to solve it. If they analyzed the reality in prewar Poland coldly and penetratingly enough, they discovered knots that they realized could never be undone. No one can fully engage himself in activity knowing in advance that he will fail, and for that reason palliatives did not attract them. To foresee failure opens the door to all varieties of fatalism. And such an estimate is never objective when it is made within the life of a society, because it springs from a collective climate at a given moment and shapes that climate. Every alleged statement of bare facts is essentially a political decision. One is caught in a diabolical meshing of gears where "yes" and "no," which suffice within the individual's small orbit, are smashed to bits. My literary generation went around with its back bent by dread and futility. The more it tried to argue away its failure, the more painfully it felt as if a duty were being shirked. What duty? Going out into the street and shouting at people that each day was bringing them closer to catastrophe? But my generation considered every commitment fruitless except the Communist. Because the Eastern giant was frightening, they stuck to their tables in the coffeehouses. Later, after the country had been occupied by Stalin's army, a phase of breast-beating followed, and they swore never again to underrate *hard necessity*.

I closed myself in with my poetry and studies, but the images festered inside me—peasants' bare feet; Silesia's slum districts; the Zyrardow textile factories, whose owner was a French capitalist named Boussac; Poland's split, as an underdeveloped territory, into a handful of rich—no more than a few tens of thousands—and millions of poor. But my attempts to write about it ended in failure. Measured by the applause from my friends who hated the system, they were successful; but I knew that they had little in common with literature. For me the so-called poetry of social protest (I published an anthology of it) had no connection with the living springs of art; it was journalism, which I wrote to redeem myself for not taking part in the workers' clashes with the police.

My theoretical articles sometimes made me out a kind of adolescent Zhdanov, but in reality my fanatical fury left me with a feeling of repugnance. I did not have at my disposal instruments precise enough to lay open the deeper layer of my thought: that the collective imagination is given shape through the discipline of form itself, and that poetry is political in a totally different sense from the conventional use of the term. I was keenly aware that art has its limits, and after my first mistakes I displayed a great deal of firmness in this belief. But I was tortured by a basic dualism in which my will and my achievements negated each other. As relations with my converted friends cooled off, my tension, at least in that area, was relieved. Their criteria were strictly utilitarian. Only one subject carried any weight with them: the Revolution, the greatest event since the beginning of man's existence on this earth.

They did not reflect upon Russia, except perhaps in terms of the legendary Five-Year Plan; the past, with all its (according to them) prejudices, they were ready to throw overboard. As for myself, I could not avoid an encounter with Russian poetry. There was a basic "otherness" in the very language, a completely different emotional attitude to people and things, a special kind of "otherness," which was really that of a self-contained civilization. Nothing is more deceptive than the apparent similarity between the Polish and Russian languages. A different man looks out from behind each, and their confrontation is like a meeting between a Sicilian and a Chinese. My acquaintance with Russian was limited to colloquial speech; the alphabet, which I learned from my father, created some difficulty in reading. My school had substituted French or German for Russian in an attempt to wipe out the stigma left by the hated former ruler. So it was on my own that I discovered Pushkin. And I was captivated by him. My native tongue was incapable of such power of expression, such masterful iambs, and I had to admit it. The memory of those lines has never been erased. Gradually, however, I began to distrust the lyricism, which seemed to unfold of itself as if born from the very sounds themselves, even though with a master like Pushkin it was the result of conscious effort.

That poetry was like a magical incantation; everything was reduced to sound. It was even free to mean nothing, since the creative stuff out of which it was made was not the world but the word. The intoxication of a chant, the intoxication of rhythm. Poetry as a literary genre wandered quite late (in the seventeenth century) to Russia from Poland; in their turn some Polish poets who were my contemporaries borrowed technical devices from the Russians. My own experiments taught me that the influence of Russian musicality is always harmful: when the ear is sensitive to a language with strong accents, the natural desire to rival it can be disastrous for weakly accented languages like Polish or Czech. The precision of line and of intellectual nuance that can be achieved in these languages is then destroyed by the wild impulse to write a tribal song or by a measured beat—in that case, the metrical ideal of all poetry would have to be Edgar Allan Poe's *The Raven*, and it surely is not.

The connection these meditations have with politics is not easy to explain. For me the Russian Revolution was personified not by Lenin but by Vladimir Mayakovsky. And quite rightly, I think, because his work welded revolutionary theory with the old dream Russians had of themselves as a chosen nation, and the two messianisms nourished each other: class as redeemer and nation as redeemer. Shortly after Mayakovsky's suicide, I imitated my colleagues and, thrusting my jaw forward, recited, or rather barked, several of his noisiest verses. We added a couple of inches to our height, flexed our muscles, and beat our chests to show our gorilla-like contempt for a decadent culture. In me such impulses soon gave way to shame. Mayakovsky was a giant, but a hollow one who, when tapped, echoed emptily. One syllogism from Thomas Aquinas annihilated him. Whether or not one accepted or rejected that syllogism did not matter; a mind trained on it could not help but be suspicious of words used as an unshackled vital force. But Mayakovsky symbolized for me the Russians' revolution and —who knows?—perhaps their whole eternally ambiguous civilization, so powerful, human, hungry for justice in literature, and so miserable and cruel in worldly affairs. It seemed as if

they spent all their strength in extraordinary feats, leaving
nothing for more modest desires of harmony and happiness,
which they branded treason and weakness. Perhaps there was
some truth to the saying that the Russians, "being able to do
more, cannot do less." The mania for the gigantic, so visible
in Mayakovsky, which cost him a suicidal shot—for no one
inflates himself or runs away from his center, his inner point
of support, without paying for it—repelled me as a kind of
lie. By the same token, Russian Communism no longer held
the value of a promise.

Although I had no reason to doubt my reactions, which were
the result of my knowledge of an area neglected by my colleagues, their scorn cut deeper than I cared to admit. In the
same way matter, with its brutality, blood, and dirt, mocks the
spirit. An article by a young Communist critic about my
volume of poetry provoked my anger, as always happens when
someone uncovers our painful secret. He accused me of wanting
to keep my hands clean. But according to him only people who
carried their thinking to its logical conclusion were free from
this sin: if they were progressive they were materialists, ergo
Marxists, ergo supporters of the Soviet Union. This was the
equation hidden between the lines. Yet the shot had hit the
mark; it had struck to the heart of my inner discord. Even
then, the outlines of the conflict that was to fill many years of
my life were clearly visible. My reasoning went like this:
thought and word should not submit to the pressure of matter
since, incapable of competing with it, they would have to transform themselves into deed, which would mean overreaching
their lawful limits. On the other hand, I quite justifiably feared
dematerialization, the delusiveness of words and thoughts. This
could be prevented only by keeping a firm hold on tangible
things undergoing constant change; that is, control over the
motor that moves them in a society—namely, politics. Marxists
dismissed their opponents by treating them en masse as "ide-
alists." Although such an indictment embraced too many elements to be philosophically correct, it did contain a particle

of truth. I was stretched, therefore, between two poles: the contemplation of a motionless point and the command to participate actively in history; in other words, between transcendence and becoming. I did not manage to bring these extremes into a unity, but I did not want to give either of them up. The article I mentioned can serve as a strong argument against believing that all logical reasoning must arrive ultimately at Marxism, such as it was then conceived. It can also serve as an argument against the so-called inevitability of historical processes. The critic did not have to write it; it was an act of will with unforeseen consequences. One never knows what pebble will tip the scales. By intensifying my fear of "having clean hands," he might have provided one of the main stimuli that later on could have persuaded me to stick to People's Poland. But after the war I found myself among the élite, and already, unfortunately, my taste for the earthly and the material had so increased that millions of exploited and terrorized people depressed me all the more violently. I relived all my earlier struggles, only more acutely. Somewhere, within some fold of consciousness, that critic's article stirred, but this time it had an effect that completely counteracted his intentions. I can generalize this incident by saying that his advice to embrace the brutal truth of life already contained the germ of its own contradiction.

The greatest ally of any ideology is, of course, the feeling of guilt, which is so highly developed in modern man that it saps his belief in the value of his own perceptions and judgments. My own inborn tendency to be overscrupulous was for eight years rather effectively cultivated by the Father Prefect. After that, various personal complications (which I deliberately pass over) aggravated the condition. At the university, while reproaching myself for political passivity, I could not help noticing that my addiction to a contemplative existence—a kind of catlike curling up in the sun to dream—was much too strong ever to be broken. "Curling up in the sun" is perhaps an exaggeration, for I spent my days working very hard. But it was only the table with my papers and books that really interested

me. I could not even go out in a kayak or on a hike without
struggling with myself. I looked at each new day as if it
were to bring the solution. To what? The secret of existence,
of a line of poetry that existed in some empyrean but had
to be drawn down to earth. I needed quiet like a mathematician
who has worked for years over nis problem and feels that the
true revelation is drawing near; it is always going to happen
tomorrow. But I did not know how to accept this style of life
with a clear conscience, and my guilt complex deepened after
the trial of a group of my colleagues in 1936; several leaders—
among them Robespierre—were jailed for a year or two. I was
not deemed worthy, though my record was bad, to sit on the
bench of the accused. My colleagues, regardless of our differences in outlook, seemed to me the embodiment of intellect,
daring, and capacity for self-sacrifice in the struggle with the
blockheaded authority of the state.

In spite of the specific nature of Polish-Russian relations, in
those years our Communists and fellow-travelers resembled their
counterparts in the West. Only after the war, with the acquiring
of direct experience, did the problem of Marxism and Communism shift from the emotional-political sphere to the philosophical, which removed it so far from the naïve opinions of
Western sympathizers that, for the most part, the possibility of
any kind of dialogue with them vanished. A secret doctrine
was created which imparted a different meaning to propaganda
slogans than what was apparently understood. In many respects
it was like the doctrine of the Stoics. If the Stoics meditated
over how man should behave in the face of an inexorable order
of nature against which it would be vain to rebel, my contemporaries saw themselves confronted by the inexorable order
of history, and similarly excluded any possibility of rebellion.
For the Party élite with whom I had contact, the Russian
system was gloomy and repellent. But since it was chosen and
anointed by the *Weltgeist*, to become a Communist was to
perform an act of obedience toward the hidden law of becoming
that is stronger than personal likes and dislikes. And so, from

the dreams spun by nineteenth-century Socialists about a perfect society, nothing had really been salvaged. Instead, the foreground was dominated by the Hegelian conviction that certain phases will inevitably be victorious over others: that things are as they are, and we are not responsible.

But I am getting ahead of myself. This was necessary to make sure that, while I reveal my first ties with so-called Marxism, I do not create the impression that my further ups and downs were at all similar to those of Western fellow-travelers.

My fate was to grapple exclusively with the secret doctrine as I sought to discover where, in which of its segments, the falsehood lay, and what is the duty of a man who encounters an obstacle that is the creation of human beings, yet seems almost wholly to elude their reason and will. For many people, the answer may be easy, as hunting a whale is easy for those who have never run up against one. For us, however, beginning with the year 1939, the problem was no longer abstract; it had become a concrete situation which required daily decisions. Like the primeval hunter face-to-face with mysterious nature, we learned painfully that if one could hope to subdue the equally mysterious element that has replaced nature in the twentieth century, it was not by force but by wiles.

Russia

———◆———

TO PRETEND THAT I AM DIFFERENT and to conceal an obsession
that is characteristic of all Poles would be senseless. I ought
rather to own up to it and try to analyze it as dispassionately
as possible. Poles and Russians do not like each other, or, to
be more exact, they harbor all sorts of uncomplimentary feelings, ranging from contempt to disgust and hatred, for one
another. Whatever vague mutual attraction exists between them
is always tinged with suspicion. The barrier seems to have
arisen from what Joseph Conrad called "incompatibility of
temper." Perhaps all nationalities, seen as wholes and not as
assortments of individuals, are odious, and their neighbors uncover in them only what are unpleasant truths about human
societies in general. It may well be that what the Poles know
about the Russians the Russians know about themselves but are
unwilling to acknowledge, and vice versa. A defensive reflex
may lie beneath the hostility with which Dostoevsky, a nationalist, regarded the Poles. Only in *Notes from the House
of the Dead* does he speak of them with respect. And even
then those fellow-prisoners, shielding themselves with their patriotism and Roman Catholicism, stressing their superiority over
their environment and their otherness at every opportunity, do
not awaken in him any warmth of feeling. Similarly for Poles,
every encounter with Russians puts them on the defensive
because it unmasks them in their own eyes.

The confused background of the quarrel is as hard to describe
as the motives for a hereditary vendetta between two families

who live on the same street. And it would have remained
a local affair had it not betokened events on a planetary scale.
Russia could have become what she was only by liquidating
the Polish-Lithuanian *Respublica* (which bordered on Turkey
in the southeast) and, starting from 1839, by converting to
Orthodoxy great stretches of territory whose population was
mainly Greek-Catholic, therefore pro-Polish and obedient to
the Vatican. Places such as Galicia under the Hapsburgs, where
the Greek-Catholic Church managed to survive, were forcibly
converted to Orthodoxy after the Second World War—a fact
that, torn from its context in the past, would be incomprehensible.

The cause of the enmity between Poles and Russians is
usually attributed to the injuries the former claim to have suffered at the hands of the latter. This is only partially true.
The roots go much deeper than either the nineteenth or the
twentieth century. All the upheavals in Europe prove that beneath the changing surface there is an unchanging core. France's
cultural continuity was not destroyed by the French Revolution,
nor Russia's by the October Revolution, nor Poland's by the
Communist seizure of power in 1944–45. No doubt every civilization receives a permanent imprint from a period that has
been of key importance for it. France, for example, owes everything to its bourgeoisie, which was already a powerful creative
force two centuries before the Revolution. In Poland during
this period, the gentry became the dominant force, and it is
the vestiges of "gentry culture" in the behavior of a Polish
peasant or worker of today that particularly irritates a Russian,
who derisively refers to him as "sir."

The sixteenth and seventeenth centuries were of primary importance. Today it is hard to realize that Polish, the language
of the ruling and hence educated class, was once a symbol of
elegance and refinement as far east as Polotsk or Kiev. The
Muscovites, like the Tartars, were those barbarians on the peripheries against whom wars were waged, and no one was
particularly interested in them. In Polish literature of the time,

there are many descriptions of Hungarians, Germans, French, and Italians, but little notice is taken of the Czar's subjects except to remark on their incomprehensible humility in the face of despotism and their tendency to break promises, or to ridicule their guile and the savagery of their customs (the French, in turn, considered Polish customs savage). The flow of ideas, like the colonization of primeval forest lands and steppes, was a movement from West to East. Practically everything people valued—craftsmanship, architectural design, literature, discussions on humanism and the Reformation—came from Flanders, Germany, or Italy. If there was also heavy borrowing from the East, it came from Turkey, thanks to the great trade route, and was especially marked in fashions in clothes and harnesses, which kept their Turkish names. Muscovy, on the other hand, as she slowly transformed herself into Russia, did not represent much of an attraction except as an emerging power. Russia was to receive her cultural imprint from the nineteenth century, just as Poland received hers from the sixteenth and seventeenth, an era when there seemed to be a void in the East, which gave Poles the idea of Russia as something *outside*, beyond the orbit of the civilized world. Consequently, their defeat at the hands of the Russians shocked them, as if they had been conquered by the Tartars: if it had any meaning at all, it must signify a punishment for their sins. But their real sin had been the centuries-long discussion of their sins—in literature, in local diets, in the parliament—from which almost nothing practical ever came.

The vanquished who shows his contempt for the victor by refusing to see any virtue in him except the capacity for blindly obeying orders is able to inflict real hurt, because he reminds the victor that he is strong only at a price. Thus Russian and Polish writers (usually émigrés in Paris) carried on a polemic in which neither side spared the other. In Pushkin's anti-Polish poems there is anger at the fanatic pride of the losers, who will not admit they have lost, who dream of vengeance, who conspire and stir up every chancellery in Europe against

Russia. These poems do more than impugn a nation trying to recover its independence. The memory of a great rivalry still lives in them: Poland's resurrection would have raised again the question of whom Polotsk and Kiev should belong to; it would have struck a blow at the very foundation of the Empire. So Pushkin foresees that "all Slavic rivers will flow into the Russian sea."

Mickiewicz, the Polish poet and revolutionist, the ally of the Carbonari, was in a better moral position than his colleague (and friend, until politics came between them), who was a semi-prisoner at the Czar's court. Mickiewicz's brutal pamphlet on Russia, written in verse that has remained a model of terseness, hits the mark so truly because the author's hatred for absolute monarchy is so closely bound up with his sympathy for its victims, the Russian people. The observations it contains are really no different from the material Gogol used in his satires, although the fact that Mickiewicz is a foreigner whose criticism is not tempered by attachment to the country does add something new. What horrifies Mickiewicz are the savage landscapes, the savagery in human relationships, the passivity and apathy of the people in their bondage. The very tribe of humanity inhabiting that land disquiets him like some formless hulk, which the sculptor history has left unchiseled:

> I meet the people: broad-shouldered/Broad-chested, and thick-skulled/Like the animals and trees of the north,/Full-blooded, hearty and strong./But each face is like their country/An empty, open and wild plain:/And from their hearts, as from underground volcanoes,/No fire has yet risen to light their faces,/Nor glows from ignited lips,/Nor goes out in dark lines on foreheads/As with the faces of people in the east and west,/Over which so much of life's troubles has passed/Of legends and events, sorrows and hopes,/That every face is a memorial to the nation./Here, people's eyes, like the cities of this country/Are large and clear; never does the soul's tumult/Move the pupil with an extraordinary glance,/Never does desolation cloud them over long./Seen from a distance they are splendid, marvelous;/Once inside,

they are empty and deserted./The body of this people is like a fat cocoon,/Inside which sleeps a caterpillar-soul,/ While shaping its breast for flight/Unfolding its wings, flexing and adorning—/But when the sun of freedom shall rise,/ What kind of insect will fly out from that shroud?

Mickiewicz's poem is a synthesis of all the Polish attitudes toward Russia. Many decades later, Joseph Conrad expressed the same dread of formlessness and moral chaos in his novel *Under Western Eyes*. Although Conrad did not admit it, that book appears to have been a polemic against Dostoevsky's Russian Messianism.

Nazism is now a thing of the past, but perhaps the opinion that Slavs are "subhuman" is not. This view, which was widespread among the German masses, applied above all to the Poles, their closest neighbors, and made it easier for the Nazis to carry out their monstrous crimes. To say that the Poles are unaware of those faults—disorder, an inability to control matter (since the Middle Ages, rickety bridges and muddy roads have been part of the standard image of Poland in European literature), recklessness, drunkenness, lack of talent for making life *gemütlich*—that allowed the Germans to acquire the pleasant feeling of their own superiority would be to exaggerate. At the same time, however, the Poles are aware of their good traits, rarely found among the Germans, whom they consider slow-witted and ponderous: imagination; a sense of irony; a gift for improvisation; a tendency to make fun of all power, which enables them to dissolve every political system from the inside (just as the Italians humanized Fascism by turning it into a sort of masquerade). Frederick Nietzsche knew what he was doing when he stressed his Polish origins.

But the contrast between these two stereotypes might serve as a lesson to the Poles in judging their relationship to the Russians. For in Russia the inability to order one's immediate surroundings—in other words, the disregard for *Gemütlichkeit*, plus graft and embezzlement of government funds—reached unheard-of proportions, and organizational efforts brought results only, when the power of the state directly benefited. Poles are often very efficient outside of their own country, and, in fact, the Poles in Russia, whether voluntary and involuntary émigrés, acted as a civilizing force. The Polish image of the Russians was always incomparably more complicated than the German image of the Poles; nevertheless a shade of contempt seasoned with pity always crept into the vision. The Poles felt superior because of their traditions, their Catholic moral code, their sense of belonging to the West. A certain leaden tranquillity at the bottom of the Russian character acted on them like a slap in the face; for a people used to intellectual compromise, this patience, this imperturbability, this extremism in matters of ideas were inscrutable. And all these feelings made the memory of defeat particularly mortifying.

To the Russians, Polish curtsies, smiles, conventional politeness and flattery were empty forms and a sham. They convinced themselves that they were superior to such shallow, self-satisfied social butterflies, with their irritating sense of honor and their proneness to heroic but senseless impulses. Perceptive enough to distinguish an older cultural formation, suffering from their inferiority to everything Western, tortured by their guilty consciences because they served autocracy, the Russians guessed the unspoken word that hung in the air: barbarians. They were fascinated by the very things that repelled them: poetry, irony, a light touch, the Latin ritual.

In their infatuation with the West, especially France, the Poles deluded themselves. For they were bound to the land of Montaigne only by what they had borrowed, no matter over how many generations. This might be considerable. But France's whole social structure was different. How could someone who was every inch a nobleman (or an heir to his culture) communicate with someone who was every inch a bourgeois? Poland's social structure brought her closer to Russia: in both countries capitalism appeared late and cut no durable traces in the psyche. Polish hopes for winning European aid, based usually on a faith in meaningless promises, constantly proved to be misplaced. Napoleon was defeated, but before he was he had managed to use Polish legions for quelling the uprising in Haiti. Today you can meet there ebony-skinned people with Polish names, the offspring of these soldiers who could not return to Europe. Yet in spite of this the Napoleonic legend determined the political habits of the Poles, who always remained certain that freedom was "the wind from the West." And they staked their next claim on democratic revolutions, hoping for the overthrow of all kings and tyrants. But the revolutions petered out with no substantial results. And the Crimean War was hardly a crusade.

During the nineteenth century the Poles developed what might be called a Cassandra complex. Except for periodic outbursts of anger, usually rhetorical, or the few fierce Russophobes among writers like Karl Marx or the Marquis de Custine, the Poles encountered among Western Europeans an inexplicable love for both Russia and the Czar who symbolized her. The Poles protested loudly about the limitless ambition and limitless possibilities that lay in the expanses of Euro-Asia. But the Allies, after hearing them out politely, went off to the Czarist embassy to get the particulars on these suspicious revolutionaries. Hence the feelings Poles have about the West are at the very least ambivalent, and deep down perhaps even malevolent.

Polish and Russian revolutionists should have been brothers in their common struggle against Czardom. Regardless of what today's textbooks say, it was the "incompatibility of temper" arising out of the disparity between their respective historical formations that prevented a solid alliance between these people, who were equally self-sacrificing and enlightened (both came from the educated class). Even the most radical Poles had great inner resistance to change because of their love for the past. They therefore often unconsciously considered the revolution as a means of conferring on all citizens the old parliamentary privileges of the Polish gentry, and not as the beginning of something that had never existed. If the revolution was to bring justice, it must first do away with the domination of one nation by another; in this case, Poland must be restored to her sovereign statehood. The striving for social justice merged with the striving for independence, but since conservatives and progressives were in agreement on the latter (though not always), radical programs lost their edge.

The Russians meanwhile had other problems. They could reflect bitterly on their sovereign (oh, how sovereign!) state. There was nothing to restrain their thoughts: neither religion, that most reliable support of the throne, nor earlier governmental systems, which were universally hated because they were equivalents of Czarist power and oppression. They were directed exclusively into the future; they wished to destroy, to change the land into a *tabula rasa*, and then to begin to build anew. The Nihilist movement, which had enormous consequences, did not catch on in Poland. Besides, even if the revolutionists of both nations had shown each other mutual magnanimity at all times, they could not have forgotten that bone of contention: Byelorussia and the Ukraine. The Russians spoke the truth when they reproached their colleagues for hoping to become heirs of that same *Respublica* that had gradually Polonized those territories and supported the Uniate or Greek-Catholic Church there. But those Polish colleagues were right, too, when they accused the Russians of accepting as just and proper the intended Russification of these countries and of imitating the language of official decrees by speaking of them as "Western Russia." The whole matter of this no man's land, since both sides regarded Byelorussian and Ukrainian simply as folk dialects, was foggy and uncertain.

At the beginning of the century, a number of Polish Marxists realized that nationalism weakens the revolutionary thrust by leading to an alliance between classes; they therefore opposed independence and made the overthrow of despotism throughout the whole Czarist empire their primary goal. Rosa Luxemburg was one who subscribed to this error, which backfired on her supporters and successors. It was as if in the 1950s one had preached revolution to the peoples of North Africa on condition that they remain an integral part of France. The "independence-minded" Socialists, of whom Piłsudski was one, gained the upper hand. Sovereign Poland came into being after the First World War, thanks to the chaos in her neighbor to the east; and the Polish-Russian War of 1920 was a popular war, supported by workers and peasants. We now know from later events on different continents, notably in the Arab countries, that certain characteristics are common to all newly established states: the violence of national emotions; the dominant position of the intelligentsia (which in Poland, unlike the peasant Baltic countries, was sociologically linked to the gentry, then in the throes of economic decline); the role of the Army. In Poland another element was the hatred the Leftists bore for the Rightist National Democrats. This gave rise to many paradoxes. The National Democrats had in the past sought reconciliation with Czardom because it guaranteed "order," while the Left had sprung from insurrectionist, anti-Russian traditions. The Left had promoted the legend that Piłsudski was a providential man; and when, with the help of the Army, he took over the government, the Leftists saw this as the lesser evil—a protective buffer against pressure from the Right. But as the parliamentary system and the free interplay of political forces were done away with, both the Social Democrats and the progressives of various shades saw the gradual breakup of their parties. Rosa Luxemburg's successors, the Communists, had violated a nationwide taboo, and their tragedy was to rampage in a blind alley. They had the same chance that a Mexican party would have if it had advocated Mexico's annexation to the United States. They were shot at by the Polish police and by Stalin, who finally dissolved the Party in 1938, summoned its leaders to Moscow, and had them executed. Thus Marx's prophecy was fulfilled in reverse: at the time the *Communist Manifesto* was published he considered the ruin of the Eastern empire and the rebuilding of Poland according to her 1772 boundaries a prerequisite for revolution in Europe.

Marx, whether we like it or not, spoke of "European civiliza-

tion." He also divided nations into "good" and "bad." On the
eastern peripheries of that civilization he placed three nations
whom he favored because their peoples—the Poles, the Hungarians, and the Serbs—were, in his opinion, creative and free-
dom-loving. He could not bear Pan-Slavism and had a violent
antipathy toward Slavs—with the two above exceptions—who,
he declared, were always ready to serve as blind instruments of
tyranny. For this reason his articles on international politics have
a strange ring to a Polish reader. They could just as well
have been written by a Pole of the nineteenth century. How
strongly those feelings are embedded can be seen today. For
out of all the nations on earth, the Poles are joined in true and
mutual amity only with the Hungarians and the Serbs.

To my generation these imbroglios seemed obscure and far
away. We grew up in a normal country whose splendors and
miseries were a domestic affair; decisions were obviously made
in Warsaw and nowhere else. The martyrdoms, conspiracies,
and deportations to Siberia that figured in our textbooks aroused
only sympathy; common sense told us to poke fun at the
Romantic pathos of a bygone era. In my imagination Russia's
presence was, as it were, subdued. The quarrel had been somehow laid to rest. We were separated from each other by the
posts along the frontier; and a natural taboo stood guard against
any thought of introducing *their* system into our country.
Marxism, revolution, yes, but not *their* brand. Let them do as
they liked at home; it did not concern us. One can look upon
such an opinion as stupid. But in this I was typical: that pro-
hibitive threshold really existed, and any politician who ignores
it commits a mistake.

Moreover, the attitudes within that area between the Germans
and Russia were not formed everywhere by the same determinants. In the northwestern and southern provinces, formerly part
of the Prussian and Austrian Empires, the main call was for
resistance to the German *Drang nach Osten.* To me the Germans, except for the cruel myth of the Knights of the Cross,
meant nothing; I did not know their language. Moreover, Kaiser

Wilhelm's Army had not left behind any particularly unpleasant memories. As I tapped a finger to my forehead, like many of my contemporaries who observed the ripening insanity of Hitlerism, I was intensely involved by the drama of the whole epoch rather than by the part played in it by those Martians whom I could not imagine from the inside. I transformed politics into a secret writing, into cosmic images.

Russia, however, was relatively, but only relatively, concrete, as a chaos and an infinity remembered from childhood and, above all, as a language. At the dinner table in our shabby, miserable (as I know now) home, Russian had been the language to make jokes in, whose brutal-sweet nuances were untranslatable. When, for example, you translate such a sentence —from Shchedrin, I believe—about two dignitaries hurling abuse at each other before a gaping and amused crowd, it really does not mean much of anything: *"I rugalis tak uzhasno, chto vostorzhennye bosyaki ezheminutno krichali ura!"** Poles, it would seem, are able to get an intuition of "Russianness" mainly through the language, which attracts them because it liberates their Slavic half; in the language is all there is to know about Russia. The very thing that attracts them is at the same time menacing. I used to perform a certain exercise which gave me a good deal to think about. One had to take a deep breath and pronounce first in a deep bass voice: *"Wyryta zastupom yama glubokaya,"*† then to chatter quickly in a tenor: *"Wykopana szpadlem jama głęboka."*‡ The arrangement of accents and vowels in the first phrase connotes gloom, darkness, and power; in the second, lightness, clarity, and weakness. In other words, it was both an exercise in self-ridicule and a warning.

My generation, however, repressed its awareness of the dangers and masked, under various disguises, the political impasse that tinged thought and word. It was unforeseeable then that the

---

* Russian for: "And so terribly did they abuse each other that every minute the delighted ragamuffins cried out: 'Hurrah!'" (Tr.)
† Russian for: "A deep pit dug out with a spade." (Tr.)
‡ The same in Polish. (Tr.)

martyrology, which had been put to rest in the museum, would soon begin all over again. Although I was constantly visited by a feeling of imminent catastrophe, it was of planetary proportions, not just those of my country. This feeling was to provide the motive for still another conflict with my environment. The majority of Poles, as early as the first month of the Second World War, took a leap backward and made themselves at home in the old, familiar conditioning. Twenty years of sovereign statehood is a short span, and whatever habits had been acquired during that time were brushed away like the dust on a butterfly's wing. Too many similarities in the situation carried them back: the partition of the country between two enemies, jailings, deportations, Siberia, reliance on France and England, Polish "legions" in the West. Conditioning also explains the rationale of émigré politicians: liberation ought to follow if Germany and Russia are defeated, since it happened that way in the First World War. However, as someone has rightly said, every drama is played only once on the stage of history; and if it is performed a second time, the tragedy is contaminated by elements of bloody farce. Many of us who had come to intellectual maturity in conditions that made us rather skeptical of national passions suffered a very painful inner split during the war years: to admit to ourselves that not only our reason but our powers of observation saw the error of reverting to old postures was almost monstrous when those postures were assumed by a humiliated and persecuted people.

From time to time we are thrown into situations that distill, as it were, our somewhat indefinite feelings; they cleanse them from everything superfluous and reduce them to a few basic lines. At the same time they are still complicated enough to function as a metaphor, which is always closer to reality than any theory. This is why, instead of trying to pin down my adolescent emotions, I want to run ahead, beyond the Second World War even, to describe something that happened at the very end. The image, whose every detail is still vivid in my memory, dates from January of 1945.

In the largest room of a country house, a dozen or so Soviet soldiers and noncoms are seated on benches next to the walls. On my knees, which are pressing through my threadbare civilian trousers, I hold a tin of tobacco and I roll up a pinch of the crumbly leaves in cigarette paper. Those men, jostling me with their arms on both sides because there is not enough room on the bench, were not in the least distinct from some mythical Russia. Perhaps to a complete outsider, who had never been thrown together with Russians before and who could not have distinguished among the intonations of voice or the meaning of gestures, they might have looked like a new and unknown species. For me, however, they were the legitimate inheritors of those same human gifts that had sustained both Dostoevsky and Tolstoy. And just as their forebears had routed Napoleon, so they had routed Hitler. Our gazes converge toward the center of the room, where a man is standing who could not have been much over thirty. He wears a long white sheepskin coat and has the type of attractive face often met in the Rhine country. The man is a German prisoner of war; a conquistador now in their power.

The corpses lying in the fields that winter, teeth glistening, inspired neither triumph nor regret. Indifferent as stones, they were part of the spectacle of punished pride; their belt buckles with the inscription *Gott mit Uns*, now trampled into the snow, I passed by in ironic meditation. And so one of those now stood before us. Behind him he had left tidy houses, bathrooms, Christmas trees with colored ornaments, vineyards cultivated for generations, and the music of Johann Sebastian Bach. Torn from his own community, now in theirs, without bathrooms, or tablecloths kept in a chest, without towels and pillowcases embroidered with maxims, without rosebeds; these men had only vodka, the medicine for misery, boredom, and unhappiness. He looked stupid there, or, if one prefers, naïve. Because it was more than just his standing alone in front of all of them, one against many; more than his being weaponless and they armed. No, it was the psychic density of that silent Areopagus that overwhelmed him. With his own people he had never created such tension; it was almost a telepathy, going around without words or signs, welding individuals into a whole bigger than themselves. He had always needed speech, a shout, or a song. But these men, perhaps semiliterate, emanated some kind of monumental knowledge of resignation. And it was just that, his inability to read anything in the eyes turned toward him, that drove him silly with fright.

Maybe I should have hated him, above all for the stupidity that, multiplied by the stupidity of millions like him, conferred power on Hitler and made of this young German the blind instrument of murder. But I found no hate in myself. I imagined him, for some reason, on a sunny slope, in a drill, pushing a wheelbarrow full of shoots from fruit trees. They did not hate him either. Because, like a caged animal, he was afraid of the unknown, one of them got up and gave him a cigarette; that movement of the hand meant reconciliation. Another clapped him on the back. Then an officer went up to him and slowly, distinctly, pronounced a long speech. It was useless because the German understood nothing, but he glued his eyes to the speaker's lips like a dog who strains to guess the meaning of his master's words. Yet from the friendly tone he concluded that they did not want revenge, did not want to harm him. "Don't be afraid," the officer stressed repeatedly. "Nothing bad will happen to you, the war is already over, you are no longer an enemy but an ordinary man. You will work for peace and will be sent to the rear right away." The pity, even cordiality in the voice, the mild, grave tone of authority quieted the prisoner and he smiled timidly: gratitude. Though no command had been given, one of the soldiers sleepily picked himself up from his bench and took the prisoner from the room. The rest fell back into their previous apathy of physically exhausted human beings. In a few minutes the soldier returned alone, dragging a white sheepskin coat that he threw next to his duffel bag. He sat down and rolled a cigarette. The melancholy way he inhaled his smoke and spat on the floor expressed the thoughts of all of them in that room on the frailty of human life: "That's fate."

Cruelty? But one has to place the incident against the background of the war. The Germans had exterminated countless thousands of Soviet prisoners, putting them behind barbed wire and letting them die of starvation. Rumors about it spread so quickly that everyone exposed to such a fate preferred to fight to the bitter end. The number of defenseless people massacred by the Germans in Poland was as large as the whole population of Switzerland. As for the Allied soldiers, they had more than once quietly managed to do away with their prisoners. Hatred and contempt usually accompanied single or mass murders of this sort; that is, in one's mind the victims first had to be deprived of their humanity, they had to be transformed into hideous puppets; and it was on these objects, subsequently, that one could take revenge.

This psychic process was systematically encouraged by the Nazis, who used it on the Jews and the Poles. But these Russian soldiers had murdered the German not out of hatred but out of respect for necessity. That necessity had taken the form either of the difficulties of transferring the prisoner to the rear or of a white sheepskin coat. It may well be that, in their estimation, to take a man's covering and let him go like that into the freezing cold would have been an inconvenient or ugly thing to do. Since we ourselves define what necessity is, we draw a line between the "necessary" and the "possible." The humanitarian comedy they had staged might be called a crime if it had not most clearly answered to their inner need. Along with their sincerity of feeling went the conviction that such an operation should be carried out with the utmost sweetness and calm.

Who knows if we have not reached here to the very core of the Polish obsession? The chain of historical causes and effects from which any collectivity is forged stretches far back into the past, and the individuals who conform to its pressures do not stop to consider what has marked them with this or that stamp. As I sat on the bench musing over the incident I had just witnessed, it did not seem to me that the final links of the chain—i.e., the political system—could be decisive. After all, a system does not grow out of a void. Even though as a finished product it could be exported, its characteristics were determined by its own native soil. I recalled certain fragments of Russian literature from the last century; I did not disdain the Polish stereotype according to which a Russian, having slit someone's throat, is fully capable of shedding bitter tears over his victim. But what came back to me with the greatest clarity was what I had read about the sects of Eastern Christianity. Because of the "Eastern" part in me, I felt a certain affinity with these sectarians who, from the ruthlessness of nature and human society, drew the conclusion that the world is in the undivided power of Satan. Only the Kingdom of God was to abolish its diabolical law, which they identified with the law of Creation. For this reason Russian mystical writers believed that fulfillment of the Kingdom of God would bring salvation not only to man but also to the fly and the ant. In practice, however, this nearly super-human sympathy cut off intention from deed. Before the coming of Christ, we are completely subject to a shameful law; therefore the revolt of our hearts is powerless. Later on, when the Kingdom of God received the name of Communism, one had at least the consolation that an earthly "iron necessity" led up to it. By submitting to it—and it required murder, oppression, and torture —one brought the Great Day that much closer.

These soldiers need no longer have had anything in common with Christianity; they need not have been Communists. Yet thanks to their childhood environment they had received a training in duality so advanced as to have no equal in any other country. Their lofty constitution, their education, and their literature aimed at an ideal of brotherhood. The "new man" was noble and pure. But only in theory, which grew up slowly, autonomously, rising like a coral reef out of the sea. The reef would have collapsed had it not been shored up by a "conspiracy against the truth." Their comedy, which the soldiers played more for themselves than for the prisoner, was a tribute to what *should* be, since they knew all the while that reality runs along quite opposite tracks.

When you cut the tie between intention and deed, then noble words, friendly embraces, tears of sincere confession—all that charming effusiveness so characteristic of Russians—are simply an excursion into a land free from the compulsion of earthly laws, a land where all men are brothers. Theirs is an authentic depth of feeling, a full acceptance of oneself and the other— although at the same time some layer of our being is not deceived, for we know that it is *only* consent. There will be no inconsistency if one denounces or kills the other immediately afterward, since we are not to blame, but the evil world. Only in the Kingdom of God (or in Communism) will the lion lie with the lamb. Such a shedding of responsibility easily turns into an addiction; and then the threshold beyond which an alleged necessity begins is very low. Evil is perpetrated without enthusiasm, but one does nothing to avoid it. Furthermore, every free act becomes suspect because it seems to mask an obedience to a material compulsion.

The Poles are closely enough related to the Russians and menaced enough from within by the weakness of their own individualist ethic to be fearful. But their history, which made them what they are, was on the whole deprived of eschatology. Their radical Protestant sects, the leaven and the promise of later democratic movements, believed that justice was quite attainable on this earth. Although many a time they forbade their members to hold office (since all power makes use of the sword), they seriously discussed how to apply the commands of the Gospel to the existing society; that is, how to organize it. In Polish literature there are no characters like Dostoevsky's Alyosha or Prince Myshkin, who symbolize the dilemma: "either all good or no good at all"; nor is there that desperate restlessness of "superfluous men" thirsting for an Aim, a God, which for almost a century in Russia foreboded revolution with its absolute goals. The key work* in Polish literature, which is as highly ap-

* *Dziady (Forefather's Eve)*, by Adam Mickiewicz. (Tr.)

preciated by the Poles as *Faust* is in Germany, has for its subject a Promethean revolt against God ("You are not the father of the world, but its—Czar!") in the name of solidarity with unhappy mankind. That revolt, however, is overcome by Christian humility and political action for the good of men (a Russian would have chosen one of the two: either humility and sainthood or action). Thus the loftiness of Polish Romanticism, if scrutinized more closely, is a good deal more down-to-earth and modest in its aspirations than Russian realism, pervaded with limitless desire.

Although I carried away a number of dualistic elements from my sojourn in high school—and perhaps, on account of that, it was easier for me than for others to understand the Russians—they were offset by other influences. What sort of influences these were can best be indicated by the title of a sixteenth-century work (which we analyzed in class): *De Republica Emendanda*. My attraction to Lithuanians is rather significant, too. Comparing them to Poles, I had to admit they had greater constancy and practicality. Their cooperatives could have been a model for all Europe. At any rate, matter counted for them—and it did for me, too.

I may or may not be fair here, but at least I am exposing my obsession. To me, the "depth" of Russian literature was always suspect. What good is depth if bought at too high a price? Out of the two evils, would we not prefer "shallowness" provided we had decently built homes, well-fed and industrious people? And what good is might if it is always that of a central authority, while Gogol's *Inspector General* forever remains the reality of shabby provincial towns? Through the Poland of my youth ran a line. On one side were the districts formerly administered by Prussia or Austria; on the other were those in which the Russians had displayed their administrative talents. The contrasts were vivid. But the Russian revolutionaries, dreaming of a *tabula rasa*, deluded themselves. Once they had established their leaders in the Kremlin they could only build out of the material of people, habits, customs that they found at hand; and still worse, they themselves were part of that human clay molded by the spirit of their land. Soviet historians maintain that Ivan the Terrible, Peter the Great, and Catherine II were "progressive" because they worked for the future Revolution. Although such notions of "progressivism" are laughable, they reveal a good deal about the Russian cult of energy that always emanates from a center of supreme power and breaks through barriers with complete disregard for spontaneous growth.

My attitude to Russia contained the germ of my later misunderstandings with my French or American friends who accused me more than once of nationalism, although they were well aware that I do not divide people into better and worse depending upon their membership in any group—linguistic, racial, or religious—and that I reject the notion of guilt by association. They were surprised at my almost exaggerated sympathy for Russians taken individually. All of these attitudes did not seem to hang together. Regretfully I had to say that I did not possess a language that would allow me to carry through the necessary distinctions. But that lack of terminology is not only *my* lack. The twentieth century, panic-stricken in the face of nationalist and racist ravings, strains to fill up the chasm of time with production figures or the names of a few political-economic systems; meanwhile it has renounced investigations of the fine tissue of becoming, where no thread should be overlooked—even the ideas of forgotten Russian sects. What apparently disappears forever is, in fact, imperceptibly transformed, and such remote phenomena as the character of Ancient Rome are still alive, simply because it was there, and nowhere else, that Catholicism took on a form. Or, to use another example, the French conquest of the territories south of the Loire in the Middle Ages was driven into the collective unconscious of the region's inhabitants as a fact, to have repercussions more than once in Protestant, and later in revolutionary and lay propensities.

When the description of countries and civilizations had not

yet been inhibited by a multitude of taboos arising from the compartmentalized division of knowledge, authors, who were usually travelers, did not disdain continuity as it is written in the slope of a roof, the curve of a plow handle, in gestures or proverbs. A reporter, a sociologist, and a historian used to co-exist within one man. To the mutual detriment of all, they parted ways. Today certain aphorisms about how countries live together irritate us because they try to express some truth that cannot be seized by reason. Dmitri Merezhkovsky said to one of his Polish interlocutors: "Russia is a woman, but she never had a husband. She was merely raped by Tartars, Czars, and Bolsheviks. The only husband for Russia was Poland. But Poland was too weak." Whether or not we find it difficult to think about the validity of that opinion, nothing prevents our at least seeing elements in it of old popular beliefs, which were not always so foolish.

Our knowledge does not develop at an equal pace in all areas; it progresses in some, drags its feet in others, or even retreats. The current fear of generalizing about racial and territorial groups is an honorable impulse because it protects us from falling into the service of people interested not so much in truth as in an expedient argument for a political battle. Only after the reasons for such a fear have disappeared will minds skilled in tracking down interdependencies penetrate what for wise men today is an embarrassing subject, fit only for table talk in a country tavern. They will not disappear until the appraisal of any civilization ceases to be a weapon against those human beings brought up within it—in other words, not soon. But when it does—because Russia's destiny was fought out on the banks of the Dnieper in competition with her neighbors—those emotional clashes I have been speaking about here, which are vital now only for those directly involved, will surely make exciting material.

Journey to the West

◆

THIS HAPPENED IN THE YEAR 1931. There were three of us, and the sum of our ages made sixty years. Robespierre, whom we, like the majority of Vagabonds Club members, tacitly recognized as our leader, marched along, arms churning like a windmill, his sinuous, knobby figure bent forward under the weight of his knapsack. He never indulged his fatigue, and to show that he despised it he turned his body into a mileage-eating machine. His severe face with its arched nose resembled the faces of monks in old German woodcuts. Elephant waddled like a tall, plump drake. I could have recognized him in the dark simply by touch. His shaggy body was pleasant to grab and pinch, and his woolly head of black hair used to provide a convenient fingerhold when we wrestled in the school corridors, for our friendship dated that far back. He had the gentleness and solicitude of a *yiddische mammeh*, which he probably got from his Jewish mother. He was cultivating a beard and encouraged its growth with caresses; besides that, his trousers were always falling down. Robespierre and I used to say that only the will of God held them up. I looked at the most fifteen, and my childishly round cheeks caused me a great deal of embarrassment.

We represented three kinds of humor: Robespierre's was dry and sarcastic, Elephant's ironic but gentle, and mine noisy. Our humor came in handy when we wanted to abuse the owners of dishonest means of communication. If a car (and there were few in our region) passed us, stirring up clouds of dust, we sang our cursing song after it, wishing it the soonest possible disaster ("She broke down, oh that proud automobile," went the refrain).

During June 1931, however, after our spring exams in law, we were setting off for regions beyond our own and we had to take advantage of an equally dishonest means of locomotion: the train. Our plan was to take the train from Wilno to Prague; buy a used Canadian canoe there (because sporting goods were half as expensive in Czechoslovakia as in Poland), transport the canoe to Lindau in Bavaria on Lake Constance, and from there paddle down the Rhine and its tributaries as near as we could get to Paris, to which we had been lured by the Colonial Exposition. Our love for maps was responsible for this plan. Though surely Vasco da Gama, starting out on his journey to India, knew more about the seas through which he was to sail than we did about our route.

The first Western European-type of small town we happened to explore was Litomyšl in Czechoslovakia, where we were hospitably entertained by a haberdasher whom we met quite by accident. In the western part of Poland I would have encountered similar small towns, but where I was from, in the east, usually such clusters of houses and streets were no more than "trading posts" for the manors and hamlets, where old-fashioned Jews carried on all the trading. Their bad paving, dust, dirt, straw, and horse manure were viewed with contempt by the inhabitants of larger towns or the countryside. My admiration for Czech tidiness and for our friend the haberdasher's standard of living is a good example of the "Western complex" that is found in all people from the East. It does not have the same intensity everywhere, of course. I was to remember Litomyšl again in 1940 on a Russian train as, pretending to be asleep, I overheard two commissars talking about the territory the Soviet Union had acquired as a result of the Molotov-Ribbentrop pact. About even the poorest counties they talked like two Alices in Wonderland. But their wonder was not friendly. There was envy in it and anger.

Prague, the first Western European capital I saw, intoxicated us with its effervescent air of laughter and music, its taverns in the narrow streets near Hradcany Castle, its crowds in Bata tennis shoes, wandering outside the city on Sundays, walking or riding with balls, javelins, discuses. My first modern crowd. Everywhere posters announced *Hikers and Lovers*—I do not know whether it was a movie or a play; in other words, tourism as a sport (unmotorized as yet) was already part of mass culture.

I spent two weeks in Czechoslovakia. Robespierre and Elephant went on to walk across the Bavarian Alps, and I remained to carry through the purchase and transport of the canoe we had tested on the Moldau. In the parks of Prague a familiar hunger assailed me. That feeling can be compared to physical hunger except that it is insatiable. The tree-lined gravel paths grated under my feet; I passed couples kissing; there was music, whispers through the foliage—a carnival of hot, jostling, embracing humanity. I was an outsider, yet at the same time so avid for their reality I was ready to devour them all, whole and entire. Had I been sitting on a bench with my own girl, I would have been part of them, but I would only have deceived my hunger. My timidity drove me into solitude, but it was not only that. My erotic desire went further than any object, my pansexuality included the whole world and, not able to be a god or an ogre who swallows the world, tastes it with his tongue, bites, I could only take it in an embrace with my eyes. Besides, like all hungers, this one disperses, too, at the limit of words.

(I would have been unable to guess then what my next visit to Prague would be like—predestined, waiting within these walls. The passage of time, love affairs, nothing was to slow my chase after that unattainable feast of a pansexual image-devourer. My plane from London was to land at an empty white airport. Snow was falling. It was December, 1950. A huge fellow with the face of a hoodlum, wearing the uniform of the Czech Security Police, opened the door to the cabin and asked for passports. The waiting room was empty. My footsteps echoed back at me. In one corner a handful of people in dark, ill-fitting suits stood whispering among themselves—some sort of delegation waiting for a dignitary. At the front entrance to the waiting room were three snow-covered cars and a boringly deserted square. I took a taxi. The tribe of taxi-drivers has a gift for discerning whom one can or cannot speak freely to; for half an hour my driver spilled out his laments and reproaches against "them." I did not answer. From Prague I took the train to Warsaw, where a portly Robespierre was now a high-ranking Stalinist bureaucrat. Colorless streets in the twilight. From some building high over the city shone a huge red star. Pedestrians walked quickly, with downcast eyes.)

Summer. From the train taking me to Bavaria I jumped out in Pilsen. To kill a superphysical hunger, the best thing is a hike. So I walked, buying only a bit of sausage and bread in the villages. Out of frugality I refused to eat dinner in a restaurant, allowing myself at the most only a glass of beer. The things I remember from that hike: the white highway, the taste of dust in my mouth, the mileage, the farm where I helped with work in the fields and the pleasant country girl—some of her teeth were missing. Then the train again, and a feeling of strangeness as I passed over the German frontier—all around me people were speaking a language I did not understand. Furious with myself, I made an act of will and entered, for the first time in my life, the dining car. There I was greeted by a spectacle for which even now I still try to imagine an explanation. Beside me sat a raw-boned man who looked like an officer in civilian clothes. He ordered a steak and absorbedly tied a napkin under his chin; then, with eyes glued to the steak, he rubbed his hands. He did not really eat the contents on his plate but, rather, engulfed them; chomping and grunting to himself, he immediately ordered a new portion. It was the same thing all over again: the ritual of rubbing his hands, the rapt gazing at the plate in anticipation of its delights, and that same speed. Most surprising of all, his speed did not diminish with each successive steak. Who was he? Where was he coming from? I have no idea why, but it seemed as if he were returning from the trenches, or from a P.O.W. camp of the last war, or that he had spent thirteen years somewhere frozen in a block of ice. I arrived in Lindau at four in the morning. A fine drizzle was coming down, and the sailboats moored at the docks near the station were rocking to and fro, their masts touching because the lake was stormy. As I stood on the shore, getting sprinkled by the waves, I did not see the Alps on the other side. Every form, even the feel of the air, was new and astonished me. What I did next shows that I was a real savage: I adjusted the straps of my knapsack and headed through the empty streets, where a milk horse was clip-clopping along the asphalt, to a "safe place." That meant the forest. For a long time I forced my way through a thicket on the mountainside, to find a place as far off the path as possible. I cut off some branches, prepared a place to sleep under a low-hanging spruce tree, and rolled up in a blanket. In the middle of a foreign country I could now sleep as if I were in my own home.

The meeting with Robespierre and Elephant took place in the afternoon. They related their adventures while soaking their calloused feet. We chose to spend the night in Deutsche Jugend Herberge, and the next morning we began our trip. The plan had to be fulfilled; to wait for the weather to clear would have been beneath our dignity. At the station we picked up our Canadian canoe, carried it to the lake, and here were seized by alarm, but we put on a good face in front of each other. A group of people on the pier were staring at the madmen; no doubt they were making bets: will they get off or not? Wind, rain, waves battering against the cement. We rowed desperately for a quarter of an hour, rising and falling like a cork, almost in the same spot. Finally the port began to grow distant. Elephant, who was sitting in the middle, was chattering from the cold and from the torrents of rain pouring down his collar. Such was our start. Not too charming. But we were not interested in passive pleasures. On the map we had divided our route into segments, and each segment had a date. By evening of that day we were supposed to be in Constance, on the other side of the lake.

For me the narrow streets of the little shoreline towns, the asphalt, the quiet, the cleanliness, the waiter's green apron in the tavern, the children in raincoats, the checkered shopping bag of a *frau* passing by were all enveloped in a dreamy majesty. I actually believed that those who participated in this order and wealth should be spiritually superior to the rest of mankind, which was slightly soiled, impulsive, and easier to understand; they should know a higher kind of love and carry on conversations of a loftier nature. A pile of horse manure in the street provoked the mental exclamation: so even here! . . . It was not easy to bring myself to accept the fact that here, at the foot of the Alps (how romantic!), a wave obeyed the same laws as waves everywhere, and that the oarsman's effort to steer the prow of his boat into it brought the same results.

We passed Friedrichshafen, the base for hydroplanes. Toward evening the lake calmed and we stuck to our paddles as dusk fell, then rowed in darkness. An oncoming ship could have crushed us, but it passed alongside, cabin lights glowing. Our goal was already close. With relief we listened to the faint lapping of water against the boardwalk on the edge of the long gulf beside which the town of Constance lies. Our boots rapped on the paving of the square and we stood in the presence of the history of the Church: before us loomed the gilded wooden structure in which the Council of Constance had been held between the years 1414 and 1418. Here we found a link with Western Europe other than through natural elements, which are the same everywhere. We had only to think back on our schooldays and the pages of the textbook devoted to the Council of Constance, which was important because it condemned the teachings of Jan Hus.

The ensuing days of our trip took us from ecstasy to ecstasy. The lake as it narrowed changed into a taut sheet, almost bulging from the pressure of a current that was already the Rhine. With every thrust of the paddle our canoe fairly leaped into the air. And our physical joy was undiminished by the almost constant downpour. Further on the Rhine carried us so fast that all we had to do was steer. Warnings of rocks or tree stumps passed incessantly from stern to stern. Yet our joy was not only physical. Every bend in the river concealed a secret which, when disclosed, took away our breath. If anywhere, it was here we could have said that we had penetrated into an enchanted land. From the steep slopes branches hung out over the green water, making grottoes which were surely apartments for nymphs. In those branches Delaware warriors from the novels of Fenimore Cooper could have been crouching. Higher up the slopes vineyards rolled by, and castles. Our glances were all the more avid because we glimpsed all that luxuriance only from the corner of our eyes, as we wiped the sweat from our faces. Sometimes, when the river's treacherousness demanded less of our attention, we rested the paddles on our knees, knowing that what was passing before our eyes would not be given us again—ever.

We flew on under wooden covered bridges that seemed like tunnels on posts. A world like the old-fashioned engravings I had loved to look at as a child. Our passion for discovery drove us onward, and we would put off choosing a town to spend the night in if the current favored us. Once it favored us to such an extent that we found ourselves plunging ahead with the speed of an express train. Some vague misgiving whispered in us that we had better start thinking about what this meant. The waterfall at Schaffhausen had for a long time been considered a wonder of nature, and my grandfather, like other tourists, must certainly have visited it—the grandfather who died in the train crash near Baden-Baden and whose album of engravings had been left behind in the house where I was born in Lithuania. Our reflex came just in time, for we stopped within six hundred feet of the abyss that sucked down a white column of foaming water. In Schaffhausen there was no cheap Deutsche Jugend Herberge, so we spent the night beneath the patchwork quilts of the local Salvation Army. The next morning we transported our canoe around the European Niagara in a rented auto.

Disaster struck further on. Near the Swiss town of Koblenz the Rhine has a few miles of rapids, and one needs to be familiar with the current. But even that helps very little, and accidents are frequent. A special police patrol on the German side of the river had the job of fishing out those who capsized. But all that we found out too late. Robespierre was in charge of the map and he guided us along the Rhine, but since he treated obstacles lightly, he looked into it rarely. We had not even tied down our knapsacks. In this seething and frothing water it did not do much good to strain our attention, because our oar strokes remained behind the river's rush. We struck, without knowing it, an underwater rock which tore open a hole the size of a fist in the bottom of our canoe. It may also have been that a patch had simply come loose in our used boat. In any case, I did not understand why the prow of the canoe had lifted so high, was getting higher and higher, and finally why something cast me out like a frog, head first. Everything changed then. I was spitting water, and movement organized itself into two systems of relationship: the heads of my companions moved further and further apart from each other and the canoe's green bottom from them, while the riverbanks flashed backward. That moment of emergence into a cosmos other than the one we were in a second before endowed sensual objects with great clarity. I was a poor swimmer then, and along with a religious effort of will I felt an astonishment that this self here, in the middle of the Rhine, was identical with that self of time past. I reached out for the grasses on the shore, longed for, washed by whirlpools, and while I struggled with the current they grew as gigantic as cathedrals.

After changing into the training suits lent us by the German river police in the town of Waldshut, we drew up a sorry account of our situation. The Germans had pulled our canoe out of the Rhine a few miles lower than the place we took our spill. They had also rescued two knapsacks—but not the one that held our passports and money. Was our journey over? Absolutely not. First of all we had to find our way to the nearest consulate and get new passports; and after that we would see. The pleasant and generous policemen lent us a few marks for the trip to Zurich. Well-rested, and warmed by the coffee our hosts had served us, we crossed into Switzerland on the ferry. There the compartment of a Swiss electric train, similar to the interior of a streetcar, impressed us more than the waterfall at Schaffhausen.

Our story was received somewhat skeptically in the consulate. They promised us an answer within a few days, after they had verified it by telegram. Meanwhile, however, our stomachs were growling. In the park we sat down on a bench and searched our pockets for small change, counting out how much we could buy. There was only enough for the cheapest purchase, cheese; and we divided it up with our jacknife into daily portions, keeping in mind the days ahead. We also made a valuable discovery: in the squares, very tasty water spurted out of the jaws of bronze animal heads. Pewter cups on chains invited the passerby to drink.

The night we spent at the Salvation Army ended badly. At dawn I was awakened by someone scratching me on the foot; a fat policeman stood over me asking for documents. There followed a few hours of arrest until we were freed by a telephone call from the consulate, but we had stopped believing in this tidy country. Our decision, the next day, to leave the city was proof that we did not understand civilization. Along the lake for miles stretched nothing but private villas with their private gardens and private docks; but to us a lake was still a synonym for nature. Weak from hunger, we succumbed to alternate fits of laughter and fury. To shut yourself up in your own house, fence yourself off from others and say, "This is mine," one had to be a pig. In this place we felt very strongly that ownership is pitiless, that it works against those whom it excludes. So we headed for the mountains, and every evening for the next few days we came back to the same forest clearing. Mornings we were bothered by the cold, but through the fog came the sound of cowbells, and we were afraid to light a fire lest we attract a man with a stick and hear shrieks of "That's mine!" Where we were from, no one cared whom the forest belonged to. It was for animals, hunters, and vagabonds.

The consulate finally presented us with new passports and lent us a sum of money to get to the nearest consulate in France, which was the one in Strasbourg, because we did not want to forgo Paris. So we set off again for Waldshut. There we found out, however, that it would take a long time to repair the canoe and even longer to sell it. On the other hand, if we were to pay back our debt to the policemen from the sum in our pockets, we would have nothing left for the rest of the journey. We made a getaway at the crack of dawn, bidding farewell to our canoe, which we left lying outside the police station as security. Our new plan envisaged a crossing on foot through the Black Forest to Basel.

Slopes overgrown with grass to the knees. Black masses of spruce. Climbing, climbing, and then a view of the valley, with its sharp church steeple. We were in excellent humor and our hike went off with jokes and singing. On the afternoon of the third day, after having done around sixty miles of mountain trails, we set foot in Basel.

We began our acquaintance with Western Europe, thus, from her center, for surely the shores of the upper Rhine are that. Ours was an introduction from the side of oaken beams hewn in the Middle Ages; of the Zum Wilde Mann inn, decorated on the outside with painted sculpture; of jutting eaves, of ironsmiths in leather aprons resembling gnomes in a fairy tale.

We were not the only ones who appreciated that taste. Young Germany was then on the move, already perverting its attachment to the past, changing it into a myth of blood and soil. One could have called that era the era of the *Wanderervögel*. We met them everywhere. In twos, threes, on foot or riding bicycles. They would gather in groups in front of a Deutsche Jugend Herberge and sing. One of them always directed. Our efforts to make contact failed. They were overly polite, overly quiet, but at the same time contemptuous and hostile to foreigners. Wrapping ourselves up in blankets in the dormitory, we listened to the breathing of the sleepers. The future was already there, among those beds. Today I sometimes think that Elephant's closest neighbor could have been the Gestapo officer who later tortured him during questioning. Elephant was not cut out to sit in jail as a member of an underground organization, or to bear the twisting of his limbs and beating of the face, or finally, with what scrap of his consciousness remained after he had broken his legs in a suicidal jump from a window, to comprehend with relief that his poor body was dying. No one was cut out for it. But the jovial Elephant was called to a life of gentle humor and friendly chats over wine. His mind was liberal and skeptical, resistant to the temptations of heroism. His death, and the death of others like him, tips the scale of guilt for those contemporaries of ours, the *Wanderervögel,* more heavily than the death of young enthusiasts.

I cannot help but consider those dormitories we slept in as an extract of Germany. For some reason I am convinced that if none of those sleepers was to kill Elephant (a "London agent," according to Europe's temporary rulers), then at least one of them, while sitting in the trenches on the Eastern front, must have heard Robespierre's shrill voice speaking through the Moscow radio.

Elephant, however, as we stood on the bridge near Basel, was pulling up his trousers, which had fallen below his navel. The bridge led to the French border town of Saint-Louis, and we were reading the inscription on a sign. France—our spiritual sister—welcomed us. The sign prohibited Gypsies, Poles, Rumanians, and Bulgarians from entering the country. The scornful glances we exchanged took care of our Western allies. We crossed the bridge.

What was France to us? Was it what appeared as we pressed on the door handle of a bistro in search of a glass of beer? The door opened onto a fragment of a movie. It was like thinking you were entering your own room, but walking into an audience with a Cardinal. A big room. Air dense with heat and smoke.

Workers holding glasses of wine in their hands; girls sitting on their laps, mouths open in song; and lots of eyes turned toward us in surprise. We retreated in a paroxysm of timidity, ashamed of our lack of worldly experience.

But above all we met suffering humanity in France. The train took us through Alsace, along the Vosges, and standing at the window we tried to count the number of dead for every mile of cemetery. Geometrical patterns, formed by rows of small crosses leaving wings of shadow and light behind them, covered the landscape as far as the line where sky meets mountains. We were not indifferent to that view, if only because the Unknown Soldier was then one of the most honored themes in the poetry we read.

Sunburned and ragged, our faces covered with stubble, we did not look too unlike living and suffering humanity, and so they treated us like their own. We found ourselves among a polyglot mass of workers, mainly Poles, roving about in search of jobs. At that time Poles in France had the status that was later to devolve on North Africans—a labor force used for the heaviest jobs and getting the least pay. Eyes winked at us significantly, elbows poked us in the side: "On the bum, eh?" In Strasbourg we had no trouble finding the consulate: steel-helmeted police, supplied with stacks of guns, bivouacked in the neighboring streets. In front of the consulate a crowd of clamoring, gesticulating men swarmed; others sat on the sidewalks or huddled in groups.

Learning comes quickly to the young. In this birthplace of freedom and revolution, it had not taken us long to see the seamy side. Robespierre's nickname came from his high-school days, when he became famous for a highly enthusiastic composition about the Jacobins; in me Kropotkin had left a deep impression. We were sensitive to the smell of misery and brutality. Rubbing shoulders with that tragic mass, we came to an opinion of our own about France, and it was close (though not in every shade) to what I hold now. France's beauty evokes the greatest tenderness. Her symbolic role as the heart of Europe will never allow her to be condemned, for from her every ash a phoenix is born. Here freedom is possible as it is nowhere else, because the pressure of social convention stops at the threshold of the private hearth and no one is compelled to live like his neighbor. Yet the price of this freedom is often indifference to the fate of the silent and the humiliated: live and die as you like. What Robespierre, Elephant, and I said to each other—that France's essence had embodied itself in capitalism or capitalism had embodied itself in France until the two became one—was not stupid. But we did not take into account the weight of past centuries and we were not familiar with those other Western countries where one's neighbor gives a helping hand, takes an interest in you—and in exchange demands conformity.

The worm of our privileged position gnawed at our consciences. For we had pressed through, finally, to the consul; he received us kindly, invited us to dinner, and gave us train fare to Paris. As students, we belonged to his sphere. And of course it was tourism that interested us, not social probing. For me, the interior of the cathedral in Strasbourg, with its gloomy immensity, still surpasses all the cathedrals I was to see later on. In Colmar's narrow streets Robespierre's German came in handy because the passersby did not understand French when we asked directions. Bursting with our impressions from Alsace, we boarded the train and immediately fell asleep on the hard benches in third class.

It was a summer morning. Four or five o'clock. Gray-pink, iridescent air like the enamel inside a shell. We inhaled Paris with open nostrils, cutting across it on foot, diagonally from the north toward the Seine. The moist flowers, the vegetables, the coffee, the damp pavement, the mingling odors of night and day. Where the wide sidewalks changed into a market place, we took pleasure in submerging ourselves in the human stream, its color, movement, gestures, and glances. We lost count of the streets, we forgot about our own existence, our bodies were simply instruments registering impressions; the promise was infinite, it was the promise of life. On the deserted Place de la Concorde, the sight of the pearl-gray expanse between the Arc de Triomphe and the trees in the park made us want to draw deep breathes. Branches of trees emerged like huge feathers from the fog. There was not a soul in the Tuileries except for one pair on a stone bench. She was bending her head back under his kiss. He had a flower in his buttonhole. Further on, through the mist, the river already shone in the sun. We walked over the Pont des Arts toward the Boulevard Saint-Michel, without bringing to those names anything other than what we ourselves saw there; and that was enough.

Today, the most amazing thing about Paris for me is that it still exists. Man's fleetingness seen against a background of unchanging nature affords an inexhaustible subject for meditation; but if the background is created by man himself, the contrast is all the more intense. That whole sea of human eyes (vainly we mask a desire that is overwhelming and orgiastic with some inadequate word, vainly we isolate ourselves with trifles from something more profound than ourselves) floods Parisian architecture year after year: certain eyes and faces perish and die, but the flood never lets up. Those eyes, whose secret I tried then to guess, have been surrounded by wrinkles, they have lost their glow, but the city is the same, and today I can walk along a street in Paris as avid as ever for something more than just an amorous adventure. At the same time, that everrenewed contact between old stones and successive generations awakens an image in me, I do not know why, of kings sleeping amid a tangle of stone lilies, like dried-up insects in winter.

We trod the sidewalks of the Boulevard Saint-Michel, licked the cool fountain spray from our lips in the Luxembourg Gardens, where children were floating little sailboats and prodding them with long sticks. The children are here today too: the same, bewitched into immortal elves, or others?

Our emotions in Paris cannot be presented simply as youthful rapture. An ambition to reach a heart that seems difficult to get at sometimes turns into love; it is similar with Eastern Eu-

ropeans. Their snobbery seasons their experience of this storied
city. They have a sense of personal achievement: "I, Stash or
Jack, have finally made it!" they say to themselves, and tap their
foot on the sidewalk to make sure they are not dreaming. Besides, they are burdened with a longing for a homeland other
than the one assigned to them from birth. Poland weighed on
us. To live there was like walking on a sheet of ice underneath
which grimaced a million deformed, nightmarish faces. The lack
of a uniform standard made it impossible to take a man "as he
is"—the forefront of the picture was always dominated by his
status: white-collar, peasant, Jew. And it was not the politics
conducted during our childhood that bred this state of affairs,
but whole centuries. Whether such a desire to escape from an
insoluble problem is good or bad I do not judge here; I only
declare that it exists and that spasmodic patriotism is sometimes
a compensation for an inner betrayal. (Are Poles not similar in
this to certain homosexuals who, frightened of their abnormality,
impose marital fidelity on themselves?)

Our low condition—we lived in the "Palais du Peuple" on
the Rue Glacière—did not spoil our delight. That sonorous name
designated the Salvation Army shelter. Lodgers were let into
the dormitories only in the evening. Each received a sort of
cabin—the beds were partitioned off from each other by a
screen. On a table near the bed was a Bible. Early in the morning
the whole company was driven downstairs for breakfast, which
could be had for a few cents. In the evening a free supper
was obtainable in return for polite singing of the psalms, and
sometimes we waited patiently through the evening service. A
skinny carrot-top blew the trumpet while a giant Negro pounded
a drum in time with the pious crowing of bums from various
countries, who fidgeted impatiently, sniffing the odors from the
kitchen.

At the Colonial Exposition, the French Empire displayed its
splendors: pavilions in Moroccan style, Madagascan and Indo-
Chinese huts (inside, an imported family went through the
motions of their daily routine for the tourists). That whole ex-

hibit was actually outrageous, as if it had been an extension of the Vincennes Zoological Gardens, in which it was held. After one tired of looking at black, brown, or yellow people in their cages, one went to look at the monkeys, the lions, and the giraffes. That, of course, did not bother the organizers of the exposition; perhaps they even chose the place for the very reason that the natives, the wild animals, and the palms went well together, just as they did on postage stamps. And we, too, childish and eager for the exotic, considered it more or less normal: if there are colonies, then it cannot be otherwise. Yet something rankled within us: petty bourgeois, red in the face after soaking up their wine, unemployed Polish vagrants in the dives near Saint-Paul, the smell of poverty in the "Palais du Peuple," the incredible ugliness of family gravestones in Père Lachaise cemetery, fit for the heroes of Flaubert. Was this a world for which we were not yet grown up enough, or did we have the right to oppose it with our otherness?

They acquired their colonial empire late, while we in the East knelt in admiration before their culture, the beauty of their books, the excellence of their painting. But who were these people here, who thought in the highest spiritual registers? While military expeditions mowed down the colored peoples, acquired countries and ports, these people here in Paris enjoyed freedom by refusing to identify with their own government, or even nation, although they, even the poor, simultaneously profited from all this power and wealth. All that collective wealth appeared to them as a natural gift. They were proving the rule: let not thy left hand know what thy right hand doeth. But their lofty words received wings, thanks to the very down-to-earth efforts of their generals, prefects, and merchants. Their revolt against the bourgeoisie concealed a secret respect for order, and they would have quaked had someone told them that if they carried their rebellion to its conclusion, it would mean no more little bakeries, no more package-goods stores or bistros with their cats dozing in the sun behind the windowpane. Theirs was always a secure revolt because their bitterness and their nihilism rested on the tacit understanding that thought and action were measured by different standards: thought, even the most violent, did not offend custom. Any other nation, had it permitted itself such a dose of poison, would have long ago ceased to exist; for France it was healthy. Only when carried to different soil did her slogans, books, and programs reveal their destructive force, among people who took the printed word literally.

But that silent understanding—which allowed them to revolt, not knowing and yet knowing that monuments would be erected to them and that their works would find a place in libraries and museums built with money squeezed from the toil of variously colored peoples—brought extraordinary results and, justly, they were admired by the whole world. An observer of this situation might have some doubts about the permanent stance of the initiates at the top of the social pyramid. If they glanced down and became infected with the suffering of the millions below, the responsibility would kill them, their art would die. If they wanted to know nothing, they would have been hypocrites, and their art, protected by an illusory purity, would have been hypocritical in its very form, and therefore ephemeral. But they were neither oppressed with despair nor hypocrites; they drew a line beyond which sound, color, or word should not go. They knew the secret of balance—a disturbing secret, to tell the truth—and perhaps artists and philosophers are not too praiseworthy if their knowledge of the fate of the humiliated and the disinherited must always remain "within bounds."

On our walks about the city we were conscious that this was the capital of a great power and our every sensation was colored by that awareness. When I arrived in Paris after the Second World War, it seemed small to me, as if the rush of history had pushed it aside: an Alexandrian town, drawing its reason for existence from the preservation of its treasures, preparing for its new function of a city-monument. A Soviet diplomat, assuming my solidarity as a Slav, said to me then: "We'll teach them to work!" His threatening tone, the triumph, the revenge in his voice, his Russian self-inebriation ("Europe is ours") offended me, who understood more of the entangled, never straight paths of civilization than he. He felt superior to them because he knew the depths of hells, while Paris had been barely touched by the wing of every cyclone—a fact that made me angry, too, although in a different way. Standing with my glass of vodka at receptions in the Soviet Embassy, I watched how Leftist luminaries of French literature and art minced around that diplomat, seizing upon his every word, nodding approval—polite little boys in front of their teacher. The magic unguent of power must have rubbed off upon me, too, a new arrival from the East, with my broad non-Western face, but I was ashamed of it.

A Russian could treat them only with contempt, because France, discreet and hidden, was inaccessible to him. I, on the other hand, penetrated her gradually, beginning with that summer in 1931. It may be that my training began with the letter I wrote to Oscar Miłosz whom up to then I knew only through correspondence. He answered, fixing a day and advising me to buy myself a suit. In the letter a money order was enclosed. I exchanged my short pants and khaki shirt for a cheap suit from the Samaritaine department store, and on the appointed day boarded the train for Fontainebleau. I was nervous because it was a great event.

In the Hotel de l'Aigle Noir, I guessed from the bowing of the staff that I was visiting a person who was highly esteemed there. I knocked, and for a long time I stood on the threshold, unconscious of where I was, uncertain whether I had not perhaps mistaken the number. His room was full of chattering birds and the flapping of bright wings. Lots of cages with African birds, the daylight coming and going on the perches, a breeze from the garden rippling the curtains.

He had thick, arched eyebrows, a high forehead, graying, rumpled hair—good hair for plowing one's fingers through. Tall, slightly bent, he seemed to take up more space than his body. His masterful air inspired respect and he himself showed respect to others; the servants valued most of all, perhaps, his attentiveness, the gift that renders one aware of the presence of another man. It was apparent who he was from the way he held his head, and from his eyes, which seemed to draw a circle about him so that the rest of his person remained in the background. His eyelids, like those of a tired bird of prey, disclosed hot black lava or, rather, smoldering coals; there was an aura of bridled violence and pride about him, an aura of the desert, which suggested an image from the pages of the Bible. "*Aimer les hommes d'un vieil amour usé par la pitié, la colère et la solitude*"*—those were words from a poem of his. He knew the language of birds, and when he talked to them as we walked along the avenues of the park at Fontainebleau, they flew from all over to sit on his outstretched hand.

He did not have a foreign accent when he spoke Polish. Our conversation began with his questions about family affairs. I noticed a signet ring on his finger, and said that I did not wear a signet because it would have gone against my democratic convictions. (In Poland, that mania was characteristic of people I despised.) "That's bad. You should remember that you are a *seigneur de Labunava.*" I fell silent, not knowing whether I had run up against a confirmed stuffiness or whether in the West one could freely admit one's origins in public without exposing oneself to ridicule. Soon I understood that by emphasizing his aristocratic origins (his biographers exaggerate this, but he himself was the instigator), he was looking for a way of separating himself from the "*temps de laideur ricanante.*"† He guarded his solitude and did not recognize many of the values generally accepted in his epoch.

Kind to my ignorance, he listened to my remarks about France. He was not an observer. He loved his adopted country in every detail, in its past, in the tissue of its daily life. "Careful, careful. As long as you must give out opinions on France, remember [we were walking along the park fence on the

---

* To love people with an old love used by pity, loneliness, and anger. (Tr.)
† "Age of jeering ugliness." (Tr.)

streetside where men in blue denims were repairing the gas pipes] that in every French worker like those there lives two thousand years of civilization." Then he lapsed into one of his furies, to which I later became accustomed: *"Vous, les Slaves, vous êtes des fainéants! Fainéants!"*‡ I remembered that exclamation well, long after his death, as I listened to the deep Russian voice saying: "We'll teach them to work!" Who was right? Does virtue express itself in the patient shaping of the landscape over the centuries, in the bustling about the vineyards, in the carving of oaken Louis XIII and Louis XV wardrobes, in the slow, rhythmic work of a skeptical and experienced people who lighten the strain of their tasks with pauses, a chat, a glass of wine—or is it expressed by sudden thrusts of will capable of raising a St. Petersburg out of the swamps on the Neva, and of releasing interplanetary rockets from the empty steppes? Men who understand their place in the world differently cannot be measured by a common standard.

‡ "You Slavs, you are idlers! Idlers!" (Tr.)

The Young Man and the Mysteries

◆

THE LITHUANIAN LEGATION was on the Place Malesherbes. I went there now and then during the winter of 1934–35, for I had lived up to my promise of returning to Paris. As is usual in poor countries, this had been possible only thanks to a state scholarship. To win it I had to prove that I was a serious student; that is, I had to finish my studies at the university, even though the scholarship was not in law but in literature. I preferred not to tell anyone about my visits to the Place Malesherbes. I considered them a very private affair, and besides prudence advised it: diplomatic relations did not exist between Poland and Lithuania, and I could have easily been labelled a "traitor," that epithet Poles are so ready to confer. It would not have helped much to appeal to reason by pointing out that both Klimas, the Lithuanian legate, and I were born in the same country, the same community even, no more than a mile away from each other. The Legation—quiet, peaceful, and democratic—was, despite the different language spoken there, somehow more pleasant than the Polish Embassy, where, even as you entered the lobby, your nostrils were assailed by an odor of contempt for anyone deprived of social prestige. To tell the truth, I hated the Embassy. It was peopled by magnificent specimens of titled fools, ingratiating to foreigners but impolite, even downright boorish, to their own citizens. Among those fools I counted the cultural attaché, a poet who was pleased to invite me a few times to his elegant apartment for breakfast, although unfortunately we had nothing to talk about. For these people diplomacy came to nothing more than snobbery, "connections" (all of them useless), and a knowledge of gastronomy. When juxtaposed with the crowds of Polish unemployed roaming about Paris, it was not a pleasant sight. My visits, however, had nothing political about them. I used to meet Oscar Miłosz there. He had already disengaged himself from his more responsible posts, which took up too much time, and contented himself with a few hours of work per day and the rank of minister. Summers he spent in Fontainebleau. On the table in his room stood a row of books in various languages and dictionaries, and on the floor lay heaps of the newest volumes of poetry, sent to him with dedications by faithful poets. He permitted me to rummage in those heaps and take what I wanted—with a few exceptions; for example, the works of Joe Bousquet had always to be returned. It was from my relative that I first heard about the heroic, martyred life of Joe Bousquet, one of the most fascinating figures in the French literary world.

For breakfast Oscar Miłosz usually took me to Poccardi's, an Italian restaurant. Our conversations there brought a new element, or dimension, to my thinking, and the mixture was a heady one. Although the gaps in my knowledge and the barbarian chaos in my mind were gigantic, my openness and the need to adore were still greater. Like all young poets, I believed that there were secret places in contemporary art, that there was a thread which would lead one to the heart of the labyrinth. Because of this belief I subjected myself to many ascetic tortures, like a man who, instead of treading on the ground, balances uncertainly on a tightrope. Now all those forced measures suddenly seemed absurd. Modern poetry, according to my kinsman, bore the stigma of an age of decadence and should not be taken too seriously: what was there to that clever weaving of words with which an author, seated in front of his window, tried to capture his scattered sensual impressions? There was nothing daring in that little game of parody, as the perspective of past centuries showed: after all, the only true source of poetry—divine inspiration—manifested itself rarely enough. The matchless Bible. Dante. Faust. And, curiously enough, Byron, whom Oscar Miłosz thought underestimated. He sympathized with Edgar Allan Poe, but regarded him as an example of blasphemous metaphysics. If literature in general found little grace in his eyes, that does not mean he discouraged me from it. On the contrary, he stressed continual exercise ("An idle pen rusts like a sword," he wrote me later on in one of his letters), but warned me that nothing is accomplished by attaching too much weight to questions of form. I would never have dared to treat him as a master to whom one brings one's works for criticism. My humility and my awareness of the great distance between us can be set down to my credit; for I saw my scribblings as part of that heap on the floor which he swept into the corner of the room with his foot. At the same time I realized that I could not imitate him—both the language and the period that lay before me imposed different laws. I was given the honor, however, of being translated by him from the Polish. He published one of my poems in the distinguished review *Cahiers du Sud*.

I could also thank him for bringing the whole epoch into my perspective. For young people, whatever happened ten years ago is already prehistory. But as I listened to his reminiscences, the whole pre-First-World-War era of literary Paris came alive. He even imparted, though seldom, certain details of his gloomy family life; they explain much of that feeling of being orphaned, that nostalgia of a lonely child, which is so visible in his works. "And madness and cold roved aimlessly through the house." His father's last years: paranoia, hair to the waist, sitting for whole days in the cellar with a sharpened axe on his lap. He spoke about his mother without indulgence: "She pursued me everywhere with that sweet Jewish love of hers. It was unbearable." It appears that he was not good to her. I do not know why, but I associated his father's long hair with the gray, womanish hair of Raymond Duncan, whom we once visited in his "Academy" on the Rue de Seine. For some reason it made his fleshy red face look a bit immodest above his Greek chlamys. As we were returning from that visit, my relative told me about Raymond's sister, Isadora Duncan, the dancer, and her friend, the poet Sergei Yesenin. Oscar recalled the drunken exhibitions in Paris of this Russian hooligan (as he called him) with evident horror. Although he felt a kind of disgust for Russians, he advised me to watch their Five-Year Plan very carefully.

I used to wonder if he lived a completely solitary life. He was fifty-seven. I knew that "elective affinities" and the friendship of women played a large role in his past, and that the recurrence of the Don Juan motif in his work was not accidental—Don Juan understood as emotional insatiability opening the door to a higher state, to *amore sacro*. Later, in various countries, even in America, I was to meet elderly women who still preserved their attachment to him. Here, he had *la baronne*, quiet-voiced and protective. I remember her parasol: the three of us are walking along the gravel footpaths in the Parc Monceau. Oscar, sensing my puppylike curiosity, said to me later: "She is a widow. She thinks it would be a good thing if I married her. But you know, it would be like putting on somebody else's boots."

He had already stopped writing poetry then, or at least what one is accustomed to calling poetry. An alchemist, an exegete of the Bible, he had set himself other tasks. Yet he was not completely indifferent to literary fame; he was certain it would come to him eventually. Unknown outside of narrow coteries, appreciated only by a select minority such as Francis de Miomandre, Jean Cassou, Armand Godoy, Edmond Jaloux, or the *Cahiers du Sud* group, he would jubilantly show me recent press clippings about himself from France, Belgium, or Latin America. But he took offense if anyone compared him to Claudel, deceived by the outer similarity of their long, Biblical phrasing. Despite his Catholicism, Oscar wanted nothing to do with Claudel, as if he scorned the Frenchman's easy success. He knew that his own writings had to wait for a new public sensibility to be born out of those ferments that bring new inner worlds to light by changing our angle of vision. The most accessible of his works was his mystery play, *Miguel Mañara*. Performed by the Théâtre du Vieux-Colombier around the time of the First World War, it had been staged since then only rarely. Rather, it was read at closed gatherings by members of the audience who divided the roles among themselves: one of the Benedictine monasteries in Belgium and a small group in Poland did this. The Polish translation of *Miguel Mañara* appeared in 1919. The first doctoral thesis about Oscar Miłosz's poetry was written in Lithuania—his chosen fatherland.

Both the earthly weaknesses and the greatness, of which I was well aware, and the marks of madness (or so I thought) in some of his pronouncements, plunged me into reflection, as a result of which the outlines of new continents emerged. It was not, however, the best apprenticeship for working with the Polish literary milieu; rather, I was kept from being part of that milieu by my intuition that its problems were unreal. For a long time that intuition was to lie in the depths of my being, unable to rise to the surface, to be expressed in words. So a sort of gap developed in my relations with my literary colleagues. I bore within me a "reserve zone" that was foreign to them, and the paths I chose later on almost always took them by surprise.

But most important of all, I saw before my eyes a man strongly convinced that it was already *very late*. My relative understood the history of mankind in categories of decline and punishment—punishment served to close a cycle. From observing the *"temps de laideur ricanante"* and from his decoding of hidden prophecies, this heir of the Rosicrucians learned that the cycle was closing and that we were entering the Apocalypse of St. John. He foretold the outbreak of war for the near future. It would be the war of the Red Horse and it would begin in Poland, or, to be exact, in the Corridor where the Poles had built the port of Gdynia. But after that . . . ?

I should explain how I listened to his prophecies. My intelligence remained disturbingly disproportionate to my development as a man, to my formation of character. I was like a child, in love with myself yet enough aware so that my conscience bothered me incessantly. Despair over my monstrous egoism—which I did not want to renounce—reached extremes of tension in Paris. It was not only adolescent *Weltschmerz.* My sins, after all, were not imagined. Who knows if it was not precisely this impossibility of bringing order to my personal problems that caused me to nourish myself so passionately for several years on catastrophic visions, borrowing from the Marxists little more than their belief in a spasm of history? The impending annihilation was sweet: it would resolve everything; individual destiny lost its significance, all would become equal.

So my relative's predictions fell on fertile ground. I was thrown into a near trance by my dread of and intoxication with the inevitable disaster, and this made me forget my private despair. True, I gained a picture of future events that went beyond the current standards and conceptions of my day. More than once, no doubt, a flicker of disbelief crossed my face because he would break off and ask, "You think I'm a lunatic, don't you?" That would happen, for instance, when he spoke about America. America was completely beyond the scope of my thoughts, as it was for most of my contemporaries; so when I heard that America was the "beast coming up out of the sea," from the Apocalypse of St. John, I mentally pinched myself to recover a feeling of reality. Atomic weapons and intercontinental missiles were equally unthinkable then, just as cannons and tanks had been for the ancient Greeks. What was the meaning of this "universal conflagration" which, according to him, was supposed to begin somewhere around the year 1944? What was the meaning of the statement that "America will be destroyed by fire, England by fire and water, and Russia by a falling piece of the moon?" After that, an era of reborn humanity was to follow, the reconciliation of religion and science and the triumph of one universal Church.

A billiard ball rolls in one direction; it strikes another and changes course. My initial movement in matters of Catholicism, pro and con, was determined by my high school and by my loathing for religion as a national institution. After conversing with Oscar Miłosz and reading his two metaphysical tracts, I veered off diagonally from my preceding course. To be sure, the tracts (or rather poems)—*Ars Magna* and *Les Arcanes*— were very difficult for me, and on top of this they aroused mixed feelings, sometimes even strong hostility. But they were to remain with me permanently as, little by little, I uncovered their meaning. These works are about how the former pupil of the Lycée Janson-de-Sailly liberated himself from the mechanistic outlook drilled into France's youth in her secular schools. Modern man's bitterness and sorrow, already so apparent in Byron, has only one source: the mind's image of matter as infinite, as subject to time without end and without beginning, which provokes a cosmic terror before a universe that exists *nowhere*. Hence the question he constantly asks of himself, waking and sleeping: *Where is space?* The Newtonian universe is a prison. In 1916 Oscar Miłosz, without knowing the works of Einstein, experienced an illumination: he discovered for his own use, through intuition, not mathematically, a theory of relativity. If space is the relation of one movement to another, it can no longer be thought of as "its own receptacle and that of other things." "*We recognize it as only one element of a three-part concept of movement, which includes space, time and matter.*" "The seeing man perceives space through the movement of light; the blind man through the movement of his hand, or of another part of his body, or of his whole body; both the blind man and the seeing person, as well as a sightless paralytic, perceive space through the idea of movement, an idea so fundamental that it is the starting point for the most abstract operations; in short, *a spiritual principle inseparably connected with the circulation of our blood itself.*" "By replacing the erroneous notion of space as a preexisting receptacle with an image of it as a dynamic simultaneity of the three elements of our initial perception, we see that space changes into the totality of matter synonymous with energy, and the idea of energy is indivisible from the idea of time. *Space, regardless of whether or not the ether exists, becomes a solid, with time as one of its dimensions; everything thus is a simple product, the spontaneous work of movement.*"

Further he wrote: "The necessity for reconciling the priority of movement with dynamic simultaneity requires our assent to the idea of a primary movement, a movement of incorporeal light, which precedes the physical light creating the universe; the conception is that of the medieval philosophical schools of Chartres and Oxford. This incorporeal light has absolutely nothing to do with any odic theory." It is not my task here to present his theological views (for him, that moment of intuition had meant a return to religion). The axis of these views is the certainty that Revelation carried in embryo all the discoveries of modern physics.

From that time on he lived as a practicing Catholic and tended to comply in everything with his confessor's advice. He had difficulty, however, with certain points of doctrine, and I suppose he suffered because of the Vatican's cold reception of his metaphysical glosses. The Church, it is well known, treats the whole Pythagorean-hermetic tradition with distrust, although it has endured in her womb with stubborn persistence, giving rise to great monuments of poetry, including Dante's. The initiated ordinarily have a powerful sense of their exceptional mission and lay themselves open to accusations of pride. But Oscar Miłosz, when describing his mystical experiences, had no illusions; he knew that his works were not for his contemporaries and that he, for whom the paternoster contained all of philosophy, had to be suspected of wanting to remove the curtain of dogma.

I did not consider myself a Catholic because that word had such a definite political coloring in Poland. Besides, it would have been false if applied to me, considering my untamed biological individualism. Nonetheless, I had brought from high school a knowledge of the abysses which, after all, would have to be fathomed sometime, and they again began to tempt me. Owing to this, and also to the delicate persuasion of my relative, I attended lectures on Thomist philosophy for a while at the Institut Catholique on the Rue d'Assas. They were held early in the morning, and I always arrived with lips burned from hurriedly swallowed coffee and thoughts full of the faces I had seen riding to work on the Métro. The audience in the lecture hall consisted mostly of milky-skinned girls with thick braids. The lecturer, Father Lallement, took a mathematical delight in St. Thomas's system, and as he drew circles and ellipses on the board, the chalk in his fingers squeaked precisely. The full lips of his pointer's face were pursed, as if he were eating something bitter but tasty.

Along with all of this, my opinion of Paris was undermined by Levallois-Perret, where the lodging house, or, rather, camp, for unemployed Poles was located. The streets that led to it were a sterile hell of industrial civilization, a place of sojourn for souls who were born into degradation and who would die in degradation. The very thought of immortality was an outrage there. In this camp (high fence, narrow gate, like the doors of an armored train) one of my colleagues worked as both manager and clerk in one person, earning the merest pittance of a salary. The real power was in the hands of a stocky ex-sergeant of the Foreign Legion, an expert at parrying knife thrusts and felling insubordinates with his fist. The inmates were thrown out of the camp in the morning. Ahead of them stretched a long, empty day which they filled digging in garbage cans, begging, or stealing; sometimes they made a few francs carrying loads. One way or another they got money for wine—indispensable when you have nothing but despair and an empty stomach. They came back drunk every evening, and in the brawls that followed, the sergeant from the Foreign Legion demonstrated his prowess.

A few Métro stops away: the luxury of the Champs-Elysées. For all I cared, that whole world could have fallen into the chastising fires, and I consoled myself that it certainly would fall. If it had been possible to drag those pomaded females from their limousines, kick them in the bottom and make them crawl on all fours, I could have taken revenge for those in the camp (or maybe for myself under a mask of justice). The setting up of machine guns aimed at the Café de la Paix I also would not have looked upon as an immoral act. But my emotional propensity for revolutionary solutions was never clothed in any decisive form, although it turned vehemently against Rightist totalitarians. I dreamed, for example, about a Leftist dictatorship minus the doctrine, or even about a theocratic Communism like the state organized by the Jesuits in Paraguay in the seventeenth century.

My acquaintance with Günther disturbed me. In spite of the mutual distrust between us, there was a disquieting affinity. Günther, a young Nazi, used to recite his poems to me. They celebrated the age of chivalry, sacrifices and blood, and they had the sound of clanking swords. I met him at the hotel near Montagne Sainte-Geneviève, where I had moved from the vermin-infested Polish student hostel in the Batignolles district. Günther and my friend, a resident of the same hotel and a student at the Sorbonne, were drawn together by common homosexual tastes. Although I did not share these, they did not bother me; I was even amused by my neighbor's constant chasing after Negroes who would then take his watch and money. The Hotel Laplace was distinguished by its permissiveness: one could cook on any sort of burners there and dry laundry in the windows. Its residents could yell raucously at each other in their unique slang—the place was inhabited mainly by Polish Jews studying medicine. It stood on the corner of a medieval street scheduled to be razed soon because the houses threatened collapse. Twenty years have gone by, however, and to this day nothing has changed. "Soon," in countries with a long past, is not measured by the calendar.

In an attempt to subdue my inner chaos, I set up a fixed routine for myself. I walked to my lectures at the Alliance Française (where final exams for the Cours Supérieur awaited

me in the spring) through the Luxembourg Gardens, and twice
a week I went swimming at the Piscine Pontoise, near the
hotel. I liked the pounding of the trampoline, the green water
in the warm sun which came through the glass roof. If the
Congress for the Defense of Culture, in the spring of 1935,
had been held in another district, my reluctance to break this
daily routine would have won out, but it was only a five-
minute walk to the hall of the Mutalité, and so there was no
excuse for not going. I was not a bit pleased when, at the
last moment, Günther horned in on my plans and said he was
going, too, because he was very curious. I felt uncomfortable
sitting next to him in the gallery; after all, I had written poems
announcing Germany as the fuse of tomorrow's historical bomb.
The speeches from the platform accused him, Günther. Curiously enough, when André Gide, Aldous Huxley, and the Soviet
writers uttered their lofty sentences about freedom, peace, respect for man, and so on, and when the hall joined with them
in a transport of pacificist enthusiasm, a wave of nausea swept
over me. Günther hid an ugly leer behind his hand. His gesture
reminded me of those other meetings I had attended in Poland
with my Marxist colleagues and our scoffing at the speakers'
old-maidish phraseology. Here, too, the toothless whinings, the
smoke screen of "declarations" and "resolutions" aroused my
anger and drove me into solidarity with Günther. In the final
analysis, Günther's anger was the same: anger at weakness
adorned with words. He preferred what he thought was more
honest: naked violence.

Above all, that heavyset blond boy was imbued with Greece
as it had been conceived by nineteenth-century German professors and with Hölderlin's nostalgia; he did not foresee what
the alleged "purity" of violence really meant. Günther did not
have the makings of a fanatic. He often ate dinner with Werner,
an emigrant from Austria and a doubtful "Aryan." His interest
in Poles he justified by invoking the sacred tradition of friendship between Stefan George and Wacław Rolicz-Lieder. Doubtless that absorption with the imaginary contributed to his early

disillusionment. As I heard later on, he soon fell into disfavor with the authorities in his country, as a heretic.

If I had doubted that the time was at hand for the accomplishing of what had to be accomplished, I would have stifled the voice within me that confirmed the prophecy. But the day of the soccer match between France and Germany—it took place just after the annexation of the Saar—I came home certain. German tourists, transported to the game by buses, filled one-third of the grandstands. Was this sport or disguised warfare? The disciplined yells and lifting of banners with the swastika— the aura in itself was so obvious, it would have been hard to remain indifferent.

I was sharply attuned to a universal catastrophe, which was not just a fear of war. At night I used to dream a fatal ray was pursuing me and that when I reached the safe shore it finally pierced me through. The intensity of that feeling was to weaken gradually over the years, and I set about forgetting it: not too praiseworthy a remedy, but a common one and due to impotence, either real or imagined. Like the natural end of individual life, the naked fact had to be veiled over by a multitude of minute bustlings and passions that were supposedly important.

I must have struck those whom I knew in Paris as over-preoccupied and absentminded. And it was true; I had such an extreme receptivity to external stimuli that every detail engraved itself in my memory with all its color and solidity; at the same time, like a lunatic, I was a passive instrument of another power that operated from somewhere inside, that was at once me and not me. There was nothing to do but submit. It transformed all my experiences into magic spells that were much too strong to be broken by putting them on paper. I wrote little, but I passed whole weeks in the power of one rhythmic phrase, which did not really leave much room for conscious aims—either good or evil. I acted like a medium at a spiritualist séance. Perhaps my passivity partly justifies my not noticing other people. To seize me, to force me to be fully present, would have been as hard as holding a water snake in one's hand. Afterward, of course, I was tormented by regret.

Art as a storehouse of impressions did not interest me as much as I snobbishly let on to others. The mornings, days, and evenings of a human community were quite enough. Certain paintings that I saw in the Louvre, though, were to imprint themselves more strongly than I could have supposed: the eye encounters shape and color, the mind is taken up with something else, but the object we have seen becomes an inseparable part of us. Likewise, I only pretended that I listened to music. At the Châtelet Theater, my attention was completely absorbed by the stage, which I looked down upon from my seat in the top row as into a well. Down there at the bottom a strange ritual was being enacted, and sound had value only insofar as it set two fields of bows in motion, like wheat bent in the wind.

I tended to avoid theatrical performances. In the first place, they would have ruined my budget; in the second, I was bored by the gestures and talk enclosed in a three-sided box of the stage. I liked various kinds of masques and interludes, things on the borderline between theater and ballet. One production made a really powerful impact on me, thanks to Ludmila Pitoëff, who was probably the greatest actress of the day. In Pirandello's *Tonight We Improvise*, Ludmila Pitoëff changed from a young girl into an old woman within a quarter of an hour. She sat on her chair in front of the footlights, and her companions, the goddesses of time, applied wrinkles to her face, erased the rouge from her lips, and scattered gray in her hair. Never before had the horror and pity of tragedy so deeply penetrated to me. My own regular subject of contemplation was the same: the devastating process of change—in individuals, in countries, and in systems. Perhaps all poetry is simply this.

One detail concerning the paintings of Van Gogh: when I stood before them for the first time (I was not familiar with his biography), a current of revulsion, as at something indecent, ran through me. "A madman painted that; you have *no right* to paint like that." It would be easy to put down my inner shriek as a symptom of petty-bourgeois prejudice. However, considering that I was well acquainted with Impressionism and Cubism, that I knew a great deal about the theory of modern art, I would say there was something more to it. I was fanatical about all works of the mind, to which I said a passionate yes or no. Not that I opposed certain schools or trends, but within the same school or trend I saw some works as "saved," others as "lost." It depended on something within the work, order or lack of order, something I sensed, and I could have been very menacing, had I been given the power, as an exterminator of "degenerate art"—though I would have understood it in my own way, which had nothing to do with the primitive views of politicians. But it was too difficult then to express my likes and dislikes aloud; I would have been unable to define them clearly. So I accepted the convention that whatever is modern is very good, and my moment of fury at Van Gogh remained a private and shameful secret.

For people from other large cities, Paris is not the same thing as it is for a young man raised in the mountains of Peru or, like myself, in the provinces. If Wilno seemed exotic to the inhabitants of Warsaw, I must have preserved some of that exoticism in myself. The collision of two historical phases and two sets of behavior within me deepened my inner split, but the injection I received was not such a bad thing: while learning the gestures and habits of Westerners I recognized that they were hollow, as if eaten by termites, and would soon collapse. Their big names, which Eastern Europe also uttered with a pious sigh, Oscar Miłosz dismissed with one snap of his fingers, and I see now that he was correct. The whole Eastern European attitude toward "centers of culture" is false; it comes from timidity. They imitate instead of opposing; they reflect instead of being themselves. Through his very existence, my relative worked a cure in me, and fortified my contempt for the shrines of the vanguard back home, where ears strained to catch the latest novelties from Paris. My contempt, however, did not dispel all my timidity. And for tactical reasons, too, it was not advisable to show it. Where else, if not in those small nurseries, where the disciples of André Gide, Léger, the Surrealists, Freud, and Marx grew up together, could I have found allies?

I did not want to return to the sad landscapes, the melancholy skies with their heavy clouds, the shrieking crows. But my scholarship was up; there was no more work to do, and I needed work not only to eat but also to give my writing a rest, not to force my hand. The year in Paris had been more of an anticipation than an accomplishment. True, a wish to escape the destiny hanging over my country came over me from time to time—all one could do there was count the grains of sand sifting through the hourglass—but I drove it off without too much trouble. In fact, that sense of future catastrophe made of my loneliness too heavy a burden and even spurred me to return to familiar people and places.

The last time I saw Oscar Milosz he was standing on the steps of the Opéra Métro station, the day before my departure. A gentle hawk, or, rather, swallow—because a swallow viewed close up has a rapacious, somewhat uncanny look like a creature from another element: immobile, a potentiality, only, of flight. Shaking hands in farewell, I asked: "Who will survive this war, if, as you say, it will begin in 1939 and last five years?" "You will survive." Running downstairs, I turned around once more; then, with the image of his narrow silhouette against the sky imprinted in my memory, I presented my ticket to be punched. Notice of his sudden death was to reach me in spring of the year 1939. Not without reason, it turned out, had I called that year, as the snow was melting, "the last."

I see, however, that I have not said what I wanted to say about this man, and that actually I have wriggled out of my task. Doubtless my inner resistance is too strong, and it would take a far deeper confession to overcome it, which is not always indicated. Through his love for sparrows in the street, for

children, for trees, and for "brother cloud," through his tears
of emotion over beauty when he recited some of his favorite
poets—and he knew an incredible number of stanzas by heart—
he was all tenderness and affection, a hermit contemplating
creation in the desert of a modern city. His anger, like that
of Heraclitus from Ephesus, exploded against the blindness of
men, and he reproached himself for allowing their pettiness to
cause him pain. His room on the Rue Chateaubriand contained
nothing more than a bed, a table, and a few books; for me
that hermitage, with its bare walls, imparted a permanent ironic
significance to the Rue Chateaubriand: just across the street,
in the exquisite pension Atala, amid tasteless comfort, resided
that poet-snob, the cultural attaché of the Polish Embassy. They
did not know each other nor could they have, so diverse were
the levels on which people of apparently the same era functioned. And the poet-snob, when I used to meet him, did
not suspect that under my affability of an awkward adolescent
I was laughing at him.

But I would have left out the most important thing if I did
not mention the lessons in strategy that Oscar Miłosz gave
me, without meaning to. One of his books begins with the
following motto from Descartes:

> . . . since a person who, without intending to lie, says that
> he saw or understood a certain thing ought to be believed
> more than a thousand others who deny it merely because
> they could not have seen it or understood it: just as, in the
> discovery of the antipodes, the testimony of a few sailors
> who had sailed around the earth was believed rather than
> a thousand philosophers who could not believe it was round.

In bearing witness, Oscar exposed himself knowingly to contempt and hatred. For, despite the enthusiasm of a few writers,
he was obviously mocked and scorned by those who set literary
fashion. From this I concluded, on my own modest scale, that
one should not run too far ahead, everything ripens slowly;
either we keep advancing one step ahead of the reader, or by
going two steps further we exceed his reach. In other words,

there is such a thing as public knowledge and private knowledge, of which writing is only a per cent. Although my ego ascribed some wisdom to itself in its efforts to oppose the world, I was sober enough to reserve that wisdom for some other time, regarding it as no more than a possibility. Thus my conclusions only suggested a technique of behavior; and later on, whenever I failed to follow those rules, I went down to defeat. Was my behavior cowardice? A foreclosing of any really great ambitions? But to each according to his deserts. Worldly and sinful, I could only go forward with my own time, working in, at the most, one or two strands of a promise that something more was to come. If Oscar Miłosz had behaved like everyone else— that is, if he had gone on producing works of "literature"—he would have won renown, perhaps a seat in the Academy, instead of being a solitary genius, a Swedenborg of the twentieth century. But, obedient to his calling, he refused to play a game. Was my shrewdness, then, a miserable fear of losing a good name? Possibly. But on the other hand, I had an attachment to "this world deafened by the noise of metal" and the humility of those who labor at a loss. I should not be condemned too much for that. Can a twenty-three-year-old youth be full of mighty and untarnished hope when he opens a book (the one with the motto from Descartes) and reads:

> In the evolution of thought and of Christian sensitivity, our epoch corresponds to the darkest time of night, that time which directly precedes the first ray of morning. I address myself to the reader who is already initiated by his sleepless nights into the terrors of that hour when the shadows decompose. The sudden melting of a glacier would have created less mud than the deposits of rotting scraps from the past sticking to our hearts. O, how old everything is, and inexpiable, and empty! Wasted days, summits unconquered, and all the baseness that is suddenly brought back. Tears, tears. But we weep later, in the full sunlight, never at the precise moment.

The Publican

◆

CERTAIN PERIODS OF OUR LIVES are difficult to remember; they are like jumbled dreams out of whose obscure depths only one or two details emerge clearly. This means we have not mastered our material and—insofar as the past is at all decipherable—have not deciphered its hidden contents. Such were the years that elapsed after my return from France until the outbreak of the war.

I walked Wilno's sloping streets—a city of clouds resembling baroque architecture and of baroque architecture like coagulated clouds. I was living in the student dormitory and was on the lookout for a job. The draft notice I was expecting did not materialize. Unfathomable criteria, known only to the Army, guided the selection of candidates for reserve-officer training schools. Probably my student's deferment and my rather doubtful political dossier rendered me undesirable in their eyes. At any rate, my military education was confined from then on to a few days a year of substitute service with shovel in hand (ninety per cent of my colleagues were Jewish workers and artisans). And I found a job thanks to Thaddeus.

I feel somewhat hesitant about describing Thaddeus and his wife because, by overlooking others who were equally good to me, I show a bias. But as an upright couple they especially intrigue me. Their quiet endurance and their scrupulous fulfilling of whatever they thought a duty suggested that a secret principle operated within them. They always chose to focus their attention on the small, the everyday, the average. The domain of their activity was usually the provinces, which explains why, coming from Warsaw, they found themselves in the eastern borderlands of the state. Their careless attitude toward fame often revolted me; only later, when I had seen with my own eyes so many reputations go up in smoke, did I appreciate them to the full. Both of them were theater people. They had started out in acting, then went into directing and organizing. Wilno could thank them for the time and effort they put into founding a school of drama there, which earned a solid renown.

Politically they were ranked with the "liberals" and "Masons" —two epithets that were far from flattering, if indeed they were not the equivalent of "kikes" and "commies." Government slogans and Rightist eloquence they dismissed with a contempt that was the more insulting for being silent. They practiced complete tolerance, behaving the same way to all people, regardless of race, religion, or nationality. Besides this they were crypto-Catholics. Crypto-Catholics in a Catholic country? But look at the majority of the Polish clergy: one of the principal organs of demagoguery was a shrill daily put out by the Franciscan Fathers—a miracle of technical efficiency, incidentally; it might have been modeled on the Hearst outfit. Thaddeus and his wife, in keeping their religious views to themselves while manifesting a sincere anticlericalism, were a rare species indeed.

Thaddeus worked for the local Polish Radio station. On his recommendation I was hired as his assistant. The Polish Radio, a corporation with the majority of its stock in the hands of the government, had a structure very much like that of the B.B.C. On the whole, the functions of employee and author were kept separate; authors were invited from the outside. Our work consisted of making program charts, corresponding with lecturers, supervising the timing of broadcasts. I found myself, thus, among the millions who live, eat, and dress at the price of selling a certain number of hours of their life. Up to then

I had managed to drift, but further drifting would have meant going into journalism, and that did not attract me.

The occupation of a bureaucrat may be very necessary; it was not long, however, before I had made up my mind (later my conclusions were verified) that bureaucrats are parasites, paid not for what they do but for being in this or that room, behind this or that desk, from morning to evening. Every month they receive salaries that have nothing to do with any completed achievement but depend on their place in the hierarchy. To hold that place they must behave in the prescribed way, since their activity is regulated not so much by the surrounding world as by the functioning of the body they are part of. As long as I warmed a chair in that office, it was one of my main tasks to write up reports to the Head Office (they saddled me with this because I was a writer). As a rule I would have gladly limited myself to two sentences: "This month nothing happened. Money is requested." But, cursing and laughing, I had to fill up dozens of pages of an office *Bhagavad-Gita*.

The basis of all bureaucracy is the propaganda that passes from bottom to top. It is meant to soothe the conscience of those at the summit, assuring them beyond a doubt that they stand at the head of a mighty, smoothly run organization and that money is being spent wisely. If, however, someone had broken down those sums of money into the acts of individual people, he could have shown that yawning, scratching, drinking tea, or concluding offensive-defensive alliances against a rival office Mafia absorbed the largest percentage of banknotes. I do not mean to suggest that the first institution in which I happened to find work was faultily conceived. It was administered according to the laws of thrift, and ordinarily engaged no more personnel than it had need of. Bureaucracy is parasitic because its activities are unproductive; they do not shape matter directly. And bureaucrats have no more reason to glory in their financial security than the prostitutes or publicans of Israel under Roman rule.

A suspicion swiftly arose in my mind that an immense number of people maintain themselves with jobs that are dishonest. At the bottom of their hearts they know this, but in their feverish bustling they try to prove to themselves and to others that if not for them the globe would stop turning. The peasant is honest because his energy is transformed into bread. The artisan is honest because he makes over wood, hide, or metal. And even a French shopkeeper, so often blamed for the high cost of food, is a titan, if his fourteen-hour workday be known: he saves his customers millions of hours a year that shoppers at state-owned stores must waste standing in lines or chasing after some product not available in their neighborhood. I was more or less thinking along those lines, while the Marxists, who dreamed of changing the state into one huge office, paid no heed to such trifles. True, they could appeal to my pride of a fallen angel who believes he is called to loftier tasks. No doubt a single translation of a French poem, labored over for a month—I tried to get up early in order to snatch some time before going to work—had more social value than a month of yawning over correspondence. But the remuneration I received for the translation amounted at the most to one-thirtieth of the monthly salary I earned simply by my presence in a pleasant environment where coconut matting silenced human footsteps and modern furniture awakened the temptation to prosperity.

Resentment, bitterness, fury: I was possessed with the whole myth of escape, of breaking with everything that was familiar, of striking off blindly, if only I could "begin all over." I might rise above myself then, shed one snakeskin that was unpleasant and shameful and of which I was constantly reminded by these houses and streets. But I had to become a clerk precisely in this provincial city, and it suffocated me. My city, as a relic of bygone days, brought tears to visitors' eyes. I was moved by it only when I could transform the jingling of sleigh bells, the steaming breaths of passersby, the rosy light on the cathedral columns into a memory, a spectacle that would vanish a while later without trace. For me, Wilno was a map of many rented rooms (my parents had long ago moved away, and I had been doing as I pleased since I was sixteen), a set of symbols of my not settling down, of my not accepting, of my temporariness; I have still not entirely unraveled the reasons for that anxiety. Here, however, I need only say that I gorged myself on the coming apocalypse almost to bursting, and if I relaxed or forgot about it, it was even worse. And I had no real friends anymore. Avid for approval but at the same time arrogant, I was haughty, incapable of simple human feelings. I could have made up for this by being open, but because I did not understand what was going on inside me, I could only pass "alongside" others. Faces like shapes of fog. If Thaddeus and his wife granted me their friendship, or, rather, their care, I ascribe it exclusively to my literary talents, not to any personal qualities. I paid them back with respect and sympathy, but their tranquillity and balance were not for me in the state I was in at that time.

Then there was my animal sexuality. This, despite the contents of the word "animal," is neither warm nor natural. It is usually the result of an inhibition, or even a revenge against one's feelings, so that the drive acts independently, without involving one's whole being. Through love affairs that were only an exchange of physiological favors, I practiced Manichaean purity, searching out women like myself, who were divided, ready to tumble into bed or on the grass with me and then return to an interrupted conversation as if the interval had been without significance. The greater the distance from the sexual act, the less attachment to it, the better. But such duality has a lot wrong with it. Because the drive is universal, its object is more or less a matter of indifference. What was to have been animal purity becomes a slavery to the prejudice of social prestige, since the choice of objects depends on whether or not winning them impresses us. Along with this I yearned so strongly for a platonic love, for an intellectual brotherhood infinitely superior to the realm of fleshly compulsion, that I would almost have been prepared to accept that proverbial lady who, in the most ardent moments, reached for a piece of chocolate. Of course, by setting up an equation of either/or and reducing sex to a thing that was not completely worthy of me (Lucifer, that proud and weightless spirit, is hostile to the body), I was deluding myself.

I would have deluded myself entirely, if not for the fact that I wrote. The written page offers concrete proof; it bears witness. And it made my head swim as if from a toothache. Rightly, I suspected myself of having fallen into some sort of psychological-political snare. Only now, however, I can see that my personal problems were a disguise for the collective uncertainty: did not Hans Castorp fabricate his fever so that he could stay in Davos on the Magic Mountain, far removed from the world, because the world terrified him?

1936, the year of the Spanish Civil War. Almost everywhere in Europe, literature was either revolutionizing itself or, and this was more common, drowning itself in a hodgepodge of sweet melancholy and impotent sarcasm. In the thirties the vanguard movements lost their momentum, giving way to more classical trends: rhyme and meter can serve various purposes, but they can also be used, like ice, to freeze decaying meat. The banner of Russian Communism did not attract me. It was in that year that I published my skeptical open letter about the "Front for the Defense of Culture." The brain-teasers of the vanguard school did not amuse me. Like a chess player who lifts a piece, then puts it back, I perceived that I could make no move and yet that this was logical. Whenever I read Marxist poets, they repelled me by their intellectual and artistic inferiority; I had burnt myself once before in that flame. Their sympathizers? Old-maid André Gide and his naïve *Retour de l'U.R.S.S.* As for the poetic shrines of the vanguard, their time was up; one does not wear short pants forever.

But when Thaddeus and I listened to the pronouncements of Warsaw politicians over the radio, there was pain in our exchange of glances. His throaty guffaw was more like a bitter realization than a laugh. And though I tried to shelter myself

in the melancholy awareness of time slipping by, it did not agree
with my temperament. My poems, thanks to the demiurge, were
wiser than I; beneath the ice of classical form they expressed
an astonishing violence.

I am very far from wanting to impose a sociological interpretation on art. It not only fails to account for everything, but
the results it gives are usually more erroneous than helpful.
However, it should be rendered its just due. Many a time while
meeting writers from various countries, I have thought about
the difficulties of mutual understanding. Every one of us is
hinged to the society we grew up in, even though we succumb
to the illusion that we are free. Only others who are not deformed by this same hump can discern what is hidden from
ourselves. There were certainly many people then who were
but dimly aware of Europe's, especially Middle Eastern Europe's,
sickness. But artists' antennae pick up every wave; and they
suffered, surprised that they did so. Even those who mouthed
nationalistic absurdities knew they were only stupefying themselves with a narcotic. Against a reality that constantly clouded
over and dissolved, I set my poetry, but my efforts were
punished with a daily feeling of distaste. That distaste taught
me a great deal. I should add that I was renting a room in
a house whose walls must have been six feet thick, on a little,
narrow, badly paved street famous for its second-hand bookstores. Its name is pleasant to recall but terribly symbolic:
Literary Alley. There an old housekeeper, a Lithuanian woman,
who looked like my grandmother, pampered me and insisted
on serving me coffee in bed.

To my relief, I was quickly ejected from my provincial
haven. Poland was not totalitarian, but neither did it have a
parliamentary system. In spite of a bevy of political parties,
the government rigged the elections to assure victory for its
own "non-party bloc." And since the so-called "colonels" were
afraid of being outbid by thoroughgoing admirers of Fascism
and racism, bad times descended upon Leftists and liberals inso-

far as they still held some of their positions. Yet already the press was unleashing a campaign against "suspect" persons.

The Polish Radio Corporation did not require a loyalty oath from its employees, at least those on the lower rungs. Loyalties varied, but obviously the higher-ups did not want trouble. All went fairly well until the Right's hatred for Thaddeus and myself exploded in a whisper campaign. Denunciations soon appeared in the papers. The outer sign of a man's abnormality is his mistaken attitude toward people "who ought to know their place," like Negroes, Jews, or Algerians; this is why the Franciscan Fathers' daily declared to the whole country that a Communist cell was operating within the Wilno radio station, and that this cell was responsible for a Jew being entrusted with the religious programs and for Byelorussian choirs being allowed in front of the microphone.

The charges brought forward by the disciples of St. Francis of Assisi were not unfounded: Thaddeus really valued that speaker, who was very knowledgeable about our region's extraordinary denominational mosaic; as for the Byelorussian songs, they are, after all, one of the most moving documents of European folklore, yet to betray, even in this way, that the Byelorussians existed at all was not the thing to do. After the denunciations in the press, the county authorities initiated the next phase: it categorically demanded my dismissal from the Polish Radio. Evidently, owing to the reputation I had acquired at the university, I was considered the chief perpetrator of evil. Thaddeus, one or two months later, met the same fate.

Serving me my notice, our station director blushed and stammered; and in Warsaw a "real" director (I say "real" because there were nominal ones, too) at the Head Office of the Polish Radio flew into a rage over these "police methods." One of Poland's characteristics is the unusually large role played by energetic women who occupy high posts in the hierarchy. The director I am speaking of was a woman whose endurance, industriousness, and precision were unrivaled by any man. From her I received a proposal to apply (but not at once) for a

position in her office; in other words, I was transferred beyond
the reach of local political bosses. Meanwhile my political adventures had not at all disrupted my plans for a trip.

I swore vengeance against the nationalists, but I was basking
in the sudden change of my routine. Once more I was master
of my own time, I could lounge in bed until late, read, write,
and I had the unknown before me—they had done me a good
turn. Now Italy awaited me. Sleet was falling in Wilno and the
buds had not yet unfolded; Vienna was still overcast, but in
Klagenfurt I rode into the sunshine, and in Venice I stepped
out into the sultry air of spring.

On that trip in the year 1937, I conducted myself as befitted
a young tourist cultivating his intellect. I visited galleries, took
notes, made diagrams of schools of painting. In the rectangular
courtyard of the University of Padua there was a plaque that I
read attentively. It bore the names of students who had studied
there during the Renaissance. I felt a certain pride in finding
many Polish names on it. The spirit of Bologna took hold
of me quickly, so similar was it to the spirit of my own city.
In Florence I climbed up to Fiesole to visit a Polish printer
whose workshop consisted of but one room where he adroitly
hand-bound ornamental volumes. Fanatically devoted to his craft,
he despised machines and machine civilization. The address of
a painter for whom I had a message from friends in Poland
took me on an excursion to San Gimignano. From the station
I rode in an old-fashioned fiacre through a green tumult of
hills; a few dozen medieval towers suddenly leaped out of that
green, like one hand with many fingers. Siena pulled the ground
from under my feet with her paintings—that feeling, as of
falling, when everything horizontal suddenly comes up to us
aslant, lasted a long time. In Assisi I did not give a single
thought to the Franciscan Fathers; besides St. Francis was like
air, impossible to imagine. I was interested in the villages in
the valley of Umbria, seen from above, and in the lake of
Trasimeno—I looked for a boat, the shape of a boat, because
wood, more so than stone, always provides a tangible contact

with the past. The land where I was born, after all, was a land of wood.

I made my way thus to Rome. Because of my inner spasm, I could not respond to Italy. A tourist needs to have quiet, which is necessary for true or even pretended delectation. The softness of the bluish landscapes irritated me, and I longed for more pungent nourishment. Signorelli's fresco in Orvieto representing the coming of the antichrist was perhaps the only thing I saw that harmonized with my mood. The fresco shows the antichrist in the form of Christ. He is pointing at his heart, from which flames are bursting. His smile of kindness seems to contain a flicker of irony, but that may be just an illusion of the viewer. What goes on at the edges of the picture reveals his true identity: torturers kneel on the chests of their victims; they are choking them with rope nooses and their knives are raised to strike.

My thirst for brotherhood, for being a part of the human throng, an equal among equals, also remained unsatisfied. Meetings with Polish painters or with tourists of other nationalities did not help. Arms gesticulating on the Campo dei Fiori, shouts, glances, a collective warmth such as I had not felt since those moments in Prague, aroused desires impossible to name. I remember a man named Francesco Ficello. Francesco sat across from me in a third-class compartment and drank wine from a bottle. He wiped it with his sleeve and stretched it out to me without a word. Then he cut a piece of cheese and gave it to me. So began our short friendship. He was a railroad watchman in Maestre. His home in the workers' suburb of Venice harbored an unheard-of number of bedbugs, which I verified for myself when he invited me to his house. Despite the bedbugs and all the poverty I rubbed up against in Italy, living in the cheapest hotels, it seemed to me that there are degrees of poverty; and even though this is no consolation for those who are poor, because they are unaware that anything lower exists, still the Italians are protected from the apathetic poverty of the North by something that comes from the very essence of their country.

Francesco, with whom I made the rounds of the working-men's taverns, told me all about the wines from different provinces and the ways to fix *frutti di mare*. His program of popular diversions also included a visit to a Venetian brothel. She was, I am happy to say, a charming girl, full of candid gaiety and warmth. For a moment I was united to her by something more than just sexual functions, which she approached good-humoredly, slapping her stomach. A human bond sprang up between us; we liked each other, and it did not matter that probably half an hour later she would forget about me. In the open window a salty-putrid breeze from the sea swelled the sheer curtains. Since every foreigner is a *tedesco*, she took me for a sailor from the German warship anchored in the roads, as a symbol of the flirtation between Hitler and Mussolini. She must have been a pious girl and surely lit candles at the altar of the Madonna.

Many years later my love for the Italians bloomed suddenly once again: I was riding in a bus between Thonon and Annemasse; that is, on the French side of Lake Geneva. A drunken old Italian woman was singing and laughing, revealing her decayed teeth, and the passengers turned away in embarrassment. With her fingers she pointed between her spread legs and croaked, *"La bestia è morta!"* Both regret and triumph sounded in her voice—the triumph of liberation from the tyrannical "beast of sex," which neither redeems nor condemns us, it just is.

Warsaw, to which I had returned from Venice, wound me up as tightly as if I were preparing to hurdle an obstacle or take an exam. Too many memories of sojourns here in humiliating poverty made me regard her as a hard and pitiless city. And in fact Warsaw differed more from Paris than Wilno did— by her tribal laws of pride and shame, by her way of judging each one according to purely superficial characteristics: dress, gesture, shrewdness. True, the anxiety that filled the penniless student as he passed an elegant shopwindow or entered a coffeehouse where the initiates sat: those who understood the mysteries of income, was softened for me, thanks to the helping hand extended by certain people already well established. For a number of years the family of Mieczysław Kotarbiński, a professor at the Academy of Fine Arts, offered me their kind protection. To his support I was indebted for all my scholarships—including the scholarship to Paris—my contacts in artistic-academic circles, and my room and board in their home whenever I came to Warsaw. That he had taken a liking to me when we met in the country at my relative's home was not strange because he helped many young people, using his personal influence with the stubborn and somewhat eccentric director of the Foundation for National Culture; that director, though a Rightist conservative, had succumbed to the charm of the freethinking and liberal Kotarbiński clan. My benefactor, a short, dark, nervous man, with fingers stained yellow from nicotine, more of an artist than a professor, has his private monument in the memories of more than one contemporary of mine. He was executed by the Gestapo in 1943, and almost everything he painted burned up along with the city. Even though their home then served me as a moral support, it would have embarrassed me to betray my greenness. So I found myself not a little nervous as I set off for the Polish Radio building. Every clerk who passed me in the lobby, carrying his papers, seemed to have achieved some unattainable degree of priesthood. The Polish Radio kept its promise, however; a contract was shoved at me, I signed, and my first salary was paid out.

I rose in my career with a staggering speed that was directly proportional to the boredom and sarcasm I began to manifest after my initial timidity had worn off. A combination of hard work and impudence is perhaps the best formula for anyone who wants to get ahead. But I was not counting my steps forward; I cared only about getting another day behind me. With surprise I noticed after a year that I had made a lot of money—

and because it was so easy, the secret of that million-plus ag-glomerate of people (I had always wondered *where* they got the money for dinner) was a little disappointing. It is worth noting that I never had the opportunity to become acquainted with a purely capitalistic system of free enterprise. In Poland, one area after another was being taken over by state offices.

My feeling of living a lie and of wasting my life reached a peak then. To yawn with, I had Joseph Czechowicz, a dis-tinguished poet, who sat at the next desk. I showed him the respect due his seniority, his goodness, and his literary merits. Before coming to the Office of Program Planning (as our de-partment was called), he had edited various journals from which he had been driven out, either by denunciations or simply by their folding up owing to lack of finances. Many a time he had struck bottom. Both of us practiced a kind of writing that was incomprehensible to most people and thus had not much to sell except our persons, so there was no point in complaining. Almost all of our colleagues possessed some sort of creative passion which they were obliged every day to restrain. Thin, nervously blinking Adam Szpak was a musicologist. Unkiewicz, always laden down with English books of the popular-science variety, waved his arms and jumped about in his chair, fairly exploding with a surfeit of ideas. Laconic, light-haired Szulc, a young man with goggle eyes and thick glasses, wrote essays on the history of literature. Henna-haired V., the Egeria of our group and the owner of an aristocratically prominent nose, hailed from an impoverished Viennese family. Her specialty was political excitement, and she broke out in a hectic rash whenever the news was unfavorable. Her husband, who worked in another department, was a Communist enthusiast, a passion that brought him, after he became a driller at a factory in the Urals, much unpleasantness—to put it circumspectly.

I often dropped in on the Literary Section, which was housed in a different building. There Thaddeus, who had also been run out of Wilno, was directing broadcasts. And there our greatest authority on ancient Greece among writers, Jan

Parandowski, had established a healthy routine for himself which I observed with open admiration. He arrived at the office late, read *Nouvelles Littéraires* or some other periodical of that sort, then went out for coffee. Such common sense I regarded as worthy of imitation, but none of us youngsters knew quite how to manage it. Parandowski's assistant and my peer—we were born in the same year—Bolesław Miciński, a philosopher by training, a poet, a lover of Kant, Maine de Biran, Mozart, and beer, who was curing his tuberculosis by gaining weight, wore himself to a frazzle in the daily treadmill.

Our female director sweated both myself and Joseph. During the incessant conferences, we defended ourselves by exchanging notes written with solemn expressions on our faces but containing rhymed buffoonery of the purest nonsense. A born technocrat, she was the type who would worry at the Last Judgment about whether everything was going smoothly. Yet she was the most intelligent of all the institution's directors. She surrounded herself with a Mafia of liberals and used Program Planning to fight a hostile current aimed at suppressing any "unsafe" intellectualism among Polish Radio employees. Her political views were naïve. She belonged to the generation of progressives who had declared themselves in their youth for Piłsudski and, from force of habit, stayed on later in the camp of the "colonels," despite the ruin of their dreams. But her openness to argument and criticism testified to her democratic propensities. If I soon became her confidante—an alliance that provoked the hatred of the opposing Mafia—it was due both to my spontaneously virulent utterances and to the perhaps erotic sympathy she knew I felt for her. She was still a beautiful woman, a light-haired Juno with the large body of a tennis player or swimmer and a cool good looks. In spite of her efforts though, it was not hard to see that our office was simply prolonging the agonies: it saved certain positions—a bit like the B.B.C.'s Third Program—but sank further and further into a swamp of compromises because of its policy of falling silent at the mention of politics.

Beyond satisfying the need to earn a living, my job, as I see now, gave me an alibi. It took me away from the literary milieu, where, uncertain myself, I found only more uncertainty. When one loses one's sense of direction and all activity seems futile, writing becomes sheer rhetoric under which falsehood, in spite of autosuggestion, is all too detectable. As proud as I was then, I could detect the falseness in my works, so I filled up my time with office work in order not to admit to myself that I was trapped. But the alibi was also driving me into a vicious circle: office workers, by the very nature of their occupations, are shielded from reality. They expend all their energy within four walls; then they need to relax. But reality's contours are equally blurred in both parts of the day, so that one loses touch not only with oneself but with the world around one. Unfortunately I was not even allowed the ordinary pleasure of taking myself seriously. The fate of my own country and of all unhappy Europe weighed too heavily on me not to have known that each day I plunged into a complete fiction. My torment, though, was perhaps exceptionally severe. Thaddeus simply directed radio plays. And Joseph, an inveterate early riser, got up at five every morning to inscribe his poems, like a medieval calligrapher, about the beauty of sensual things and about the impending catastrophe.

In the beginning of 1939, Mark Eiger (Stefan Napierski) began changing apartments. Mark was the degenerate scion of a family of wealthy capitalists, owners of cement factories. He had all the earmarks of Middle Eastern Europeans of his type: money, a knowledge of foreign languages, a large collection of books, a neurosis, and homosexuality. In comparison with this pale, thin rodent in glasses, I was, despite my inner complications, a specimen of vital, primitive strength. Mark's mother, Diana Eiger, resided in her own villa, kept a full staff of servants, and supported Jewish charitable organizations. To make the stereotype complete, Mark's sister was a Communist: a considerable number, if not the majority of Communist leaders, had similar social origins, and in jail. Mark, of course, was a poet; he translated Rilke, Stefan George, and Trakl; he moved in elegant circles that took their cue from Weimar, Berlin or Paris, circles I approached with the dislike and hostility of a poor barbarian. Married for a while to Tuwim's sister (Julian Tuwim was then Poland's Number One poet, although today one can see that Joseph Czechowicz's poems contributed more to the development of Polish poetry), Mark officiated in the journals that made or broke reputations, but was looked upon somewhat scornfully there because of his excessive cerebralism. I had read Mark's reviews in high school, but without understanding much in them because he could never condescend to write in a clear style. When I met him, his camel-hair coat, plaids, and thermoses intimidated me, much as did the material splendor of other "greats" such as Jarosław Iwaszkiewicz. The only difference was that the latter's poetry I liked, while Mark's I had quickly put down as lacking in any true talent. His wealth stuck out like a sore thumb. Our country's financial inequality was paralleled by the conflict between literary generations: our elders *still* had money, we already did not.

One can say anything about Mark except that he was stupid. After having published many of his own books, on the whole second-rate, he sought a way out of the impasse in modest but effective activity. He established a bimonthly devoted mainly to young authors. *Atheneum*, as the title suggests, did not count on a wide circulation. It acquired only five hundred subscriptions and a high reputation, while the editor himself supplied the funds. As I followed the course of Mark's will to resist the general disintegration which masked itself under a chauvinist vigor, I came to like him very much and his funny quirks ceased to bother me.

What possessed Mark in 1939 when he embarked on that round of household moves? In the city's new districts, pleasant though high-rent apartments were easy to find then. Mark would sign a contract and move in with books and cat, only to grow disgusted with his new dwelling a few days later. Either the airport was too close and the planes disturbed him, or the neighbor's radio was noisy, or the view from the window was depressing. So he broke his lease and dragged his insomnia and migraine headaches somewhere else. In this way, it seems to me, his attempt to drive the terror from his mind took its revenge. Common sense would have advised an escape to France, Switzerland, or anywhere, no matter where. But no one in Poland escaped; they were ashamed, so they soothed their dread with artificial reassurances. And Mark, who was a patriot, fabricated a substitute for wanderings, searching for that unattainable place that would be as safe as a mother's womb.

Soon after the German Army occupied Warsaw, Mark was arrested and sentenced to death—for economic espionage in Germany. To the Nazis he was a capitalist who held stock in a huge cement works, and a Jew. How could he have explained to them that he knew not one iota about the economy, that he was a writer, that if he had gone to Heidelberg, Marburg, or Baden it was only to search for the landscapes dear to German poets? Each of us ought to meditate over Mark's last moments as if over our own weakness. If we are to believe his fellow-inmates, he did not have the strength to walk, but had to be carried, a quivering sack of terror, to the wall and placed in front of the machine gun's nozzle. In our prayers we should not only ask for a good life but also for an easy death.

Travelers who have visited Warsaw since the Second World War cannot imagine that on the same space a completely different city once stood. Such instability contradicts their notions of order. For many Poles, those outer changes worked an imperceptible inner transformation. In 1939 the old Warsaw vanished spiritually; it vanished physically when the Nazis destroyed it at the end of the war. Although the blueprints for reconstruction were dull, the city managed to preserve something of its old color—like the popular habit of poking fun at authority—but it never regained the lighthearted gaiety once peculiar to it while its brutality grew even harsher.

It remains now for me to give a short account of what became of the various people mentioned in this chapter. Joseph perished on the ninth of September during the bombing of Lublin. A few hours' delay in my departure for the front, completely nonsensical, for that matter, would have meant my being there with him. Adam Szpak, the musicologist, carried the soul of a hero in the fragile frame of an intellectual; as a Jew he was caught and killed in Warsaw by the Nazis for shamelessly living outside the ghetto and, even worse, acting as a carrier for the clandestine press. Szulc, the young literary scholar, died in Auschwitz. The science enthusiast, Unkiewicz, turned out to be useful in People's Poland as the editor of a popular-science journal. Eagle-nosed V.'s husband, lost in the expanses of Russia, was let out of his prison in the Urals to join up with Anders' army; in this way he visited Persia, took part in liberating Italy, and subsequently brought his wife to that country. Thaddeus is a theater director in Poland today. The philosopher, Bolesław Miciński, died of tuberculosis in France during the war. Jan Parandowski, our long-time president of the P.E.N. Club, a philologist indulgent toward human excesses, brought to postwar Polish generations the gift of a new translation of the *Odyssey*. Jarosław Iwaszkiewicz was destined to figure among the "greats" not only before but also after the revolution. As for our female director, she conspired madly with the underground in Nazi-occupied Warsaw, and for her loyalty to the London government-in-exile the authorities of the People's Republic condemned her to life imprisonment. Twelve years later she was freed: a political error.

The Peace Boundary*

—◆—

IT IS NOT MY INTENTION to write a commentary for Goya's draw-ings. The immensity of events calls for restraint, even dryness, and this is only fitting where words do not suffice. The thread of one man's destiny alone would be enough to ensnarl us in a hopeless tangle of individual and historical complexities. It would take an epic breadth to cope with them, but, most likely, broad panoramas of this era will be rare, since World War II was fought on a different scale than, say, the Napoleonic Wars; and, besides, the demands placed on a writer by the develop-ment of sociology and psychology are now much greater. Yet if I were to present a personal story with a purely subjective slant, I would solve nothing because I would be leaving out the most interesting part. Again, I must repeat here that this is not a diary; I am not telling what happened to me from day to day or from month to month. To do so I would have to recreate certain hazy states of mind that are still not clear to me. I shall limit myself, therefore, to a few scenes as if I were working with scissors and miles of film footage. The frames I cut should be intelligible to a wider audience, not just to fanciers of Ex-pressionism.

When the blitzkrieg began, I felt a need to carry out orders

* In 1939, both Nazi and Soviet propaganda used the high-sounding term "peace boundary" when speaking of the line, known in history as the Molotov-Ribbentrop line, agreed upon by the two powers (in a secret protocol of the non-aggression pact signed August 23) to demarcate German and Soviet areas of influence in Poland. Needless to say, its use here is ironic. (Tr.)

of some sort, and thus to relieve myself of responsibility. Unfortunately, it was not easy to find someone to give orders. But very soon I was wearing something like a uniform made up of ill-matching pieces, unable, however, to revel in any more glorious deeds than taking part in the retreat. The shock of disaster followed immediately. Yet for me that September of 1939 was a breakthrough, which must be hard to imagine for anyone who has never lived through a sudden collapse of the whole structure of collective life. In France, the blitzkrieg did not have the same effect.

I could reduce all that happened to me then to a few things. Lying in the field near a highway bombarded by airplanes, I riveted my eyes on a stone and two blades of grass in front of me. Listening to the whistle of a bomb, I suddenly understood the value of matter: that stone and those two blades of grass formed a whole kingdom, an infinity of forms, shades, textures, lights. They were the universe. I had always refused to accept the division into macro- and micro-cosmos; I preferred to contemplate a piece of bark or a bird's wing rather than sunsets or sunrises. But now I saw into the depths of matter with exceptional intensity.

Something else was the mixture of fury and relief I felt when I realized that nothing was left of the ministries, offices, and Army. I slept a deep sleep in the hay barns along the way. The nonsense was over at last. That long-dreaded fulfillment had freed us from the self-reassuring lies, illusions, subterfuges; the opaque had become transparent; only a village well, the roof of a hut, or a plow were real, not the speeches of statesmen recalled now with ferocious irony. The land was singularly naked, as it can only be for people without a state, torn from the safety of their habits.

Regardless of the words I exchanged with the people in whose company I found myself escaping toward the East, I already saw the future differently than they. No one in Poland, neither then nor later, believed in Hitler's ultimate victory. Characteristic of Poles is the strong conviction that God intervenes personally in the affairs of history to side with the just, and therefore evil is doomed to failure. Armed with such a conviction, the Poles had many a time thrown themselves into hopeless struggles and were subsequently surprised when God did not help them and they lost after all—although this did not shake their belief in a final triumph. I, too, dismissed the probability of a German millennium, but semiconsciously my mind worked differently. There was too much of the Manichaean in me to accept the thought that the divine finger would insert itself into the iron necessity of the world's course.

What mainly set me apart from my traveling companions, however, was that they were unaware of either the scope of the tragedy or its durable effects. They placed their hopes in France, a consolation to which I, with my year in Paris behind me, responded as to a fairy tale. The only ones who completely grasped what had happened were the Communists (including the Trotskyites), but they were thrown into an embarrassing situation by the Red Army's friendly meeting with the German Army and by the dividing up of Poland's corpse. Whenever I came across any of them, we recognized each other by our jeering attitude toward our environment, which was not unlike the way sober people treat pathetically gibbering drunks. But our sobriety was relative. It did not go beyond a feeling for the proportions of the cataclysm. The Communists were bolstered by a variant of the belief in Providence; that is, in the fundamental and hidden rationality of the historical process, which could not possibly be on the side of the Nazis. To a certain point I admitted the validity of their arguments, especially when they appealed to the dialectic of the world: too sly to be overpowered by the blind and stupid force of the sword. But how and when revenge would come no one dared to prophesy. Doubtless the key was to be sought in Russia. Contact with that country, however, was so painful that several Communists even escaped from the Soviet to the German zone. My lucidity, which in the beginning had produced relief, soon gave way to a torpor or malignant fever, and for several months

I was tossed about by fantastic circumstances, as if my will had fled. I shall pass over those adventures because to describe them would require an entirely different language than is used in this book.

If at the beginning of 1940 I found myself once again in my home town, I must ascribe that both to circumstances and to a dark instinct. It acted like a doctor amid a universal rupture of all ties, and advised me to recover my bond with my family and my native region. Wilno, like all of Poland's eastern territory, was occupied by the Red Army after the defeat, and a few weeks later was ceded to Lithuania in token of friendship. The friendship was not exactly disinterested: Lithuania, like Latvia and Estonia, had to accept Soviet military bases. Nevertheless, the three tiny countries owed their independence to the cautious game between two giants, and their three governments dodged desperately about to avoid embittering either Germany or Russia. The prewar era was still alive here—normally stocked stores, restaurants, coffeehouses, punctual trains. In Wilno, newspapers in various languages, including Polish, appeared, though not without a struggle with the censor's office. It was hard for me to recognize that dreamlike city—not only because a different flag was flying on the castle ramparts and the names of streets and signs had been changed. Crowds of Polish refugees, whom Lithuania received hospitably even though she dreaded a grimace from her powerful neighbors, had turned the city into a feverish tower of Babel. There was a flourishing trade in currency and passports, contagious gossip, waves of panic, overflowing post offices where heads of rabbinical schools, officers of the defeated army, diplomats without assignments, and all those with relatives and friends abroad were sending off telegrams to France, England, and America. Departures by plane via Stockholm were becoming more and more difficult. New refugees flowed in constantly, risking, in the case of capture at the border, a trip to Stalin's concentration camps. Once they reached that desired island of safety, they quickly realized that the island was a sinking floe and escape had been cut off.

The Hotel Europa was typically situated for our town. It stood at the intersection of the two most colorful streets: Dominican Street boasted mainly Catholic churches and monasteries, while German Street had, ever since the Middle Ages, served as the main artery through the Jewish district. It was here that Felix and his wife lived. The disasters I had been living through drew me to the court that surrounded this man; so it will be in place if I sketch his portrait here.

Felix resembled a Japanese, with his black hair, sallow complexion, and filigreed refinement; he was always impeccable, elegant, and fragrant with cologne. He came from a Jewish family so rich that he had, it seems, no occupation, although he had completed his technical studies in Belgium. Just before the outbreak of the war, he sold his apartment houses in Warsaw and went into exile with a large suitcase loaded with dollars and gold. He also took his young, attractive wife, together with her furs and jewels. Their relationship was built on alternate scenes of hatred and tender reconciliation. His wife, profiting from her physical superiority, would beat him or, if he put up resistance, would threaten to commit suicide and run toward the window. Felix then fled and shut himself up in the bathroom—not to see. A few minutes later, friends (who usually played the role of arbiters) would knock on the door of the bathroom, from which a weak voice came: "Well? Did she jump?"

Felix was an inveterate alcoholic but he did not like to drink alone. Quite the contrary, he constantly needed a choir around him to tell fairy tales, anecdotes, and jokes, which would make his existence pleasant. He appreciated intellectual refinement, hence his attraction to artists and poets; these found in him a perfect teat—that is, a man who graciously allowed himself to be milked. Since many of them had wandered hither from Warsaw, he soon gathered an impressive court and his feasts drew a few dozen people.

The drinking usually began at eleven in the morning. As the

day advanced, however, it did not take on an extreme form. The poets J. and S., who set the pace, were too much the seasoned drunkards to fall into oblivion. They sipped vodka from large tumblers, continually refilling them to the brim, and carried on a ceaseless palaver throughout the entire day and far into the night. Next morning the hangover had to be cured, so the whole thing started all over again. Thus time, meaningless and hopeless, was experienced differently than in naked reality; it was transformed by alcohol.

Our gatherings were an uninterrupted "feast during the plague," and those assembled knew full well that death stalked beyond the doors and had to be outwitted. That company suited me because it lived without illusions, practicing a macabre humor and laughing, while that was still possible, at the bloody comedy of the two empires that surrounded us. S., for example, lectured on his theories of Hitler: the Führer was only playing the fool for his nation's benefit; after screaming himself to death he threw off his uniform with disgust, put on English flannels, smoked English cigarettes, drank whiskey, and expressed the highest contempt for Germany. The war between the Soviet Union and Finland also gave S. the opportunity to tell many stories, such as the one about the adventures of a Soviet soldier who took a wall clock, the largest wristwatch he had ever seen, from a Finnish hut and carried it around in his knapsack, bent double under the weight. Felix listened greedily to the anecdotes and limericks that we thought up under the influence of vodka. He could veil over his fear with them, but most likely he had always feared existence.

I could not relax. When one is in a state of exceptional nervous tension, alcohol has little effect and neither unsteadiness nor vomiting disrupt the precise functioning of the brain. Objects seemed to wound me as if they sent out sharp rays piercing the skin, and I hurried down the street with averted eyes, desiring only to be seated at Felix's table as quickly as possible; there, past and future were at least partly obliterated. I could not read, I could not write, nor could I participate in discussions that were mocked by events. I could only, and unsuccessfully at that, try to regain some sort of quiet, either vegetative or animal.

My new companions took refuge in subjective time through fornication, which both men and women considered an effective way of forgetting. But not all were satisfied with the ordinary forms of that activity; they searched for newer varieties. For instance, J. said to me that doing it in church was very pleasant. I guessed his motives: sexuality must be seasoned with evil; if all taboos vanish and there is nothing to break, it loses its appeal. J. was bored with the natural; he desired a prohibition, something to give mystery to sex to make it worthwhile. Looking at his partner, a slender girl with a tendency to blush, I imagined how she yielded to his advances somewhere in the empty nave of a church, modestly lowering her doe's lashes. I, for several reasons, observed a strict purity. What inclined me to that was my faithfulness to a close person who had remained in Warsaw and my somewhat magic view of the connection between all things: the sexual act was equal to saying yes to the world. The precarious safety, the dangers ahead, called for preparedness. I felt that fate was not to be tempted by pretending to accept the present. Besides, in moments of personal difficulty I usually feared sexual freedom as something that must draw down vengeance, since it leads to a forbidden release of energy. So I deliberately cultivated an unbearable nervous tension and mitigated it only with vodka.

The sudden death of one of our companions, the poet S., occurred in circumstances that suited quite well the phantasmagoria we upheld. It also suited S.'s macabre mind. S. was thirty. He died *in coitu* as a result of an injection that a certain rich lady, and a rather pitiless hussy, had herself given him in bed. When we visited him at the morgue in St. Jacob's Church, where an autopsy was performed to establish the cause of death, we were moved by the beauty and harmony of his features, whose defects, arising from a thyroid condition, had completely vanished. Afterward, we all accompanied him across town, walking in the huge funeral procession. His name was known to all readers of the Polish press, and he was given a splendid funeral.

City cemeteries are usually gloomy patches of stony space, but not in Wilno. Rossa Cemetery, where we had chosen a plot for him—not far from the grave of a nineteenth-century poet, Syrokomla—spreads over steep hillsides overgrown with ancient trees. Here, on All Souls' Day, thousands of candles and oil lamps are lit on the graves; they burn and flicker in the wind through the branches on the slopes above and in the ravines below. And here, under a large basalt stone, lies the heart of Piłsudski, the creator of between-the-wars Poland. We had done what we could for S., thinking all the while that maybe he had not met the worst fate. Then we began the funeral repast, drawing up a chair for his ghost, in front of which one had the urge to place a filled glass.

It would be easy to call us all degenerate. We were, however, people of the most diverse kind, drawn together by accident. In effect, there was a certain wisdom in our behavior, stemming from the awareness that in some traps it is better to behave passively than to frustrate oneself with sterile thrashing around. Felix, by selling his goods and spending his gold on the pleasures of entertaining, was bearing testimony to his superiority over those who clutched at their already useless wealth. His drunken gatherings were lighthearted, in keeping with the morrow that would demand nonchalance and the casting off of every burden. They were a farewell to the historical phase that was passing away forever in this part of the world.

The summer of 1940 arrived, and I witnessed the end of Lithuania. Poland had gone down amid flames and uproar; here not a single shot was fired. The German Armies were just then entering Paris. In the coffeehouse on Cathedral Square, I lazily contemplated a streak of sunshine on the table and the print dresses of the women who passed by the window; many of them had arrived here with only the knotted bundles of run-aways. Already they had managed to purchase things, taking advantage of the well-stocked stores where you did not have to use ration cards or stand in lines. A sudden heavy scrape of metal on the pavement roused my curiosity, as it did everybody's. People got up from their tables only to freeze in their tracks as they watched the large, dusty tanks with their little turrets from which Soviet officers waved amicably. To connect in one's mind what could have passed for a simple military exercise with the hard fact of occupation demanded an inhuman effort, as one can imagine, when beautiful weather, newspaper kiosks, flower stands, and a little dog sprinkling the trunk of a linden tree, make it seem incredible that the decisions of unknown politicians can disturb the normal run of things.

To the uninitiated observer, nothing special happened that day. Only toward evening, megaphones began to blare and patrols of Asiatic soldiers paced up and down, their thin bayonets, like awls drawn out to a thread, sticking up three feet above their heads. But the population, thanks to the proximity of the Polish counties that had already been occupied, was initiated—except for a few hundred naïve Communist enthusiasts. The fear, as it mounted from hour to hour, seemed to become almost a physical, tangible presence.

I went down to the river, sat on a bench, and watched the suntanned boys in their kayaks, the revolving rod of a tiny steamboat's engine, the colored boats, which you rowed standing at the back, using one long oar. I was sorry for my city because I knew every stone of it; I knew the roads, forests, lakes, and villages of this country whose people and whose landscapes had been thrown like grist into a mill. I experienced nothing of this sort when Hitler conquered Poland because in my heart I could not regard National Socialism as a durable phenomenon. A wolf is no doubt a dangerous animal, and should he bite, consolation is no help; yet together with the image of his fangs and claws another image rises within us: of automatic weapons, of tanks, of planes, against which the wolf is powerless. For me the Revolution and Marxism were the equivalent of this higher technology. National Socialism was too pure an evil, and it had already, at least in theory, yielded to Lenin's more diabolical sheaf of both good and evil. My thinking, of course, was not that cold. It was simply that the sandbars in front of the electric-power station where children were standing with fishing poles, the river current, the sky, all spoke to me of an irrevocable sentence.

In the days that followed I noticed that many people, who had up to then passed me indifferently in the street, now bowed to me with smiles of the sincerest friendship. Because I had the reputation of being a Communist, they calculated on my being powerful, and now was the time to win my favor. Doubtless one should have written a few enthusiastic poems in honor of the imminent annexation of the Baltic countries, by means of "elections," to the Soviet Union. Those bows gave me much malevolent pleasure, although the sense of power they afforded was not of a kind these foresighted individuals imagined. I concealed my plan to play a better joke on them.

Politically I was closest to a small group of Polish Socialists who had maintained contact with Stockholm from formerly neutral Lithuania—Swedish Socialists lent effective help in passing on conspiratorial material—and with America, where their ideological comrade, Oscar Lange, was lecturing at the University of Chicago. That Lange was later on to become the first Ambassador of People's Poland in the United States was one of the surprises of the usual political *contredanse* performed in stormy times by various public figures. It was in that group that I met Sophia.

Sophia could have been fifty or sixty, she was black-haired (dyed), intelligent, vehement, and smoked like a chimney, tearing her cigarettes in half for economy's sake and stuffing them into a glass cigarette holder. As a liaison carrying money and documents she had already made two illegal trips between Wilno and Warsaw. Without further ado we came to an agreement to set off together the next time, and not to wait long since the journey would be difficult and the border was "hardening."

Our protracted discussions over the map will go uncelebrated

by those who cannot appreciate the peculiar talent, which all
totalitarian states seem to have, for multiplying barbed-wire barriers along boundary lines. The simplest thing would have been
to go straight to East Prussia; there, however, without knowing
the terrain and without being able to pass for local residents,
we would be easy prey for the Nazis. The only advisable thing
was to head for a Polish county wedged between Lithuania and
East Prussia, which was part of the territory annexed to the
Reich. If we managed to get across the Russian-German border
successfully (knock on wood), then on the other side of that
county we would catch up with the old boundary (still patrolled) between Poland and East Prussia. From there we would
push our way across East Prussia to her southwestern edge,
where we would force our third border into the Polish counties
that were now also part of the Reich. Our fourth and last
border-crossing would bring us into the German protectorate,
with the cities Warsaw and Cracow; that is, into the Government-General. The reason for these rather insane obstacles raised
by the Nazis within an occupied country was q ite clear: it was
a question of immobilizing the skittish human animal, of cutting
off his possibilities of escape from one place to another in the
face of danger.

It would be a lie if I were to claim that I made my choice
as one looks at two sides of a scale, measuring the pros and cons.
Had I begun to think in this way I would have probably under-
taken no decision at all, because my imagination would have
reminded me of the people I had known who had been caught
trying to cross the borders and who had been sucked into the
great funnel of jails or camps in the north. I was aided by
vanity, or pride, which showed in the contemptuous curl of my
lips: who are these people anyway, I said to myself; why should
they deal with me as they please and assume that everyone
will bend to their wishes because they have power? For personal
reasons I had long had the intention of going to Warsaw, so why
should I defer to necessity now and condemn myself to life
imprisonment within a system that, who knows, might never

fall? Besides, the passivity and the nascent servility around me demanded some kind of deed in order to break the spell; and after my long vegetation at Felix's court, I could take no more idleness without aim or achievement. What would have happened had they shoved a piece of paper at me and ordered: Either write a political ode or spend five years in camp? But I refused to admit a single thought of failure as I planned my flight.

The preparations took time and required complete secrecy; we could not betray ourselves to anyone, and had to pretend we were overjoyed by the new order. I took part in the "elections"; that is, my face wore a serious expression when I dropped my card into the ballot box, having written something on it in pencil that I shall keep to myself as a voter's privilege. The result—ninety-nine per cent for a single slate—had been foreclosed, like the unanimous demand for Lithuania's annexation to the Soviet Union.

Nor could I say goodbye to my friends because the gossip would have made the rounds of every coffeehouse in half an hour. So I did not say goodbye to Felix. I shall have to recreate his subsequent adventures from the accounts I heard later on. Felix was scared. One night a crony of his, the lawyer X., first persuaded, then helped him to bury his treasure in the garden. Anxiety, however, seized Felix the next morning. He was worried about whether the place had been well chosen. That night the two of them again went out with shovels, but found nothing. It could only have been sheer coincidence that the lawyer, from that moment on, swam in money, while Felix's drinking companions had to pass the hat to buy a train ticket to Manchuria for him and his wife. Felix's departure bordered on a miracle, since the authorities granted rights of transit only to the possessors of Japanese visas at a time when it was already impossible to obtain such a visa.

It seems that a certain foresighted Rabbi helped them out of the fix: in his unfathomable wisdom he had collected absolutely all possible visas (even unnecessary ones) while all the consulates had still been operating. The Japanese visa, which the experts had copied from his passport, sold for a high fee, but it was marked by one defect: no one in the city knew the Japanese alphabet, and therefore could not have guessed that each visa contained the name of its first owner. When the five-hundredth Silberstein passed over the Manchurian frontier, the Japanese began to worry. Whether the story is true or merely an anecdote, Felix, at any rate, made it to Shanghai and from there to Australia. He enlisted in the American Army and perished in an auto accident in Hawaii. I shall do no discredit to his memory, perhaps, if I make the conjecture that he died in an unsober condition.

Sophia irritated me when she announced, two days before we were to leave, that guides cost a great deal and we did not have enough money; she suggested we take a third partner, who, in exchange for the privilege, would finance our expedition. He was a pharmacist, driven to Wilno by the war, who dreamed of returning to his family. Would I agree? There was something strange in her tone of voice. Either the candidate was offering her an exceptionally large sum and she was arranging a deal on the side, or she was foreseeing that he would get us into trouble. Somehow the sweetness in her voice was too unlike her. I tried to object: in that case our two passes are worthless, because there is not enough time to make a third. I had obtained those German passes, which guaranteed transit from the little town of Suwałki in the Reich, via East Prussia to the Government-General, with great difficulty. Produced by a local printing press, they were counterfeit from start to finish, including the magnificent seals with the swastika—those seals proved that our university's Fine Arts Department was training skillful artists. Actually the passes did not guarantee anything, but still. . . . Sophia's proposal meant that not one border but four would have to be crossed on foot. Naturally, she argued that we risked even more with my uncertain passes. Finally I succumbed to the mathematical argument, when she set down the cost in figures on a scrap of paper.

The first time I set eyes on our third man was the morning

of our departure at the railroad station. I saw immediately what had caused Sophia's strange expression. Sophia, in a kerchief and carrying an old knapsack, looked like a country schoolteacher; nor did I, with my homespun bag and the face of a native, stand out. But the pharmacist—a grayish, bloated face, faded-blue little eyes sneaking fearful and suspicious glances in our direction. The sluggishness of a hippopotamus, the very carica-ture of a bourgeois. He was dragging a huge suitcase tied round with a leather strap.

The landscapes of my childhood rolled by beyond the train window, and quickly, but more strongly than if I had deliber-ately brought it to mind, the name of a station forever linked in my memory with a true and tragic love of my boyhood years leaped out before my eyes and passed. Above all, how-ever, I was aware of the man across from me, or, more precisely, of my own wounded self-esteem. After we had exchanged sev-eral remarks, I decided he was a pig and a pitiful fool. Was such a one as he, then, to be my comrade in action—an action that was more or less equal to a manifesto of independence? Was it not a punishment to humiliate me? There was I, an intel-lectual who might have stayed on with unhappy but at least thinking beings, and I had to escape with him, a know-nothing, doomed by history for caring only about his stinking money and family bedding. Over there, I thought to myself, west of the line guarded by the two armies, history's sentence will catch up with him, in a different way, perhaps, but it will. At this decisive moment, which has been ripening for so long, when there is nothing in Europe but Hitlerism and Stalinism, when one must declare oneself for either one or the other, I am only deluding myself with the hope of an indeterminate third solution because I am unable to base it on anything. On anything except my disgust—and then to be disgusted by this fellow here! If we are caught, this man will be my cellmate, my neighbor.

Our departure had been timed so that we would arrive in the afternoon of a market day, when it was easier to get lost in the crowd. The name of the town was more Catholic than Lithua-

nian: Kalvaria. We had a "contact" there—a local farmer. Among
the flour sacks in his barn we listened to his review of the
situation. The border at village X was impossible, village Y too;
one could try near village Z. That cart in the yard (unharnessed
horses were munching in their feedbags near it) had just come
from there and we could ride back in it, but it would pick
us up half a mile outside of town because the NKVD patrols
were stationed at all the exit thoroughfares and were checking
documents. We readied ourselves, and within a few hours, at
a given signal, we began to steal through orchards, hedges, carrot fields, and cabbages. I carried the pharmacist's suitcase because after the first few minutes he was already panting and
out of breath. Drenched in sweat, I cursed the idiotic predica-
ment that had turned all my smuggler's shrewdness to no use;
if such a cavalcade, with that suitcase, were spotted by an in-
former even from a distance, it would have meant the end. The
idiocy dragged on as we trudged over the sandy road that led
toward the border. Our cart was moving along close by, but
for the moment pretending it had nothing to do with us.

As soon as I was lying on my back in the hay at the bottom
of the cart, gazing up at the sky overhead, where clouds, rosy
from the setting sun, floated lazily, I felt the inner calm that had
eluded me for so many months. No conflicts, no hesitations,
no fear even—fear was only in my nerves, it did not penetrate
further. My mind was disconnected, it did not disturb my inner
harmony. I listened to the voice of my organism: my body
believed deeply in Providence and submitted in advance to its
decrees; whatever happens to me has been destined to happen,
so why be troubled? To this day I wonder to what extent that
voice in other people signifies an acceptance of everything, and
to what extent it is untrustworthy. It helped me to control the
pounding of my heart so that, as we passed the NKVD camp
in a forest glade, I phlegmatically chewed on a blade of grass.
Beria's soldiers, who looked like rough-hewn stones in their
long military coats, were lined up in rows, singing.

Here the terrain changed from flatland to hilly countryside.

The road wound through a ravine, through groves of pine and alder, over hill and dale through orchards, then we were in the village. We pulled up in front of a hut, were quickly hustled into a dark entrance, then ordered in a whisper to climb up to the loft and pull the ladder after us.

Those forty-eight hours we spent in the hayloft could have supplied the material for a theater play with a cast of three. We were forbidden to speak out loud, to knock, to rustle the hay. Because there was no window, the roof was our only observation point; from time to time, peering through it with one eye, we saw the point of a bayonet carried by the NKVD soldier patrolling the village street. Sophia unburdened her ire by taking it out on the pharmacist. Nothing, perhaps, can equal the cruelty of a woman if she despises a male. For that matter, the pharmacist's every gesture, his every word, his very person even, was provoking. He drooled with terror and infected us with his fear; he did and undid his leather money-belt that was stuffed with dollars, turning his back lest, accidentally, we were to count his wealth; he treated us like two hoodlums from the underground to whom he had entrusted his valuable life; he did not know how to walk or even how to eat bread and sausage quietly; he did not know how to take care of his other needs either. Sophia squatted discreetly in a corner, I hid behind a rafter. The pharmacist restrained himself and suffered until suddenly, right in front of us, he undid his trousers, took out his member, as wrinkled as an elephant's trunk, and poured forth, bleating with pleasure, completely indifferent to everything save the relief of emptying his bladder. Sophia observed this unblinkingly, then turned away and said: "Slob!" The name stuck.

Since we spoke little, she ostracized him from our society by a terrorism of silence. My cautious attempts to appease her or to make her realize that Slob, too, was a human being did not come from love of my neighbor but from my sense of outrage at the earth, as an exceptionally terrifying place: if even the goodness of women is an illusion and what they really value in us are only cavemen virtues; i.e., strength, efficiency, energy.

My calm, and my enterprising spirit, though they had earned me Sophia's friendship, were not qualities with which I hoped to merit the warm feelings of others. They ebbed and flowed independently of my will, and who knows, if Sophia were to meet me in another chapter of my life, whether I would not become an object of her ridicule? I mentally arraigned her in an antifeminist court, and felt a tinge of contempt for the low urges that had crept out from under the surface of her so-called culture. My thirst for justice, however, came to naught. Because whenever I showed Slob the least sympathy, he began to whine and snivel and, worse still, mistook my gesture for evidence of solidarity with him against Sophia. Complete wretchedness compounded with complete lack of tact.

This seething behind closed doors was interrupted now and then by sounds from below, none too agreeable for our overstimulated nerves. When our farmer cleared his throat in the agreed way, we let down the ladder and he climbed up to us for a council of war. His talk was better than a map—much more detailed than anything we had. The village stood on a high bank over the marshes; that is, over the basin of a semidrained, postglacial lake. The end of the low ground was already on the German side. "In spring and autumn the water gets pre-e-e-etty high—boy oh boy, the Jews that drowned here running from Hitler! But you can get across now." Guards keep watch on the shore. Of Russian talents he had the highest opinion: "They are real woodsmen." He told us that they go out in fives, sit down in the grass, and, after a rest, move on further; a naïve person would assume that no one remained behind, but they have just relieved their comrades who were hidden there, leaving two from their group and taking two. We should wait until Sunday night, when there will be dancing in the village. The girls promised to help. They would keep the soldiers talking or do something to distract the guard at the entrance to the marshes—he was the most dangerous.

Even before the war this village had derived much of its income from contraband; then, however, neither Polish nor Lith-

uanian guards were known for their alertness, and even if one
fell into their hands it meant, at the most, no more than the loss
of one's goods or a few months' arrest. That evening we were
joined by two young boys, already seasoned professionals. They
had scarcely opened the door of the cottage, taking care that it
did not creak, when they broke into a run, and we after them,
with Slob wheezing excruciatingly. In one sprint we reached the
path to the bottom of the ravine. Our guides often stopped to
listen here, and with good reason, for at every turn I was
startled by the sight of strange statues standing in front of us:
these were irregular, glacial rock formations, tall and bright in
the moonlight and casting black blotches of shadows. From afar
they looked like people; close up they were no less fearsome,
because a man could have been hidden behind each of them.
When water at last began to slosh over our shoes, I drew my
breath with relish, savoring the smell of osiers, marsh rosemary,
and wet moss, the smell of my native land.

I felt at home in such swamps, and I have always been affected
by their somewhat melancholy beauty. The smooth sheet of
water shone with an oily gleam between clumps of vegetation,
and here and there on it a motionless piece of dry leaf floated.
We broke into it and sank up to our knees, then up to our thighs.
Slob still strained our tempers because he splashed, caught himself on bushes, and fell behind, forcing us to go back and pull
him out of the brambles. When the water reached our waists, he
managed to fall in up to his neck or go under, calling out in a
hoarse gurgle for help. In the moonlight I caught a glimpse of
his exhausted, inhumanly mud-smeared face. Sophia preserved
her sense of humor. In a mutual effort, we rescued her from a
treacherous quagmire where she had sunk up to her shoulders
and was afraid to move for fear the mud would suck her in.
Almost naked in her clinging dress, she smiled: "I lost my
panties!"

Once a signal of alarm stopped us: only the hiss of air bubbles
from the peat we had trampled . . . but then the sound of
heavy, splashing steps. They did not sound too far away. A

while later, though, our guides said: "Beast!" A moose or a deer was coming from East Prussia. He could be happy because for him every man was a danger; he did not have to worry about changes of governments or systems.

Those few miles we had to wade through took us many hours. The stars were growing pale and dawn was already blowing in the air when we stood on dry ground. We, vague shadows between the white birch trunks, were in Hitler's state. Around us the loose rustle of leaves, the fairyland of a midsummer night's dream, and within me the triumph and strength that comes of victory in spite of all obstacles. I was struck by the weirdness of the scene: at a time when Oberon's horn should be sounding in the forest and Titania awakening from the spell Puck had cast on her, our guides, lying on the moss, were diligently counting their dollars. After being taken to a friendly hut in the first village, we made at once for the hayloft and fell asleep on the spot.

The peasant cart rattled along the highway under a fine rain. Our route took us from the north to the south of this country of windswept highlands, lakes, and spruce forests that were familiar to me from before the war. Just before the little town of Suwałki, our driver turned down a road that cut through the fields and around the vegetable gardens until we reached a side street where he stopped in front of a small one-story wooden house. The fullness of being human is difficult to achieve; but to this day the inhabitants of that little house, a young droshky driver and his wife, who was suckling an infant, are proof to me that it is possible. Their fear struggled with their sense of duty toward their neighbor, and it was precisely the obviousness of their inner battle—although they tried to hide it, showing us brotherly kindness—that clothed their persons in a special pathos.

I exposed them and myself to danger by going out for a walk around the town. But in the course of that half hour I grasped the essence of the Nazi régime. My footsteps echoed in the empty streets; I met a few old women. All the Jews had been murdered or jailed, and the huge army garrison that had stood here before the war no longer existed. At first I attributed the depopulation to that, but then the funereal black banner of the S.S. and my visit to the pharmacy explained the real reason. There behind the counter, dressed in a white coat, stood a boy whom I recognized as the owner's son. When he saw me his face turned ashen and he began signalling with his hands not to come nearer, as if he were seeing a ghost. I did come nearer however, and the boy, trembling, threw me a few words. I returned, restraining my speed with a nonchalant swing, trying to act as if I *had a right* to my liberty. The entire male population of the area, with a few exceptions, had been deported to forced-labor or concentration camps. The rains still had not washed away the bloody patches left behind from the mass executions on the towns' squares. As I found out later my fifteen-year-old cousin, a resident of that part of Poland, found himself, more or less around that time, behind barbed wire in the camp at Oranienburg-Sachsenhausen. Two years later he was dead.

We would have to risk taking the train to the station at the East Prussian border. One must keep in mind that to the south lay Russian-occupied territory; therefore there was no other way. At dawn our droshky driver took us to the railroad station. We shivered both from cold and from fear, which the empty platform hardly allayed. Our next "contact"—the restaurant in a border village—turned out to be a good one. We were received hospitably and told that documents were examined aboard the train, on the Prussian side, but that we could avoid it by paying; a messenger was also dispatched to arrange for it. At night we crawled over pasturelands, under wire fences, bumping into cows in the dark. A Polish farmhand, doing forced labor for a German *Bauer*, was waiting for us at an agreed spot in a buggy harnessed with a pair of strong horses. He chose back roads to avoid the highways; after some twenty miles we arrived at the third or fourth station on the line, just in time for the morning train.

While riding in the train through East Prussia, we did not speak to each other in order not to call attention to ourselves. I had time then to think about the little painted houses, the cleanliness, the order. Terror and destruction were for export, not for home use; on the contrary, they served to enrich one's home country. Wretched humanity beyond one's own frontiers was simply material to be cut and shaped as one pleased. I sorted the stories that the young farmhand had not grudged us during our night ride. Almost all the farms here had been allotted Polish prisoners of war or deportees for forced labor, and the luck of the Poles varied according to the kind of master they received. I was able to guess from a few details that our driver's liberty to use the horses for purposes not of the most loyal sort derived from his status with the *Bauer's* wife. He had assumed all the rights and duties of her former husband, who—ironic vengeance of destiny— had perished on the front in the Polish campaign. But the young Pole hated with a quiet peasant hatred—like all his countrymen here he had to wear the letter "P" sewn on his sleeve—and he had already singled out a farm to grab as soon as the war was over. His belief in victory, that summer of 1940 at the apogee of Hitler's power, was inflexible and irrational. East Prussia would fall to Poland: that was that.

Trouble awaited us in Ortelsburg. The next crossover point, Sophia confessed to me, had a bad name: be careful, there was something fishy. Since Slob was about as much help as excess baggage, Sophia and I dropped into a smoke-filled little dive to rack our brains over a beer. Somehow we were going to have to find out from someone how to get to the border villages; but we could not trust any Germans. I latched onto a little man with a red nose, a Mazurian in a railroad employee's uniform, and began to pour cognac into him. His usefulness added up to zero because he slipped at once into an alcoholic stupor. Yet I rank him as one of the enigmatic wise men. While staring numbly at the table, he would repeat stubbornly every so often: "The Russkies will come." In that tippler dwelled a powerful, skeptical mind. Immune to official propaganda, he had come to his own conclusions, based on some sort of personal observations and intuitions, which were highly offensive to the German millennium.

Since we were getting nowhere, I decided to make a last attempt—which testifies to my instinctual attachment to the Catholic Church as a supranational institution, or at least to my opinion of its servants as people who relatively seldom serve Caesar: to seek help from the parish priest. Of course I knew, as I inquired about the address of the rectory, that I was taking a chance, but sometimes chance just needs a little help. As soon as I had opened the door, my foolishness overwhelmed me. A double chin above a starched collar, fair-haired heads of children, a catechism lesson, his eyes and the children's reflecting surprise and dread at the sight of a dirty, stammering Polish bandit. In half a minute the Church as a supranational institution fell to pieces. I closed the door and walked down the street whistling.

We abandoned our search and took the train to Willenberg, the last station on the southern border of East Prussia. There my stubborn insistence on having counterfeit passes made in Wilno proved not to have been in vain. Sophia had wandered off somewhere, and Slob and I were waiting for her when suddenly a gendarme loomed in front of us and asked to see our documents. I gave him my pass while Slob cringed, almost shrank out of sight, pretending to wrestle with the strings of his knapsack. Our Wilno artists knew their craft, for the big fellow in the green uniform merely waved his hand: never mind, it was O.K.

Then we had a hard time renting horses to get to an out-of-the-way village named Kleine Leschinen. Forest and more forest, then the lonesome house of a rich *Bauer*. He was a Mazurian called Deptuła. He did not invite us in but ordered us to wait in the nearby oak grove until sundown, and he would send us a boy guide. The sun was setting, the birds sang with flutelike sweetness, and I had forgotten we were there for a purpose; I was busy swatting mosquitoes which the cigarettes we prudently cupped in our palms failed to drive away. Shouting and gunfire almost above my head broke into that silence as if all hell had been let loose. Because of its intensity, that moment when those glaring smudges of uniforms dashed shrieking toward us seemed interminable, but it had all happened so swiftly that, before I could think, my hands had gone up and the nozzle of an automatic was digging into my chest. In that position, I caught sight of Deptuła. He came out from behind the trees slowly and, sucking on his pipe, stood gloating over his work. The memory of his small black eyes tormented me for years after the war with the desire for revenge. Although as a Mazurian he probably never left that region, I stifled the temptation to take a trip up there and give myself at least the satisfaction of letting him feel my power over him.

But vengeance was in the air everywhere then, and nothing came of it but universal despair and bitterness. In the autumn of 1945, the few days I spent in a certain village near Danzig left me with feelings of loathing and sadness. Germans were being evacuated from the area then. Some woman named Müller, who had tried in vain to defend herself by pointing out that she had harbored allied prisoners, committed suicide there, together with her children, by jumping into the Vistula. More or less at the same time, my mother died of typhus in this village; she, in turn, had lost her Lithuanian homeland in the East.

We were herded along at a fast clip through the forest. One arm breaking from the cursed pharmacist's suitcase, the second, under cover of darkness, maneuvering in my inside pocket to tear up some incriminating pieces of paper. Pretending to cough, I stuffed them into my mouth. The taste of the print was repulsive. At the police station in Kleine Leschinen, they did not search us, and Sophia, lying down on the cell floor, which was spread with straw, declared that as long as the Gestapo had not been called in, all was not lost.

Here the commandant enters. The terrible bellowing that came from the throat of that fat Bavarian might have been cause for alarm, but at the same time something playful lurked in the creases around his eyes. He did not remain indifferent to the stream of conversation that poured from Sophia, who, suddenly transformed into a *grande dame*, related a moving tale that was totally false. Doubtless the exceptionally favorable circumstances of life in this corner, certainly one of the quietest of wartime Europe, had taken the edge off his disposition. Next morning he told us he had telephoned to the Gestapo in Ortelsburg and that we were to be handed over. But his subordinate, after taking us in a horse-drawn buggy to Willenberg, needed no encouragement to accept my invitation to stop at a bar; after half a bottle of cognac he started showing me photos of his family and giving me to understand that the time had come to take ourselves off. We crawled under the barrier at the frontier. No one stopped us.

We moved along slowly from village to village, over sandy roads which the wheels on the peasant carts churned up quietly. Once we caught sight of a local concentration camp that stood on a plain. A column of prisoners was just returning from work. As they passed through the gates, their singing, which contrasted sharply with their gray, extinguished faces, cut me to the quick. Guards armed with rifles and whips completed the procession. We were shown the greatest friendliness, free from any trace of fear, in villages inhabited by descendants of the petty gentry. They simply did not acknowledge a foreign occupation. Compared to peasant villages, theirs had more carefully constructed buildings and all the residents bore the same name—that of their common ancestor. To avoid confusion, everyone tacked a nickname onto his surname.

In the little town of Ostrołęka my fatal curiosity once again drew me out on a little walk, away from the house where a fat woman, who quartered meat for the black market, had treated us to hospitality. My need to store up details of the human landscape in my own memory was invincible. Wooden fences plastered with German notices plunged me into a reverie on the metamorphoses of reality; that dream consisted mostly in amazement at the infinite number of changes that one man may see in the course of his own lifetime. Suddenly roused by the sound of a human voice, I saw in front of me a leather-coated officer of the Gestapo. Something barked and hit me in the face. My cap fell, I bent over to retrieve it, and when I had straightened up, the echo of his curses was still hanging in the air while his back disappeared into the distance. I did not understand. I lacked the following information: on seeing a German, all local people were obliged to step aside and take off their caps. "Ach, you are lucky!" said our hostess when I told her about my accident. "You are lucky he did not check your papers!"

The territory annexed to the German Reich ended just beyond the little town. Never in my life had I crossed a "green border" like this one, although I had seen a good many since my childhood. The theory went that the best time to cross was at noon, because all the guards ate lunch then; the theory was known to everyone, including the guards. Through a forest of pines heated by the sun, groups of men and women, bent over by the load of their sacks and bundles, advanced in extended battle order, crouching behind trees, crawling along the moss, then making a run for it to the accompaniment of shots from all sides. These men and women were peasant smugglers carrying food products to be sold in Warsaw. Although I had changed into a wild rabbit and was painfully out of breath, I appreciated that spectacle of a moving forest where there was safety in numbers, as thoroughly as if I had been sitting in a movie theater. That whole horde then crammed onto the train, hens cackled from baskets, geese honked, piglets squealed under the benches, people talked about prices and policemen, the coach smelled of cheap tobacco. We were in the Government-General.

Some may find this description of one journey too detached, as if the physical discomfort of a whole night spent wading in water on the peat bog did not personally concern me, or as if my cheeks after being struck by the Gestapo officer did not burn. I doubt, however, that my detachment is due to the passage of time, which mitigates all painful experiences. Intense feelings or a groan torn from me by the strain did not ruffle a deep-seated indifference, a self-forgetfulness that could perhaps better be described as the sensitivity of a camera, ready to register everything that is visible. As I crawled on all fours over the pine needles, I enlarged in my disinterested imagination a drawing of a twig or an ant carrying its load, and shots rang out against the background, for example, of a line from Paul Valéry: "*Ce toit tranquille où marchent les colombes.*"

The world was imperturbable, magnificent. I loved it because with every turn it offered itself to me ever new, ever different, and I sailed with it as once I had with the Rhine River, meeting the unexpected at every bend. Both what I had read and what I myself had written about the Great Finale paled now, and after a long quarantine I felt that I knew how to live for the day and for the hour. An unsuspected shape of existence could almost be discerned: an existence from which the superfluous, including the future, was removed, and yet, for all that, was no worse. And this descent, if we apply the measuring rod of social prestige, to the level of black slaves in colonial countries had put the highest form of liberty within my reach.

The G.G.

———◆———

FOR A STUDY OF HUMAN MADNESS, the history of the Vistula basin during the time it bore the curious name of "Government-General" makes excellent material. Yet the enormity of the crimes committed here paralyzes the imagination, and this, no doubt, is why the massacres in the small Czech town of Lidice and in the small French town of Oradour are given more notice in the annals of Nazi-dominated Europe than the region where there were hundreds of Lidices and Oradours. With the hanging of Governor Frank by a verdict of the Nuremberg Court, one chapter of total war appeared to have come to a close. Its cruelties are not interesting. But the system introduced into the Government-General had nothing to do with the necessities of war; in fact, and this was obvious to every spectator of the events, it ran counter to the interests of the German Army. The colossal energies that were mobilized to implement this system—that is, wasted on purely arbitrary goals—ought to fill us with awe at a century in which ideology prevails over material advantage.

The colored peoples did not suspect, when they were subjugated by the white man, that they were already avenged at the moment of their fall. Their conquerors returned home with their greed and converted it into an idea of supremacy over inferior races—even white races. That idea acquired a life of its own and was found not only among advocates of naked force but also, in a veiled form, among many democrats.

In the experimental laboratory known as the Government-

General, the Nazis divided the local population into two categories: Jews and Poles. The former were scheduled for complete extermination in the initial phase; the latter, in the next phase, were to be partially exterminated and partially utilized as a slave-labor force. The objective for the "non-Aryan" category was nearly one hundred per cent realized, as is borne out by the approximate figure of three million slain. The plan for the "Aryans" was fulfilled more slowly, and their number only decreased by about twelve per cent.

At the same time an economic revolution was set in motion, and it had durable effects: all of the large industrial plants and most of the large landed estates were confiscated and turned over to German administrators. After that the Communist revolution was easy—all the state had to do later on, when the Germans fled, was to take over those enterprises that now belonged to no one. There were even more important changes that affected both the white-collar and blue-collar segments of the urban population. It became increasingly difficult to earn money because the Polish administrative apparatus no longer existed, having been replaced by one that employed only the colonizers; and it was no better in industry, where wages were a mere formality. They were so out of line with prices that a week's salary bought food for only one day.

As a result, masses of people were driven into illegal activities, economic as well as political. There were certainly moral reasons why the Resistance movement in Poland developed on a larger scale than any other in Europe, but the disemployment of the intelligentsia, who had previously staffed commercial offices, universities, schools, radio, and the press, was equally significant. Not only office jobs were eliminated, but the entire school system was liquidated—with the exception of the elementary grades (a race of slaves has no need for learning); and the publishing of books and magazines was prohibited. In a short time, however, the Poles erected an underground state—with underground financing, administration, school system, army, and press. The occupier's struggle against this mass movement was reminiscent of the adventures that white rulers had had on other continents, and it cost the Reich many losses in manpower and war matériel. Thus in Berlin it became common usage to read the abbreviation "G.G." as *Gangster Gau;* the adversary always has to be a gangster and a thief.

Two conclusions can be drawn from this system. One is that nineteenth-century science fostered a completely naïve picture of history by creating contempt in the popular mind (nourished on brochures) for more complicated factors than mechanistic, material ones—in a sense, Hitler took Darwinism, "the struggle for existence" and the "survival of the fittest," too seriously, and by identifying history with nature he ignored the limits of blind force. That naïve outlook was overcome in Marx's analyses, and all the errors of his successors may be due to their neglect of his intention. Although the Nazis borrowed several ideas from the East, such as propaganda, political police, and concentration camps (it is not hard to imagine where the sign *"Arbeit macht frei"* on the gate at Auschwitz came from), they saw the secret of power only in monstrous crimes because they were too inferior intellectually to go beyond vulgarized biology. The loathing these men showed for intellectuals was a defensive reflex against a real threat; they guessed the danger lurking in any analysis of effective political action.

The second conclusion is unflattering to the professors who, busy with their facts and figures, treat them as valuable in themselves regardless of their interpretation, or, worse, who serve them in a nationalistic sauce. Generations of German professors had studied the Slavic world, but all their graphs and statistics were useless. From the point of view of German interests, Nazi policy, after the take-over of Poland, the Ukraine, and Byelorussia, was nonsense.

The four years I spent in Warsaw were no exception to the general rule, and every new day was a gift that defied probability. When I arrived, walls were being built around one-third of the city, into which the Jewish population was being herded. The gates to the ghetto were not closed yet, and we could still visit our friends. To discourage "Aryans" from such visits, signs were hung on the gate: "Jews, Lice, Typhus." But if those who were locked behind the walls had only extinction to look forward to—either from hunger, or from a bullet, or later from something vague that soon acquired the more concrete form of gas chambers—those outside the walls, who were swept away in the street round-ups that populated Auschwitz, and who had lost all prospects of earning an honest living, also knew they were running a race against time. Life, as for primitive man, once more depended on the seasons of the year. Autumn was the hardest because potatoes and coal had to be gotten for the long, hopeless winter. With spring, dreams of Germany's imminent defeat would make their appearance.

During those four years, I, and many like me, unlearned Western civilization, if what it teaches can be boiled down, more or less, to respect for money and the feeling that one has some kind of rights. Practically everyone I knew found himself in the financial situation of artistic bohemians, and all of us had the role of criminals hunted by the police. There were no grounds for being certain that one would eat next week, but this was accepted serenely. My friend, the novelist George Andrzejewski, invented a "theory of the last penny" which I can recommend to everyone as tried and tested. It propounds the following: at the very moment when you have nothing in your pocket but your last penny, something *has* to happen. And it always did.

The steps I took to encourage destiny a bit give some idea of the possibilities that were open to us then. I began by trading such things as Players and Woodbine cigarettes and whiskey (war booty from Dunkirk; it circulated on the black market), as well as less elegant articles like blood sausage and ladies' underwear. Today this sounds amusing, but my despair, if I returned home without a sale was genuine.

Shortly afterward, I began to sell a completely different sort of product: my new volume of poetry, printed on a ditto machine and laboriously sewn together by Janka, my future wife.

As far as I know, it was the first literary work published in occupied Warsaw. More or less at the same time, on George's initiative, a typewritten literary journal was put together, and we filled it with anti-Nazi articles.

One day I heard that workers were needed to dig out the remains of the French Institute's bombed library. The rescue effort was sponsored by the University Library. Like all libraries in Poland, it had been closed to the public and subordinated to a German central office, but its personnel had been kept on. Despite the salaries, which were below starvation level, the Polish employees loyally stayed on—besides, librarians are a special tribe; they are capable of feeding themselves on their very love for books. Having been assigned to a team of workers who loaded and transported the packing cases, I saw my opportunity and clung to the library for good. Now I could take home piles of books in various languages and immerse myself in reading. I owed my chance to become a porter to the new director of libraries, a tiny German Slavicist who had decided to protect himself at all costs from going to the front until the end of the war. With this in mind he and his adviser, a Pole by the name of Pulikowski, had elaborated a gigantic plan, requiring at least ten years to accomplish, that made both of them indispensable. With unshakable logic, the plan envisaged the rearrangement of the book collections from Warsaw's three largest libraries and the transport of millions of volumes by horsedrawn cart so that one library would contain Polish works only: the second, foreign works only; and the third, works on music, theater, and art. It was an undertaking to match moving the Alps, and in its *systematisch* approach faithfully duplicated the whole Government-General—except that its madness was bloodless.

The Polish personnel regarded the small docent with disdainful indifference, reserving the whole of their hatred for his adviser. This man must have experienced great inner turmoil. Raised in Germany, married to a German woman, speaking only German at home, he believed, it seems, that the New Order was permanent. My colleagues, porters and clerks, in the library warned each other of the traitor's approach by clearing their throats. Many a time, as we sat back on our heels to rest or crouched in an alcove to smoke a cigarette, he would try to sneak up on us, treading softly in his rubber-soled shoes. His overseer's zeal, however, did not protect him from death in 1944. Who killed him—whether Germans or Poles—I no longer remember.

Physical labor, interspersed with moments of reading, agreed with me, and I prospered on potato and carrot soups. I was grateful to the war for one thing: the end of my bureaucratic career. In the dark recesses of the stacks no police could have ferreted out the underground publications stuffed between the volumes, and that was convenient. Riding through the city with a load of books, I warmed myself in the sun, stretching out on the packing cases; I felt as if I were melting into a fascinating city-jungle with its waves of panic and intermittent bursts of gunfire. In winter we sometimes made a detour to one of the employee's houses, where we warmed up with a shot of pure alcohol. I grew attached to our whole collective there at the library, with its Polish head, the historian Dr. Lewak. Of course the trifling pennies we received as salaries were not enough, and beyond the initial period, when I looked for the moral support that comes from belonging to a group, I showed up only now and then for work in order not to lose the right to keep myself supplied with books.

The underground state grew in strength little by little, and, like all writers, I began to receive small grants from clandestine funds. The source of such funds was the high exchange rate of the dollar on the black market. Dollars came through secret channels from England or were parachuted from planes, and you could tell whether or not there had been a recent drop from the way the black-market rates fluctuated. The literary commissions increased, too. I worked with a clandestine unit whose name should come as a surprise, considering that such people are usually thought of as undisciplined: an actors' unit. Theater in Poland, however, has never been a purely capitalistic enterprise; in any case, its members have always seen themselves as high priests of art—and that imposes duties. This clandestine group prescribed a code of behavior for an actor toward the occupier and forbade acting in Nazi-licensed spectacles. It won high respect in Warsaw from the time when a certain actor, who had begun to collaborate, was shot in his own apartment. The group was headed by the distinguished director Edmund Wierciński, who with the help of his fellow-actors was preparing a radical reform of the theater for after the war. They were debating the repertoire and ordering translations of plays or original works. This activity served my literary workshop well. The actors themselves worked hard, and to this day their excellent clandestine performances in private homes or monasteries are still fresh in my memory. Edmund's wife, Maria, who was also a director, set a record of her own as a propagator of subversive poetry: she organized over one hundred and fifty clandestine poetry readings.

The breakthrough which the year 1939 had been forced me to revise my habits. Time was precious; not to use it as I should, to drift as I had before the war, would have meant shirking my most important duty. After all, I had run from Stalin's state to be able to think things over for myself instead of succumbing to a world view imposed from without. There was complete freedom here, precisely because National Socialism was an intellectual zero. However, I had to solve the problem of hope, or, rather, to find a position from which hope and despair were equally irrelevant. My chances of survival and of seeing with my own eyes what came out of this caldron were negligible. With some effort, I finally obeyed Martin Luther's advice: when asked what he would do if he knew tomorrow was going to be the end of the world, he said, "I would plant apple trees."

The library books convinced me that my Polish, French, and Russian were insufficient. I had had enough of French harping on Arthur Rimbaud and Stéphane Mallarmé. So I resolved to discover Anglo-Saxon poetry and began to learn English. After I could read with a dictionary, further progress went swiftly. (In German I understood, and to this day understand, almost nothing except *Hände hoch!* and *Alle Männer 'rrraus!* Not much, for the language of Goethe.)

Since I, like everyone else, was tortured by the why of Europe's fall, I tried to clarify my thought by writing about certain philosophical aspects of literature. I intended those essays—on Daniel Defoe, Balzac, Stendhal, André Gide, Tolstoy, William James, and two Polish authors (Stanisław Ignacy Witkiewicz and Marian Zdziechowski)—as a book. A few were published; others, such as an attack on André Gide, I preferred to leave in manuscript because of their obsessive nature. In those days, however, they filled more than a private need, since they were read at clandestine gatherings where they provoked serious discussion. Despite the lack of any legal publications (Poles were forbidden to publish even translations from the German), intellectual activity flourished; there was development; and by the end of the war many of us could compare the distance we had come from our old selves to the passage of a whole geological era.

The anthology of poetry I put together had a more immediate function. It contained poems, then circulating in handwritten copies, from the pen of local or émigré poets. Called *The Independent Song*, it appeared in 1942 in a nicely printed little edition; the publisher considered it the success of the underground market. That same year, I was pleased to be able in a small way to defend France's good name, which Nazi propagandists had dragged in the dirt. The whole affair proves how difficult it is for totalitarian systems to combat the word, which slips over borders more rapidly and more effectively than people on the outside imagine. While publishing *A travers le désastre* in Canada, Jacques Maritain did not suspect that his work, which was aimed at the Vichy government, would reach distant Poland. A certain Dutch merchant brought it to Warsaw. In my translation and with my very pro-French introduction, the text was set in extra-small type and printed in a vest-pocket format. My further penetration into English poetry also turned to my advantage: commissioned by the actors' organization, I pored over Shakespeare's *As You Like It* for several months, preparing a new translation since, in Edmund's opinion, the existing translations did not lend themselves well to stage delivery. Bucolic Shakespeare proved to be first-rate therapy. On Edmund's suggestion, backed by a fee, I also wrote a *Prologue* for the reopening of the Warsaw theaters after the war. What happened to the manuscript, whether any copies were rescued from the fire in the city, I have no idea. The tone of the *Prologue* (a dialogue between a humanist and a politician) was, I think, somewhat too elevated, since the relentless march of events was to bring defeat to the humanists.

The proliferation of the underground press irritated both George and myself. The death of many printers, editors, and carriers went unredeemed by the scant value of these miniature weeklies and dailies. Communiqués about Allied victories were scattered among articles that led the public astray with their false optimism. For this reason we were in favor of publishing books. They afforded space for analysis and were easier to distribute. Usually a book received an innocent-looking cover with a title like *A Handbook for Grain Cultivation*, and it was always antedated. But in our attempts to secure funds we rarely succeeded, for censorship functioned in the underground, making sure that all toed the London-government line, which did not look kindly upon speculation about the future; that is, upon any sort of ideological "tommyrot" from intellectuals. Yet, if only for ourselves, we wanted to gain a clear perspective, and to do that we chose the form of letters. Every time we met (George and I lived at opposite ends of town) we exchanged our philosophical epistles. A whole volume thus unfolded, a document of immediate reactions to historical reality.

Although these activities kept me busy, they were marginal. What really interested me was poetry, or, to be more exact, the extremely difficult task of discovering its new and vital patterns. From the stress of daily tragedy for millions of human beings, the word had burst and fallen to pieces. All previous forms had become meaningless. The emotional gibberish so widespread then made me feel ashamed, of myself, too, whenever I wrote something that might flatter those who were waiting for just such outpourings. This is why I dislike a couple of my poems that became popular in occupied Warsaw. No more than three years later I dug through to deeper layers, greatly aided by my meditations on English poetry. This did not mean imitating, for the disparity in experience was too great: T. S. Eliot's *The Waste Land,* for example, made somewhat weird reading as the glow from the burning ghetto illuminated the city skyline.

So I spent my time among books and papers from which my earnings came. There was also "The Firm," an institution a bit too colorful to pass up here, mainly because of its founder. When we studied law together in Wilno, W. was mistakenly evaluated by all of us. He was a tall, anemic youth who spoke very little, as if every sentence cost too much physical effort. The son of a miner from Silesia, he had a definite Leftist bent, but at the same time was extremely pious. I roomed with him for a while in the student dormitory. And from then on I always remembered him as a man kneeling at his bedside, hands folded, engrossed in either morning or evening prayers. True, even then I was puzzled by his mysterious ability to combine contemplation and action. He took an energetic part in politics at the university; and when he stepped onto the platform, this quiet boy suddenly became a leader, capable of polemics and violent invective; then, instead of his usual half-whisper, he barked in a hard, metallic voice. Valued as an organizer and a strategist, he performed various functions in the Leftist-liberal bloc. No one, however, could have foreseen his later metamorphosis into a trader worthy of the Wild West.

He founded The Firm in Wilno during the fall of 1941, while the German Army trudged toward the Volga. In a few months his profits soared from nothing to millions, and soon The Firm had two branches: one in Minsk, the capital of Byelorussia, and the other in Warsaw. Granted proper Nazi authorization on the ground of being "useful for the Army," the outfit was supplied with all sorts of passes and permits and allegedly traded in goods. In fact it dealt in the black-market purchase and sale of currency. The greater part, if not all, of the truck shipments consisted of weapons for partisan detachments. In this W.'s talent for high diplomacy nearly reached the level of genius, because his trucks moved unharassed through the forests of Byelorussia, which were controlled by partisans of varying colors. As a financial power The Firm secured privileges for itself from the Germans through bribery, paying out a regular bonus to a few dignitaries; it also maintained its own workshop for making false documents, and ran an effective rescue operation for those threatened with arrest—especially Jews, many of whom owe their lives to it. The Firm often transported them, carefully packaged, from city to city. Was W. a merchant-conqueror, a politician, or an apostle of love of one's neighbor? It would be impossible to separate these three qualities of his.

The Firm's headquarters in Warsaw, where the major activity had shifted as the front moved gradually westward, did not look much like a commercial enterprise. In a large room, amid the disorder of tires, crates, engine parts, and drums of gasoline, truck drivers slouched with their feet up on sofas, chatting lazily in a Wilno dialect and smoking cigarettes. This brigade, composed of "my boys" from Wilno suburbs, knew the complex organization inside and out. It was a team of completely trustworthy men who were treated by their boss as equals. In the second room W.'s partner, K., hung on the telephone. He was a fat Latvian Jew with a black mustache, armed with Aryan birth certificates to the tenth generation.

W. made a lot of money, which he invested as if he were playing a lottery; and he was right in judging all objects and values as fly-by-night, since the apartment houses in Warsaw, for example, were soon burned down, and the lots they stood on nationalized. He did choose to put money into manuscripts of books, since he intended to found a publishing house after the war. Not only did he buy a couple of my manuscripts, but he named me his agent. We made up contracts carefully, although I could never quite suppress the feeling that I was participating in some sort of make-believe and that sums of money passed from hand to hand simply to circulate.

As agent, I endeavored to bring about a merger between two nonexistent publishing houses, both of which relied on the black market for income. Negotiations were protracted, as they usually are when what is at stake is a treasure on a nonexistent island. The high point of my effort was a dinner, to which both parties had been invited, at one of the more elegant restaurants run by unemployed actors and painters who knew how to create settings of charm and grace. We drank the best French wines and cognacs, were entertained by a singer who played the accordion, but instead of sealing the agreement, that feast turned out to be the preface to further, hopeless quarrels over the percentage of shares. Yet all three of us knew that underneath those financial wrestlings was laughter. W., his would-be partner, and I belonged to the same Socialist organization—an offshoot of the group in Wilno which operated at the beginning of the war. When I took the oath (I swore to be "loyal to the people" or something of that sort), it was also to the sound of bottles being uncorked and in a similarly arty restaurant; I remember that two of Poland's best young composers, Lutosławski and Panufnik, furnished the entertainment, playing on two pianos.

To live with one's cowardice is bitter. Unfortunately, I did not know how to get rid of it. Perhaps in other Nazi-dominated countries the very act of publishing anti-Nazi works was cause enough for pride, but not in Poland. Here the whole collectivity made demands and exerted pressure. Yet the danger was no greater than walking down the street. When everything is outside the law, nothing is outside it, and prohibitions have no meaning. One Sunday afternoon I saw a family: a man and a woman pushing a baby buggy; the Gestapo car rolled up to them slowly. The man, seeing a revolver nozzle aimed at him, put up his hands; they thrust him into the car and moved off to further hunting—for sport. To play Providence, to be able to point your finger at someone and say, "That's the one," is no small treat for human vanity. People caught in this way filled the delivery quotas for the death camps at Auschwitz and Maidanek; their names could also be read on the lists of those shot or hung at "hostages'" executions.

There would be no point today in trying to convince myself or others that I had any sort of talent for heroism. I admit it openly: I turned cold with fear even at home if I happened to meet our apartment manager's eyes with their veiled threat, knowing that he suspected one of our guests was a Jew. (The "people"? The "people" cared, above all, about saving their own skin.) The manager once drove away two Jewish children who used to eat dinner at our house, and they were afraid to come any more. They slept somewhere in unfinished houses or in ruins; I spotted them once: the older boy, a ten-year-old, was sitting on a pile of bricks, reading a newspaper to the younger. But out of shame I did not go up to them; I did not have a penny on me and had nothing to give them. Such homeless children, runaways from the ghetto, were shot down in the street by people in green uniforms who left the corpses for the municipal authorities to bury.

A desire to regain their dignity drove practically all young people into the service of the underground army, known as the Home Army (A.K.), whose hierarchy was controlled by the London émigré government. Many of its divisions operated in the forests; others specialized in assassination attempts on high German officials who were responsible for crimes against the Poles. Because of the extreme difficulty of such counter-terroristic acts, the conspirators, like the Japanese suicide pilots, had to give full consent to their own death. The Home Army built up an extensive network, and among the feats of its intel-

ligence section working for the Allied cause, not the least
was the discovery of the first German experiments with the
V-2's. For most young people in Warsaw, membership in the
A.K. meant obedience to the orders of one's immediate superior,
classes in military theory, or, if possible, practical training in
the art of warfare.

Even though the actors' group was connected in various ways
with the army, I did not join the A.K.; nor were my literary
colleagues, on the whole, eager to rush into the fray, gun in
hand. By the age of thirty, one has already acquired a certain
number of habits, not necessarily good ones. The individual
invariably argues: "I don't want to die," which can be translated
as "I have more important tasks ahead of me." In other words, if
the individual says this, he shows that he lacks the humility
necessary for cooperating with others. I realized in the first
phase of the war that a resolve that breaks through our smallness is born only out of a powerful emotional impulse, which
in turn is inseparably bound up with a belief in the purpose
of our sacrifice.

These reflections may seem cynical and brutal. Yet, I never
even asked myself if it was my duty to plunge deeper into
conspiracy. Not only did I now lack the impulse, but I was restrained by my passionate hostility to the leaders of the Home
Army. The political fantasy of prewar Warsaw—with its slogan
"We will not yield an inch," with its conviction that if the
Germans struck, the Polish Army would occupy Berlin in a
matter of days—was only amplified by the defeat, and the
whole conspiratorial apparatus fed on an illusion, pumping into
itself a gloomy national ecstasy. There had to be a bright tomorrow, but whoever dared to hint that it depended upon the
choice of political systems and on the international power game
exposed himself to dangers that were not always platonic.

Beneath the smooth surface of common hatred for the occupier, a struggle was going on for control of the future. In
other words, prospective posts were assigned not according
to merit but to political acceptability. As a result, despite the

existence of a Council of Parties that included Socialists and Populists, there was a tendency on the part of the military brass to return to the prewar Rightist pattern. The country, as before the war, was to be a "rampart" in the East, backed by its Western Allies; no one could suspect otherwise. But since events continually gave the lie to this hope, the air was poisoned by the fumes of self-delusive and illogical thinking. My individualism may not have been a virtue, but at least it protected me from succumbing to collective moods and impelled me to turn away from what I considered spasms of the dying past. For that matter, writers, unable to find their way out of the snare, were the first to rebel against this exalted self-befuddlement. Beginning in 1943, some of their works showed a clearly satirical cast.

We always meet those whom we are ready to meet. The city offered him to me no sooner than my need made his appearance necessary. We had known each other fleetingly before the war, because of his tie with philosophical circles in Warsaw. The University's philosophy seminar often met at the home of my close friend Bolesław Miciński, the philosopher-poet. I once went to a lecture my future teacher gave on phenomenology after his return from Prague, where he had completed his studies at Charles University. But now I saw him differently. His closest friends called him Tiger because of his rapacity in argument, which reduced others to the status of grass-eating animals. A master of flexibility, of innocent ambush, of apparent absentmindedness, he fell upon his victim in one leap, and annihilated him with his irony, usually expressed in the form of parody and pantomime. Had it not been for him, my strenuous efforts to resist a lyricism of self-pity (as well as to reject the political stance imposed by my environment) might have come to nothing. As a catalyzer, he was indispensable.

Juliusz Tadeusz K. and his wife, Irena, rarely left their house; by Nazi racial laws, he was a *Mischling* and she deserved immediate removal from the face of the earth. They earned their livelihood making cigarettes. The tobacco on the black market came from peasants who cultivated it illegally. Fermented and cut in small processing plants, it could then be rolled in cigarette paper or in tubes. With practice, one could work up an almost machine-like production speed; finished cigarettes were put in boxes of a hundred. In addition, Tiger edited a journal for one of the numerous underground organizations (to make it more amusing, it was an organization of noncommissioned officers) and wrote political articles. Both of them sought peace and wisdom in Plato, whom they read in Greek.

It is difficult to achieve a distance from events, living in a mechanical slaughterhouse whose conveyor belt unceasingly carries off bodies of butchered human beings. In such circumstances, the future is annihilated and one compensates for its loss by creating an illusory tomorrow where truth and justice will triumph. This is precisely why almost all the inhabitants of Warsaw could not step past the threshold that victory over the Germans stood for: a promise of paradise. That the war was only an episode they might have understood, but to understand this and to know it with one's whole being are two different things. Tiger never dissociated the war from what preceded it or from what was to follow. What prompted him was not philosophical indifference but philosophical hatred.

Hatred for people who live badly. Hatred not only for the Nazis—even less for the Nazis, because they were condemned in advance to a dreadful punishment—but also for most of their adversaries, the Polish patriots. During great catastrophes one should try to live well; that, for him, was the only guarantee of salvation. What does that mean? It means not sinning in thought against the structure of the universe, which is meaningful. One sins by falling into hallucinations, by absolutizing impermanent values, by despising our mind, which leads us toward a mathematical ordering of cause and effect. Tiger had suffered many humiliations from those who rallied round the Fatherland and who were enemies of everything that appeared to threaten it. Did their heroic struggle against Hitler change them? Not in the least. They shared the same cult of action and the same contempt for the intellect. Taking them as an example, Tiger built up his own theology of history as of a being that occasionally shows a foot or a finger—and woe to those who disregard the sign! Poland's underground was self-sacrificing as perhaps no other in Europe. But for just that reason, Tiger watched it with horror and pity, realizing the full extent of the tragedy. Call it dialectical skill, or political imagination, or a sense of historical humor, he foresaw, as if in a crystal ball, that a sad future lay in store for the conspirators. The mocking impersonations he did of his superiors in the underground organization of officers and noncoms used to undo me; the more skillfully he played a part in front of them, the better he penetrated them. True, some hunch put them on their guard against that demon of intelligence: at first they agreed to publish his book on democracy, written under the pseudonym of Michael Psellos (he liked the works of English historians on Byzantium), but on second thought they withdrew their offer. Tiger also predicted what would become of the émigré government after the war: in England two rival newspapers would combat each other, the *London Bee* and the *Scottish Hornet;* "and they will spend the rest of their days that way." Externally, he was careful to keep up faultless appearances. Whenever he met the priest who lived next door, he always bowed and greeted him vigorously: "My respects, Father!" He used to say that paying homage to an ecclesiastical person created an excellent political image.

A democrat of the Left, he kept a tactical distance from the Communists. The latter, as agents of a foreign power, were avoided in Warsaw like lepers. Contrary to other countries of Europe, in Poland the Communists not only did not set the tone of the Resistance movement but, due to their stigma, could only scramble about on the sidelines. One sometimes had the opportunity to talk with a couple of them in literary circles, but they were in an unenviable position and used poor arguments. When asked about the year 1939, the deportations, and the concentration camps, they shrugged their shoulders: "What's a million people more or a million less in the light of historical evolution? A trifle." Tiger, however, forbade me to speak badly of Russia because in doing so one might offend the Ear. According to him, a gigantic, majestic Ear—History, Providence, or Fate—they blended together in his thinking—bent over the world. Tiger must have been born a Hegelian. It was normal for him to speak in metaphors, and here he meant that we should not harbor enmity toward Russia, for in so doing we lose our ability to judge soberly and to face up to future events. Open conflict broke out between us. I reproached him with an evasion of knowledge, for he did not even know Russian. I wanted him to step into the future with open eyes, but he, of course, had already put an equal sign between the words "real" and "good," and this made me angry.

Wisdom, yes, but shameful, because in thus conversing with each other we could not warn anyone, and the Home Army (like Mihajłović's army, except that Poland had no Tito) advanced toward its unhappy fate. By "warn" I do not mean the foretelling of a Communist victory. No one then saw clearly what was to come. The whole thing was unfolding on much deeper levels than the slick surfaces of newspaper articles, and it was because of this that the barriers between people were insurmountable. Some attitudes are foredoomed, so detached are they from reality. Thus, instead of arguing, all Tiger had to do when assailed by their musty odors was simply to imitate a pure maiden who embroiders her flag and sings a patriotic song about Polish uhlans. One cannot live by crippling one's awareness, by doing violence to oneself in order to remain on a level that has become intolerable. That epoch required, at the very least, a new sense of touch. This has nothing to do with afterthoughts; that is, with the question of whether the country could have avoided later misfortunes. By touch, I perceived a wall. And I realized, having profited from Tiger's cautionary whispers, that we do not necessarily have to bloody our fists on that wall or to bow down before it in humility. But no politician could have seen this, and the Socialists who were too intelligent to believe in their own manifestos bored me. Right or wrong, I considered my poetry a kind of higher politics, an unpolitical politics.

Pity, sympathy, and anger gave that poetry directness. Despite the circumstances, and despite the images of ruins and destruction taken from my surroundings, it was a triumphal poetry. It celebrated the holiday of my coming into health, for the first time in my life. A recovery from that powerlessness when everything, both in the world and in us, is so obscure and tied up in knots that we lack the courage to be sharp, like a diamond cutting glass. I had written poems on "social" themes and had been bothered by their artificiality. I had practiced "pure" poetry and had been no less irritated. Only now had the contradiction vanished. Now even the most personal poem translated a human situation and contained a streak of irony that made it objective. Something had gone on inside me after I admitted a brutal truth to myself: Poland's prewar society, which had shackled me with its subtle collective censorship, meant absolutely nothing to me, and I was indifferent to its latest pathetic and messianic embodiment. Virtue had gagged me up to then; one had to throw it off and proclaim that what appeared to be the end was not the end of either tradition or literature or art. I knew I had wasted years thrashing about blindly in some kind of quagmire. But finally I had worked myself out of it. To track down and root out of oneself all vestiges of the past—what disruption and what temptation to regret! But also what purity of air, what nakedness, what readiness to face the future!

My liberation had a political significance for which Tiger was responsible: the country's sufferings and the "national front" had screened my hatred for the Right, but now it burst forth openly. I differed sharply, however, from the Communists; they assuaged their grievances with doctrine, which put a wall between them and the concrete: hence the weakness of their writing. Doctrinally I was very far from them. An inner political liberation may be filtered through our being in various ways. The "naïve poems" I wrote then have a somewhat deceptive simplicity; they are really a metaphysical tract, an equivalent, in colors and shapes, of the school blackboard on the Rue d'Assas where Father Lallemant drew his Thomistic circles.

I also accepted my none-too-enviable place on earth and the dark instinct that led me to Warsaw. Had I emigrated then, I would probably have remained stuck in my prewar phase. Had I struck off for the East, my protest against inhumanity would have driven me back into undiscriminating Polish patriotism, and I would never have broken through my shell. Here, I had had a decisive experience. In 1943, I set down my future duties quite clearly: neither the "pure poetry" of Abbé Bremond and its later theoreticians, nor Russian Socialist realism. This experience also anticipated my later reserve toward Western literature. By fusing individual and historical elements in my poetry, I had made an alloy that one seldom encounters in the West.

Little by little the time was drawing near for the destruction of Warsaw. The uprising was a blameworthy, lightheaded enterprise; it completely confirmed Tiger's diagnosis—although two hundred thousand corpses do carry weight, and no one can tell what shapes the legend may take, or what influence it may exert during the decades and centuries to come. Moreover, the last week of July, 1944, explains some of the reasons for it. Handfuls of people stood on street corners, watching with a quiet smile as trucks were loaded with wardrobes, mirrors, rugs —the contents of German offices and private homes. They were fleeing. No one was afraid of them anymore. The posters that had been tacked up, ordering all males to report for work on the fortifications, were received with jeers. You could already hear Russian artillery fire. Rumors of an armed uprising were greeted joyfully: a chance to throw oneself at one's tormentors and take revenge. . . . Soon, however, came news that there would be no uprising. One of my Socialist colleagues told me that to take any sort of action now, when Mikołajczyk, the premier of the London government, was flying to Moscow, would be nonsense. Stalin was too clever to negotiate with anyone using such a trump card, and whoever tried to outsmart him would never be forgiven.

The military leaders (caught between two fires, because the Russian Radio broadcasts called for the taking up of arms) did not enter into such subtleties; as a result their judgment was incompetent. The command was given so suddenly that it found most of the units without weapons. Their intention was probably no different from that of the men who started the gun battle in Paris as the American Army was approaching. The outcome was entirely different.

That day, the first of August, Janka and I were walking over to Tiger's for an afterdinner chat and a cup of tea. I had something terribly important to discuss; namely, my new translation of an English poem. On leaving for a walk one should never be too sure of returning home, not only because something may happen to one personally, but also because the house may cease to exist. Our walk was to last a long time.

Ten carefree minutes under a cloudless sky. Then, unexpectedly, everything burst and my angle of vision changed as I found myself advancing on all fours. This outer-city district, where vegetable gardens and sparsely scattered houses bordered the fields, was so thickly planted with S.S. troops that the insurrectionists never managed to capture it. Machine guns fired at anything that moved. Not far away some friends lived; but when neither running nor walking is possible, three hundred feet is a whole journey. Heavy fire broke loose at our every leap, nailing us to the potato fields. In spite of this I never let go of my book—first of all out of respect for social ownership, since the book bore a call number of the University Library; secondly I needed it (although I could stop needing it). Its title: *The Collected Poems of T. S. Eliot,* in the Faber & Faber edition.

It was dawn of the next day by the time we crawled up to the island; that is, to a small modern flat with beautiful flowers in the courtyard; the open spaces around it made it seem completely cut off from the outside world. Yet during our two weeks of forced internment we did not run out of groats or potatoes or even coffee. From our host's bookcase I dug out a volume of sociological essays about prewar Poland, *The Young Generation of Peasants,* and plunged into a sorry reckoning with my own and my country's past, from time to time dropping flat on the floor as bullets traced long patterns across the plaster.

A kind of well in the cellar, which was connected to the fire hydrant, figured in one humiliating experience. The well was big enough for two to stand in comfortably, but there were eleven of us—all the men in the house. We hid in it when the rumble of huge S.S. tanks sounded in the vicinity. The women closed the metal cover over us, and inside we immediately began to suffocate. It was quite theatrical: in the light from the electric bulb I saw the mouths of fish thrown up on the sand and heads withering on stems of necks. A struggle also went on between those who preferred to suffocate and those who wanted to lift the cover. I suffocated, but with a nervous giggle. And anyway I did not know how real the danger was until one of us was picked up by the S.S. one day. He died running with upraised arms in front of a tank, along with a group of unlucky people like himself who were used as a human buffer in an attack on the insurrectionists' barricades.

Then the houses nearby caught fire and began to smoke. Since we were on the edge of the city, the only logical way out was across the fields. After much debate, our island crew divided up. Those who opted to remain behaved unreasonably. Our group, having made it over vegetable gardens, oat fields, and stubble, took shelter in an isolated building not far from the airport, a storehouse for grain. From the attic, we had a magnificent panorama of a white city on a plain over which billowed masses of black smoke pierced through with red tongues of flame. The noise of battle reached even to where we were:

the rattle of machine guns, the laborious hammering of tank artillery, the flat sound of antiaircraft guns, bomb explosions. Since our neighborhood was the closest to us, I could make out our house, where my desk, the witness of so many inner struggles, stood. Under the artillery fire its façade wrinkled like a face rapidly growing old. It was probably then that all my worldly goods fell through to the floor below. At night, dots of varicolored lights moved over the city: they were Germans firing, and very effectively too, at Polish and British planes that were flying in to drop supplies; they were coming from Italy. We passed several days and nights in the granary, while the nearby highway was patrolled by so-called "Vlasovians" (soldiers from auxiliary German Army divisions) recruited from various nationalities of the Soviet Union. To be more exact, they were taking advantage of their idleness to learn how to ride the bicycles they had captured. Of all things on earth, this, for some reason, seemed to me the most extravagant. They had chosen the slaughter of civilians as their vocation because, as their officers had told them in order to justify such a pleasure, Warsaw was a "bourgeois city." Those bodies of dead women we had passed in the fields were their work.

Among our group hiding in the warehouse there was one specimen who looked as if he had just emerged from the Tertiary, or at least the Victorian, era. A corpulent man with a short black mustache, he was wearing a black suit and a bowler. He raised his finger, sniffed, and said: "Bad. It smells of a corpse in here." And he was right. We could not prolong our rodent's life there, flattened out between sacks of grain. Opinions were again divided: some held that it was worse to go, others that it was worse to wait. Since we belonged to the latter, we set out as grasshoppers were singing by the empty highway in the warmth of a sunny afternoon.

Is it possible to surround a city of over a million with a cordon of guards? We found out that it was when we were caught and put behind the barbed-wire fence of a camp. "Camp" is saying too much: it was nothing more than the yard of some construction firm, with sleepy German soldiers guarding the gates. Every morning the daily catch was sent to a camp in the nearby small town of Pruszków. There people were sorted into transports, men and women separately, and sent off to concentration camps in Germany. At all costs we had to get out of there. I wrote secret notes to our companions in the granary, handing my appeal for help through the fence and trusting to the local children of that Warsaw suburb.

Human solidarity. Rescue showed up that evening in the form of a majestic nun. She commanded me severely to remember that I was her nephew. Her quiet, authoritative tone and the fluency of her German forced the soldiers into unwilling respect. Her conversation with the officer lasted an hour. Finally she appeared on the threshold: "Hurry up, hurry up." We passed through the main gate. I had never met her before and I never met her again. Nor did I ever know her name.

Intermezzo

———◆———

IN NOVEMBER OF THAT YEAR, as we walked along the empty highway, we heard only a shrill wind singing in the telegraph wires and the screeching of crows. The landscape was perfectly empty—flat fields as far as the hazy horizon line. After a ten-mile hike, we came to a little town near a railroad, or at least to the signs of a settlement: a few tall trees. Those trees, which stood naked and black over clay pits filled with lifeless water, seemed so terrifying to me that I turned around once more to fix them in my memory. Nothing mirrored better the loneliness of that land and the defenselessness of man. They were not a piece of nature, they showed no sign of human care: they simply rose up from the bare ground, as if petrified, into a colorless sky. If they had ever grown, it must have been in spite of the goats biting off their bark, in spite of the boredom of that province where trees were out of place. They stood so apart, so cut off from everything, as if they had been meant to serve as a last image seen by all those who had been executed here.

I had left behind me the village where I spent my time digging potatoes for a peasant named Kijo. A return to an elementary existence. And yet what was Poland, after all, if not thousands of villages and that hard indifference to history's upheavals? No matter what happens, the plow must till the soil; wheat and potatoes must be harvested. As for the humanists today who expand on the subject of work dehumanized by automation, if they were to spend every day bent over a hoe they might temper their judgments somewhat. Because when all is said and done, the peasant family in a primitive economy works out a fairly involved system of timesaving movements, and my ambition not to be outdone by them drove me on at a pace similar to that of a Detroit assembly line. I drew considerable profit from it, though, because my days and nights were peaceful. I loved the morning fog, geese honking at dawn, the icy well-water streaking over my body, the chimney smoke trailing low before evening, and the whole dale, with its little river under the alder trees, where the village lay. That microcosmos sufficed and I respected its code, which forbade the residents of that little valley to concern themselves with intrusions from outside. These occurred at night. Were they partisans, who collected clothes and sheepskin coats in various huts, or bandits disguised as partisans? Or were they escaped prisoners of war? No one spoke about it in the daytime. As there were no Germans around, power was in the hands of these night visitors because they were armed.

I violated their code only once, when a little man with a sack came to Kijo's one evening. Kijo took him to one side, whispered a few words, and loaded up his bag with something. When asked who that was, he answered reluctantly: "Those are our little Jews. They're from over yonder. They have a dugout in the forest." What Kijo meant by "the forest" in that woodless country was a small birch grove—which should fill every man with awe at the human being's talents for survival. I do not think that Kijo reflected over the question of racism or of a Christian's duty to oppose it. For him, people like himself, his own neighbors, had not ceased to be themselves; he simply continued as before, trading with them as of old, loyal to the ways of that closed community, which counseled flexibility in the face of pressure from outside powers; that is, avoidance of their madness, if this does not go beyond a reasonable caution.

The past and the future were useless to me, even though I thought about them a great deal. The Sunday clothes and clusters of people heading over the meadows toward the little church with its steeple, the wooden benches polished by long use, the big prayer books—they were placed now in a new time, more tangible than the Napoleonic and other epics. But that village and all others like it were defenseless. And their misfortune dated back much further than bombs and airplanes. Because I tried to reach to the roots of that calamity, I, like a conjurer of spirits, continually communed with the seventeenth century—the century before the disaster. Baroque angels in church, and baroque, perhaps, the hoe in my hands. Warsaw I outlawed from my thoughts: a large piece of plain had simply slid into a chasm, burying people and buildings.

Once, some sort of business took me to a gentry estate about a mile and a half away. I knew that peculiar Polish institution by heart, so that myriad associations immediately sprang from a half-phrase, a glance, a curl of the lips, and I had so mastered their meanings that I could have written a novel on each of them. Along the pathways between the buildings and in the garden there were a great many young people strolling in shiny officers' boots. With every word they celebrated the conservative national ritual. I found it rather pleasant to be in the position of a boor; that is, a man of unknown origins, perhaps lowborn. For them culture had come to a standstill in the Sistine Chapel, in Leonardo da Vinci's *Last Supper*, in good manners and brilliant social conversation; religion, philosophy, and art, therefore, had to carry the stamp of an old name, of an authority, like the English trademark on one's clothes. They would have been offended if someone had instructed them that what really counts is today, or, rather, what we are going to do today with any inheritance we have. Now, as they nursed their myths for a while longer before they went down to ultimate defeat, I asked myself if my resentment toward them did not arise out of my own wounded self-love: they recognized only those who were already esteemed. But to demand that they know how to appreciate worth in someone less crowned by success would have been futile. One gained their recognition by flattering conventions, by lowering oneself and pretending to be more stupid than really was the case. Everything essential was too difficult for them. I shook them off me gently: let the dead bury the dead. Free to face tomorrow, I repeated to myself: They should worry, not I.

The empty highway, the black trees, the puddles in the badly paved streets of a little town—and suddenly a wave of despair such as I had forgotten while working at Kijo's. It was not only because of the helmeted policemen and the danger of Nazi manhunts. In this country it was only the village that had some kind of form, defined by need and the tasks of the four seasons. The towns, on the other hand, were clearly a botch. (I cared less about the few larger cities; besides, nothing much was left of the principal one except smoking ruins.) One gets a feeling of having one's feet on the ground, of being supported, when the imagination can cling to a piece of territory filled with human settlements arranged in such a way that each of them appears livable. But here—tumbledown fences, chickens flying off in a panic at the approach of a peasant cart, apartment houses from which the Jews had been taken to be exterminated—it all gaped with nothingness and decay. It was hateful to me. Ruins multiplied by ruins made a desert, and I felt that I had no place to lay my head. My hot blood revolted against that inertia of bungling and neglect.

It goes without saying, however, that if our environment clashes too violently with our passion for being modern and constructive Fausts, an opposite reaction will occur: a desire to turn our backs. Revolution? Revolution is fine, but it would change nothing here because, if we go by its Eastern model, such trampled fields usually supplied the lifeblood for a few gigantic enterprises. The disorder of the place thus was simply an introduction, a foretaste of cracking walls and leaking roofs —minor details. As I walked down the street, alert and tense, the years and decades ahead presented a prospect of complete futility. Once again, everything I had been feeling up to that brief respite (in self-defense?) at Kijo's began to accumulate and oppress me so that I was ready to declare—I admit it openly—that a curse hangs over this particular piece of Europe and nothing can be done about it. Had I been given the chance, perhaps I would have blown the country to bits, so that mothers would no longer cry over their seventeen-year-old sons and daughters who died on the barricades, so that the grass would no longer grow over the ashes of Treblinka and Maidanek and Auschwitz, so that the notes of a harmonica played under a gnarled pine tree would no longer float over the nightmarish pits and dunes on the city outskirts. Because there is a kind of pity that is unbearable. And so one blows it all up, at least in one's mind; that is, one is possessed by a single desire: not to look.

Tiger 1

———◆———

MY FRIEND Tiger had prophesied in Warsaw that after the war I would do a lot of traveling. I laughed it off, but he said: "You don't have to believe me." To have seen the crown of an African king on my head would not have surprised me more than the fulfillment of his prediction. Me in America and on motor trips via the New York-Boston highway to Cape Cod's oceanside forests. . . . There was a certain flavor about the letters "D.P." on my Chevrolet license plates. For millions of Europeans then, they stood for that dreary and lowest of fates: "Displaced Person," but here they simply replaced the words "Diplomatic Personnel." In the little blue book that listed the names and addresses of diplomats accredited in Washington, I figured as the Second Secretary at the Embassy of People's Poland. And I was almost ready to grab every passerby and beg his pardon for my appearing as someone I was not. We always feel ourselves from the inside other than people see us—the clothes we wear are not our skin—but this revolt against the roles society imposes on us has many pitfalls.

I could fill many pages describing the Red Army's passage through Poland or my conversations with its officers and soldiers. I could also meditate over the cyclone that ruined families, fortunes, and whole classes, or try to explain why, after the overthrow, a non-party poet warranted the privilege of being sent to America. Adventures with Polish censorship or the internal affairs of a "Red" embassy in the United States would also provide tasty morsels. But all of that, it seems to me, can be dispensed with. I want to get to the heart of my five years as a writer and a diplomat for a people's democracy. And the heart of it was my philosophical star, Tiger.

He who would minimize our conflicts and decisions by ascribing them exclusively to Poland's geographical position and the terms of the Yalta agreement, which had delivered the country over to the administrators of the Eastern section of our planet, would be making a mistake. The scene of our speculations and concern was not only Poland but the world. Poland, however, had given us a bitter knowledge incommunicable to people in the West, whom we watched smiling inwardly. We could seek compensation for our suffering only in a malevolent wisdom that was manifestly higher than theirs. In our dialogues, we made deliberate use of metaphors and allegories. Powerless and ruined Greece, our beloved Greece, stood for Europe, and we often spoke of France as Alexandria because she had become stylized in the antiquated rituals of her grammarians and rhetoricians. As for the United States, was it not Rome, avid for peace, bread, and games?

It took some time before Tiger and I caught up with each other after the war. I had been living in Washington quite a while when I received a letter from him, postmarked Paris. Both he and his wife had been deported from Warsaw to camps in Germany, and after the entrance of the Allies, they had worked there as translators from German to English for the British Army. Later they took up residence in the Latin Quarter in Paris. At first they considered themselves refugees; but before long they decided to declare their loyalty to the new Poland. An exchange of letters prepared for our encounter, which I looked forward to very much.

The air in America, even summer in Washington with its 98° humidity, did not make me lethargic. It exhilarated me. The air in Poland is always oppressive; one breathes in elements of melancholy there that constrict the heart, and one always has the feeling that life is not completely real; hence the constant yen to drink vodka in the hope that an inaccessible normality will be restored. But even in Western Europe things had never seemed so concrete to me, so weighty, so filled with a material, temporal value. I did not need moss-covered ruins or medieval churches or Roman aqueducts; the little white houses in the green grass and the sound of power lawnmowers were enough.

Washington, D.C.—an impersonal machine, a pure abstraction —I reduced to the branches of the tree outside my window and the singing of birds the color of vermilion. But I liked New York, I liked to melt into her crowds. Most of all I got to know the American countryside, which restored me, after a prolonged interval, to my boyhood. Like all Europeans I had painted for myself a false picture of technology's reign in America, imagining that nothing was left of nature. In reality her nature was more luxuriant even than the wooded regions where I grew up, where the farmer, plowing with a wooden plow, has for centuries been wreaking effective destruction. Outside of New York City, the asphalt highways were like swords thrown into the thickets to signify that man belonged to a different order, that he was fundamentally a stranger to the snakes, turtles, chipmunks, and skunks who perished under the wheels of cars while trying to cross the unnatural band; the place where their line of march intersected the line of the driver's will somehow resembled the encounter of human destinies with the intentions of the godhead. I plunged into books on American flora and fauna, made diplomatic contacts with porcupines and beavers in the forests of Pennsylvania, but I was most drawn to the Northern states: Vermont and Maine. Maine spruce trees shrouded in white fog at sundown and sunrise were not, in my eyes, substitutes for my Lithuanian spruce. Had I used them to satisfy my nostalgia, it would have robbed them of their own individual beauty. But the waist-high grass showering me with droplets of dew, the fallen trees with their tangle of roots, the hidden presence of the moose and the bear—what a surprising kinship of emotional tradition! This America of trees and plants, fragrant with the hay reaped on

forest meadows, fitted over me smoothly and I ceased to be
a foreigner in her. None of us "Easterners," regardless of how
long he may have lived in France or England, would ever be
a Frenchman or an Englishman; but here, at barn dances where
everybody, both grownups and children, danced together, one
could forget. I realized then that the popular legend about
America, cut off by an ocean as if by the waters of Lethe,
was justified.

I wanted to forget. In my dreams, fragments would come
back to me: a road between the pines above a craggy river
bank, a lake with a string of ducks on it; but people above
all, uninvited guests, shadows, mostly ordinary men, unintelli-
gent, modestly ambitious, cruelly punished for wanting only to
live; various peasants, Jews from ramshackle little towns, a colleague from my high-school and university days—a pedant, a
plodder, the owner of an idiotic collection of empty cigarette
boxes, dreaming of a career as public prosecutor, tortured in
some Siberian camp; another, a bald lecher with batlike ears, who
told enthusiastically about a garrisoned small town: "We came
to Skidel and . . . paradise, I tell you, not a town! Every house
a brothel!" They shot him as he stole over the same border
I had crossed in 1940; after hearing about it, I could never
rid myself of the image of his short, fat fingers clawing at
the moss in a death spasm.

All the same, America was difficult to get used to. My
circumstances brought about an acute recurrence of my old
sickness, which I may have suffered from even in high school.
As far as I know, it does not figure in any psychiatric handbook. It consists of a disturbance in one's perception of time.
The sick man constantly sees time as an hourglass through
which states, systems, and civilizations trickle like sand; his immediate surroundings lose the force of reality; they do not
last at all, they disintegrate; in other words, being is unreal,
only movement is real. Those who plant flowers, till the fields,
build houses are deserving of pity because they are seen as
participants in a phantasmagoric spectacle, and to him they are

no more real than to a demon who flies up to their windows at night and peeks through the pane. They are foredoomed because the order in which they have established themselves and which shapes their every thought and feeling is, like every order, ripe for destruction.

It may be that not only individuals but whole nations suffer from this illness, if their misfortunes have lasted a long time and they cannot tolerate the sight of others who are dully complacent. Their envy drives them to seek solace in visions of the punishment awaiting those whom Fate has unjustly spared. Perhaps the classic example of such an incurable was Alexander Herzen. In 1847 he left Czar Nicholas I's empire for Western Europe, which in the same year he judged thus: "The world we live in is dying; it ought to be buried so that our heirs may breathe more freely; but people think they must cure it and they postpone death." "The aged world has grown stooped in its aristocratic livery, especially since the year one thousand eight hundred and thirty; its face has taken on an ashen hue." "This is the *facies Hippocratica;* it tells doctors that Death has already lifted his scythe." The world around him seemed senseless because only upheavals, ruin, and apocalypse made sense. "In Paris boredom is gay; in London boredom is safe; in Rome boredom is majestic; in Madrid boredom is stuffy; in Vienna stuffiness is boring."

A hundred years after him I had, as one can see, a few things in common with those poor Russians. I could not stop my mind from coursing through the ages like a projectile, seizing general characteristics and lines of development, speeding up the processes of becoming. In other words, I was troubled by an excess of what Americans so strikingly lack. No doubt this is why Tiger claimed that I had a dialectical mind. Dialectical or catastrophic? It is not quite the same thing, but almost. In any case, from it came my power of discernment, my capacity for seeing time brutally condensed, and my pride in dominating the anthill immersed in the daily bustle; that is, in the meaningless. I walked the streets of Chicago

and Los Angeles as if I were an anthropologist privileged to
visit the civilizations of Incas or Aztecs. Americans accepted
their society as if it had arisen from the very order of nature;
so saturated with it were they that they tended to pity the
rest of humanity for having strayed from the norm. If I at
least understood that all was not well with me, they did not
realize that the opposite disablement affected them: a loss of
the sense of history and, therefore, of a sense of the tragic,
which is only born of historical experience.

All their aggressiveness had been channeled into the struggle
for money, and that struggle made them forget the bloody
lessons of the Civil War. Later on, every one of them had so
trained himself to forget, that during the depression he regarded
unemployment as shameful proof of his own personal inability.
I esteemed these men; I was an admirer of their America. At
least no one here could justify his laziness by sighing: "If only
nations were not predestined, if it weren't for the Czar, if it
weren't for the government, if it weren't for the bourgeoisie
. . ." But, paradoxically, that triumph of the individual had
wrought an inner sterility; they had souls of shiny plastic. Only
the Negroes, obsessed like us (Oh, what a morning when the
stars begin to fall!), were alive, tragic, and spontaneous.

For someone like myself, who had heard and kept at the
back of his mind the prophecy: "America will be destroyed by
fire, England by fire and water, and Russia by a falling piece
of the moon," an evening such as the one I spent in Columbus,
Ohio, was unhealthy. Sunday. A deserted main street. Flickering
lights on billboards and movie houses. To kill time before my
train left, I went into the only little theater there. The pure
vulgarity of that burlesque show, stripped of aesthetic drapery,
plebeian, was fit for immigrant workers' camps of the last
century; even apes would have understood the copulative movements of the girls on stage. A diversion for lonely males. But
in the bar across the street the lonely were deprived even
of the consolation of stammering their confessions to the bar-
tender, for all eyes were riveted on the television screen. Was

this the highest that *l'homme sensuel moyen* could reach when left to himself, undismayed by the cyclones of history? The inside of the train, which I boarded a while later, was decorated with large reproductions of French Impressionists.

And then there was that constant masquerade of "Communism and Anti-Communism." I could tell them a thing or two about Communism, but I had to put a seal over my lips. And anyway it would not have been worthwhile; the same words meant something else to them and something else to me. I spotted the Achilles' heel of their system: that selection of mostly unqualified politicians and statesmen. Worse still were those lady enthusiasts at our receptions in the Embassy, admirers of progress in the East, hens pleading for a few kernels of lying propaganda. A perverse, comic masquerade. For what really preoccupied me were studies on T. S. Eliot and W. H. Auden, anthologies of American poetry, the work of Faulkner and Henry Miller, the poetry of Robert Lowell and Karl Shapiro, periodicals such as *Partisan Review* or Dwight Macdonald's *Politics*, and exhibits of modern art. It was not American diplomats who dispensed information about intellectual America (so little known in Europe then), but a Red.

Millions of people who care about money. I cared about it little. I was not born into a class that knew how to prize it and I had walked out of too many burning cities (literally or metaphorically) without looking back: *omnia mea mecum porto*. Soft carpets, gadgets, neat little houses I associated with flaming destruction. My superiors interpreted that somewhat aristocratic detachment from earthly goods as a sign that I would not succumb to capitalistic temptations.

The Embassy was a dog collar, a waste of time, a tedious place, and just as at the Polish Radio before the war, if I showed some diligence it was rather ironical. My lunch hour brought relief. I ate quickly in the cafeteria and then browsed through the new books at Whyte's Bookshop—I have always been an addict of reading in bookstores. If I could not wiggle out of a cocktail party, I put in a ten-minute appearance and then escaped. During those years in occupied Warsaw at least I acquired the ability to do solid work. Here I returned home around seven, ate supper, took an hour's nap to separate myself from the day's nonsense—then wrote until 2 A.M. In the morning I dashed to the office at breakneck speed, cursing the red lights. I yawned all day and waited for evening.

Only that double life could have earned me the right to breathe and to walk the earth like everyone else. Because from the moment Janka and I disembarked from the British liner on the shore of the Hudson River, it all seemed like the highest outrage. The gigantic city itself was an outrage because it stood there as if nothing had happened—it had not received a single notch from a bomb—and the people in the streets of Manhattan were free from what flowed in me like molten lead. The absurd paperwork that piled up on my desk and the letter lying on top of it, from a camp near Archangelsk, was an outrage. The letter had been received in Poland by relatives of the prisoner and sent to me with the request for a package for him. I had to live with the image of camps and trainloads of prisoners heading toward them. So orange juice, milk shakes, and a new shirt were outrageous. The constant lying of my colleagues and superiors, our mutual feigning of half-wittedness and innocence, was outrageous. And so was my unexpected meeting on Fifth Avenue with a Warsaw actress who had worked as a cocktail waitress during the German occupation. When asked what happened to her husband, she replied with a shrug, "Imagine! Joe was one of the first to run up to that German tank that was loaded with dynamite in the Old Town district [giggle]. Blown to pieces! They must have picked up the head and legs on the balconies! [giggle]."

Yet I was a completely different person than I had been before the war. The pen in my hand was different, and no matter how painful the world was, I felt no urge, as I had before, to escape into a lofty art. On the contrary, my extraordinary situation, which no American could have grasped, gave me an impetus and I knew I would have been poorer for not facing up to it. I do not want to pretend that I was tranquil or composed, because mentally I thrashed about in a furious sort of inner debate. But I was convinced that as long as we live, we must lift ourselves over new thresholds of consciousness; that to aim at higher and higher thresholds is our only happiness. While living in the Government-General, I crossed one of those thresholds—when we finally begin to become the person we must be, and we are at once inebriated and a little frightened at the enormous distance yet to be traveled. During my nightly vigils, when I accomplished so much work (for that alone society should have paid me), I constantly thought of Tiger, and I was aware, through the very possibility, through my very openness to the world, of how much I owed him.

Words cannot describe the fascination with someone's personality or an intellectual friendship. Tiger did not resemble the professional philosopher who divides time into intellectual activity and "all the rest" of life, which is given over to habit and prevailing custom. He philosophized incessantly and with his whole body: he was all movement, impersonating, parodying—now with love, now with hostility, now with mockery—various attitudes and opinions. He did not argue, he danced philosophical systems by transposing them into the behavior of their adherents. For me, he incarnated a truth that Europe was discovering anew: that philosophy, despite the university departments, is not mere speculation; that it both nourishes itself on everything within us and impregnates our whole being; and that if it does not help us to judge a man, a piece of sculpture, a literary work, it is dead.

The Marxists taught much the same thing, and they had attracted me as a young man because I sensed in them something vital and bracing. At the same time their dogmatism repelled me. I met Tiger in the way a river, hollowing out a bed for itself on a plain, meets a second river; it had been inevitable, a foregone conclusion. And it had consequences for me, of course, that were both political and artistic. Because "Tigerism" was a philosophy of action. Yet it was such a difficult one that only a few worthies, selected by the master himself, could hope to gain access to it. To practice it one had to cultivate "historical humor"; that is, one had to master a skill, like swimming or running, rather than a body of knowledge capable of being set forth in theories. Reality, according to him, was a changing, living tissue; it was woven out of countless interdependencies in such a way that even the tiniest detail germinates infinitely; and at the joints that keep its structure mobile, man is able to insert the lever of a conscious act.

Before the war, Tiger had frequented artistic circles, for the subject of style was paramount in his phenomenological analysis. It would be no exaggeration to say that he regarded the choice of one style or another as a matter of life or death. The fate of humanity, according to him, does not depend upon the foolish moves of its politicians but upon revolutions so discreet that scarcely anyone perceives them. With unequaled virulence, he cudgelled modern art almost in its entirety, because no matter how one looked at it, it derived from Romanticism, and Romanticism was Enemy Number One; it was damp, tearful, and, by necessity, always led to inner falsity. Thus Heraclitus's maxim "A dry flame is the best and wisest soul" seemed to contain the future of the earth. Tiger, with his usual flair for caricature, ridiculed Chopin: "Drowned maidens being dragged, from whose hair, ploom, ploom, ploom, water drips," and insisted that he would only listen to music "when a dozen or so little Germans"—here he blew out his cheeks and tooted on an invisible flute. These metaphors for the initiated connoted much more than a taste for Mozart. Tiger really cared about only one thing: salvation. And woe to those who think that in the twentieth century they can save themselves without taking part in the tragedy, without purifying themselves through historical suffering.

I sent the results of my nighttime jottings to him in Paris with the fullest confidence in his judgment. He did not always see the highest merit in my work, but then not just anything could satisfy a reader of Plato's *Republic* and Browning's *The Ring and the Book*, and this made every word of praise from him all the more valuable. My natural secretiveness delighted in our conspiracy; with malicious tongue-in-cheek, I wove my sentences perversely, hoping to win his approval. For it was we who were really changing the world, slyly, patiently, from within; we were the worm in the apple. And for precisely this reason my superiors had no cause to doubt my loyalty, or to fear that I would cross over to the émigré camp. I had come a bit too far from prewar Poland and her compulsive intellectual patterns. It is probably difficult to explain to students trained exclusively in Euclidean geometry just what non-Euclidean geometry consists of. Similarly for us (Tiger, me, our mutual friends) it was hard to convey our vision of the death of an epoch—an epoch in which inert matter, under the mask of spiritualism, tyrannized over men's minds; an epoch in which philosophy and poetry, disdained for "having nothing to do with life," were no more than accessories, flowers, an adornment of salons.

My post—as diplomat in the service of a bankrupt state—obviously did not entitle me to feel superior. Those people, however, who showed a more or less open disgust toward us (who had sold our souls to the devil) did not see the extent of the moral problem. And it could not have been otherwise, as long as they separated "serious" activities (struggle for power, drawing of borders, international treaties, and so on) from the individual's physiological existence. While they argued about Roosevelt, Truman, and Stalin, I would shrug my shoulders: "That's not what it's about." In despair they asked me what, then, was it about? Silence. I was not a politician, and despite my daily dose of press clippings I did not measure time by a political yardstick. On the other hand, I would have been threatened with moral disaster had I chosen the South Sea Islands, where I could have looked forward to nothing but "birth, copulation, and death," and where the price of turning one's back on the action was an empty heart. Like a sportsman, I kept in condition by being present in the collective work, present in

the literature of my language, not as one who partakes in its
lasting accomplishments (it is not up to us to decide that) but
as a sharer in its moments here and now.

Many were amazed at my cunning or my insensibility to
totalitarian atrocities; they saw my stance as the height of hypocrisy. But it was not, perhaps, hypocrisy. In the teaching of
"Ketman" practiced by Mohammedan heretics in Persia (it is
not unlike the Jesuit *reservatio mentalis*), a distinction was made
between the goal toward which we fervently and passionately
strive and the veils by which the prudent screen it from view.
After an era of liberal loosening up, the human species, or at
least the greater part of it, was once more entering a period
when, unfortunately, refined methods of keeping silent were
needful. I pass over the usual cynics bred in such circumstances;
their subterfuges are shallow. On the long list of my short-
comings I would not include cynicism. In spite of its great
cruelties, I praised my time and I did not yearn for any other.
Nor did I pine for Poland's prewar social-economic order; anyone who dreamed of its resurrection was my adversary. In this
sense, my service at the Embassy coincided with my conviction.
However, I wished my country a considerably better fate than
that of a Stalinist province. Similarly, I wished something much
better for Polish literature than the half-witted police theories
that had gradually come to enmesh it. I drew strength from my
friendship with Tiger, from the wrath and sarcasm of that passionate pilgrim. He believed that it was our duty to carry the
precious values of our European heritage across the dark era,
even though one were to be surrounded for whole decades by
nothing but absurdity, blood, and feces. Wear a mask, throw
them off the scent—you will be forgiven if you preserve the
love of the Good within you.

I have no intention of covering up our wretchedness. We
were held in political pincers of a kind that previous generations,
happily for them, had rarely known. Tiger, to someone who
judged only his exterior without entering into more complex
motives, might be pitiful, perhaps even contemptible. But let

his would-be accusers not fall into the trap of their pharisaic
virtue, which can be upheld only as long as they see a simple
contrast between white and black. Tiger was filled with a great
dread. In truth, he was a Franz Kafka abandoned in the middle
of a planetary cataclysm. To defend himself and what he loved
from the intellectually inferior, he had only his intelligence, and
he never doubted that it would triumph, although the moment
of its public unveiling was still far off. Thus he behaved like
those insects who resemble a piece of bark or a blade of grass.

In his letters from Paris, when he still had refugee status, he
jokingly described his talks to émigré groups. Did he lie in those
lectures? Not exactly. The double meaning in speeches about
freedom probably eluded his listeners. He used to complain to
me that "Fascists pay too little." As I read this—or another
aphorism: "A system that cannot guarantee us a few francs
a month is doomed to extinction"—I never attributed it to self-
interest on his part. If the émigrés, instead of raving about "pure
politics," which led nowhere, had founded research institutes,
publishing houses, and subsidized the intellectuals, they would
have shown they were worth something. If the capitalistic West
had known how to support people like Tiger, instead of leaving
their success or failure up to chance, it would not have been
what it was. Tiger and his wife, both bookworms, had modest
needs. "Fascists pay too little": the humorous wink disguised an
intricate reasoning. If they pay us (philosophers, poets, artists)
too little, it is because they hold us in contempt, which proves
they are reactionaries destined to lose. Their defeat will be accomplished through us, as a just punishment for the iniquities
of exploitation and colonialism.

Powerless Europe in 1948 had already been described in the
Book of Joshua. The inhabitants of the land of Canaan trembled
when the Israelites arrived on the Jordan, because they knew
that the Lord had delivered Canaan over to the newcomers and
that nothing could resist His will. At the sound of the Israelite
trumpets, dismay filled the hearts of Jericho's defenders. Now
the trumpet of Communism resounded so loudly in Paris that

the more discerning were convinced that efforts to resist the
verdict of historical Providence would be futile, and they decided to imitate the harlot, Rahab, who saved herself and her
family by aiding the Israelite spies. Or, if one prefers, there are
other chapters of Biblical fulfillment from which to draw analogies. The citizens of the declining Roman Empire, eaten up
by boredom and inner emptiness, wandering over a wasteland
touched by drought, felt weak in the face of Christian fanatics
announcing the good news of the Last Judgment. Thus when
Tiger spoke of "Christians," it was understood he meant Communists. The allegory was justified insofar as the idea of inevitable progress or of a hidden force behind the scenes—implaca-
ble toward all who disobeyed the Teacher's commands—took
its origins from Christianity: without Christianity, after all, there
would have been no Hegel or Marx. The sacred merely underwent secularization, the immanent replaced the transcendent.

In any case, should not the wise man have drawn conclusions
from the inevitable? Of what use were the courage and energy
of Julian the Apostate, who endeavored to resuscitate the cult
of pagan gods? He who resisted change then was certainly not
a friend of humanity. The convert, on the other hand, served
the Good if he built a bridge between Christianity and Plato.
Was that not the position we were in? Tiger, of course, adored
Hypatia, the last pagan philosopher of Alexandria, not the dirty,
terrifying mob of Christians who tore her apart. And yet, he
said, the future did not belong to Hypatia but to the Christians.

Tiger envied my placement in the right camp, although it
was due not to my merits but to circumstances. He implored
me to restrain myself, for there was no lack of heartrending
shrieks in my letters to him; it is unpleasant to be surrounded,
as I was every day at the Embassy, by shrewd fellows who
fidgeted nervously whenever you chatted with them, so anxious
were they to run to their typewriters and punch out a report on
some unorthodox remark dropped by their colleague. Today,
reflecting on Tiger's political maneuvers in Paris, I see many
reasons for his behavior. I think about it as if I were plunging

into my own life to snatch from its tangle of many threads that most essential strand of my own destiny.

It does not matter how we name the basic opposition: heaviness and lightness; life taken as it is and life shaped anew; matter and spirit; walking on all fours and soaring in flight. What was my mutiny as an adolescent and then as a young man if not a refusal of that directionless existence of "hogs"? As a child I safeguarded myself against grownups by my passion for nature, my aquariums, my ornithological books. To grow up and destroy that élan which they, in their sobriety, disdained seemed awful to me. My almost unhealthy conviction that sexuality is evil may have had its source not only in the teachings of our Father Prefect but also in those moments when, as a child, I observed that it is precisely sexuality that makes fools of adults, weighing them down, depriving them of the capacity for disinterested enthusiasm.

My hero was the brave nineteenth-century naturalist, such an ardent collector of insects that on his wedding day he forgot about his beloved waiting at the church; he was discovered in his tails, high in the branches of a tree where he was just about to lower his top hat over a rare species of beetle; at this sight the bride-to-be fell fainting into her mother's arms and the enthusiast of knowledge remained a bachelor forever.

In choosing poetry later on, I remained loyal to the pledge I made to myself: that I would never be like them and succumb to the force of inertia. Through poetry, in other words, I wanted to save my childhood. But what fiery sword protects the artist? Only his faith in an objective value. For those who live passively, values melt away; they wane in the encounter with what is considered the "real." Herein lies the secret of their impotent lives. And hence the traditional alliance between artists and revolutionaries. Because revolutionaries, with or without success, also search for objectively grounded values. They are saved by their violent "yes" or "no," by their upsetting the somnolent routine into which spiritual heaviness imprisons us. Their deed is equivalent to the creative act of an artist; it lifts them above themselves by demanding full surrender: no one puts words on paper or paint on canvas doubting; if one doubts, one does so five minutes later.

If Tiger in Paris leaned to the side of the Communists, it was because philosophy for him was an art, an incessant effort to acquire oneness (of the same sort that the scholar in tails and top hat achieved while perched in the tree). Being in the right camp was a calculation, yes, but of a higher order. Because he who does not constantly overcome himself—i.e., does not learn and does not act—disintegrates within; but if a man is to grow, social reality must be flexible, not rigid, not established as it is in the West. And nothing other than that chaos of new forms, after all, had made me decide to stick to People's Poland. It was my shield against those who spend all their time earning, spending, and amusing themselves.

It is worth noting that Tiger, although he scoffed at Romanticism, was himself a Romantic. His hatred for the "hogs" was a hatred for an unphilosophical way of life, or to put it another way, for *l'homme sensuel moyen*. The latter had to be made into a philosophical being, even if he had to be terrorized into it. I understood, more or less, that our friendship was nourished by my old resentment toward nature, my fear of her cruelties —*nature* meaning both the one outside us and the one within us. I could disapprove of my pride and my contempt, which masked my fear, but I doubt whether any kind of psychoanalysis would have cured me of impeding my feelings, which I constantly filtered through irony, because nature builds a trap out of them and lures us into animal satiation that lets us pass our lives without leaving a trace.

L'homme sensuel moyen in Poland had every reason to yearn for distant America because to him it really was heaven, while the dictatorship of the Party was hell. It made me ashamed to think of Kijo, on whose farm I had once dug potatoes. Now I was as far above him as the old aristocrats with their jabots and swords. Had not the Romantic dividing of people into those called to the things of the spirit and those who are ordinary breadwinners been grafted onto the new social relationships, thus confirming the common origin of Romanticism and Marxism? Tiger could declare his love for people, but only "people" as an idea; in reality he feared the man in the street, who was insensitive to the subtleties of the intellect and absorbed in his biology. That boor should not be allowed to touch him; one had to intimidate the boor. In the capitalist system he becomes a bit too bold if he can jangle money in his pockets. I was less subject than Tiger to that fear, thanks no doubt to my rural-patriarchal remembrances from childhood. My tradition was more "populist" than his, and through that I was exposed to the temptations of common sense. Economics, for example, was not translatable for him, as it was for me, into images of plows, horseshoes, buckets, varieties of crops. In fact he had no notion at all about economics. Primarily, he was concerned with the need for defense against the primitive thinking of the Rightist intelligentsia and against its biological penchant for nationalism. And I was with him in this because of my own hostility to the Right. Give them a parliamentary multiparty system and they would start flexing their muscles, while he, Tiger, would stand before them naked and defenseless.

At the beginning of summer in 1949, I boarded a plane for Europe. Flying over Newfoundland, where the snow was just barely melting, I thought of the countryside around Wilno. It would have been covered over with the same gray moss of coniferous forests dotted with the clear eyes of lakes. Then, in the icy twilight, the black ocean was below us with white plumes of icebergs. In the morning, the emerald color of Ireland. After America, Paris reminded me of sleepy Bruges, which I had visited before the war. Instead of canals there was the Seine, where swans could have glided and ivy could have completely enveloped the old stones. For me, there was a close connection between that tranquility and the vogue for Existentialism and Communism. They were just talking in their sleep. I munched *hors d'oeuvres* while exchanging polite clichés with

a crowd of "progressive" writers at various receptions, but I
did not attempt to break down the wall that stood between me
and them. Their warmed-over Jacobin ideas did not coincide
with any reality; they were social diversions. It was not my
place to enlighten them or to betray what I thought of them.

But how sweet to recover my past in the narrow streets near
the Panthéon, where once I had walked to my classes and to
the swimming pool. It was a Proustian experience. While my
footsteps and Tiger's echoed in those streets, I was both the
new and the old me; I felt the strangeness of time passing and
of the city, unchanged by time, waiting for our encounter. In
the familiar wink of Tiger's black eyes, I read the whole distance
I had covered from my days of a student and a beginning poet
here, groping about in a magma of words and feelings, as yet
unprepared for the dryness and agility of an intellect such as
Tiger's.

Our friendship was not an exchange between equals who give
and take mutually from each other. He wanted to dominate me
completely, so he hoisted himself onto a teacher's platform and
from there directed a threatening finger at me. He did it jokingly, but he was quite serious. I accepted the position of an
inferior, a faithful listener, although some of my silences shook
his self-assurance because they told of my reservations. This
tactic was in keeping with my hygienic habits: one should
yield as much ground as possible to one's partner, since what
cannot be defended is not worth being defended. Even so, we
found ourselves more than once raising our voices against each
other. But I felt at home with his historicism, so I profited from
those lessons. Yet my inner castle did not fade; on the contrary,
it acquired clarity, thanks to the contradiction. In America, the
contradiction inclined me toward *movement*, while in Paris,
through my conversations with Tiger, it drove me back toward
being, and I tried to diagnose my case. Whoever commits himself to movement alone will destroy himself. Whoever disre-
gards movement will also destroy himself, but in a different
way. This, I said to myself, is the very core of my destiny—

never to be satisfied with one or the other, only at moments to seize the unity of these opposites.

Tiger had just entered the French Communist Party. Later, after his return to Poland, this proved to be a thoroughly useless step. Not to go back would probably have been impossible for him; perhaps if he had known how to put himself across in book form, he could have found something to do abroad; but he wrote with difficulty and his language conveyed nothing of that dance, that mimicry, that brilliant acting-out of his ideas. To express himself bodily he had to have a group of friends responsive to every allusion, people, that is, who shared common historical experiences. He could find that only in Warsaw.

To prepare himself for his journey into lands he knew to be gloomy, he decided to limber up by rubbing himself with the ointment of slogans. For instance, I knew he was repelled by the saccharine, humanity-loving stanzas of Aragon and the rest of the French Communists. But now the sentimental speeches, articles, and poems did not infuriate him; they moved him, because Zeus (historical Providence) had given them his blessing. True, his emotion was more like that of a father surrounded by prattling children: "Not bad for seven-year-olds, not bad." He could manage nicely rounded sentences of praise for something, and immediately after (even though we might have been completely alone) whisper *into my ear:* "Trash!" He used to say that there was an "odor of brimstone" about Communist meetings, and the shiver that ran through him when he smelled that brimstone came from the pleasure of intellectual penetration: Evil is a test of what is *real.* Thus when the unpleasant subject of concentration camps cropped up in our conversation, there were always two stages in his response. First he would wither and contract: although he was splendidly informed about the millions of people behind barbed wire, he did not want to "weaken"; that is, to imagine the extent of their suffering. Then he would break into yells: he accused me of common sense (which is reactionary), of sympathy for fools—and here, for a second, he was sincere, for it afforded him satisfaction that fools

—i.e., unphilosophical creatures who could threaten him, delicate Franz Kafka—were being oppressed. That would never happen to him, of course, because he was clever. It seemed as if cruelty, if it were abstract enough, strengthened his convictions: the more shadow a thing makes, the greater and more powerful it is. But if he kept himself pumped up with the lives of the saints—Thorez's autobiography, *Le fils du Peuple*, lay on his night table—for balance he read Arthur Koestler and Orwell's *1984*. Such a reading diet provided him with the necessary "historical humor."

What is this monster, historical necessity, that paralyzed my contemporaries with fear? I was stopped by that question. It should be remembered that, not being a so-called Westerner, I harbored some strong resentments. We can rub our hands now; those Westerners will get what they deserve. They did not prevent the build-up of Hitler's war machine, although it lay in their power. They did not come to Poland's aid, although they had sworn to. At the Nuremberg Trials, General Jodl admitted that the Germans escaped disaster in September, 1939, only because the hundred and ten French and English divisions failed to take action against the twenty-five German divisions left behind on the Western front, and Marshal Keitel revealed that the German General Staff had been amazed by that inaction. One could have interpreted the Allies' behavior, both then and later, in two ways: either as a series of mistakes on the part of their statesmen, or as the inevitable consequence of a mysterious paralysis. If, however, one applied the popular saying "When the Lord God desires to punish somebody he takes away his reason," one was but a step away from recognizing a general law. I did not spend as much time pondering that problem then as I did later; there are monsters that cannot be subdued in hand-to-hand combat. One must tear oneself away from their gaze and look into oneself. I was prevented from that then by my human situation. And, to tell the truth, I was more taken up with how things actually were than with establishing general laws. The fact was that we were firmly lodged inside a totalitarian system.

The reasons for my quarrel with Tiger went deep into his as well as my own past; doubtless the concrete traditions I had brought out of my childhood, when I used to wander through the forests with a gun, and my mother's peasant-Lithuanian practicality disposed me to look rather indulgently on the too slick, city-bred flights of his thought. This is just what bothered him. It may be that I was better anchored in history than he, although he was superior to me in the agility of his mind. I did not approve of the plus sign he placed next to the idea of necessity. What has to be (if we ourselves do not fool ourselves into believing it has to be) simply is, but there is no immanent divinity that guarantees the moral glory of what is irreversible. If there were, we would have to pay homage, for example, to that Mohammedan guard in a Stalinist jail who advised a Polish prisoner to sign what was asked of him, exclaiming: *Allah dayët polozhenye!"** By this reasoning, Allah invested Stalin with power; therefore whoever respects Allah yields to power. But the prisoner did not believe in an immanent Reason embodied in the secret police, and he resisted. In so doing, he pushed back the boundaries of necessity.

The problem with choosing between madness (a refusal to recognize necessity) and servility (an acknowledgment of our complete powerlessness) is that one act of obedience can be the start of a downward slide. A man cannot bear the thought of being crushed by a physical compulsion; therefore he deifies the force that rules over him, investing it with superhuman traits, with omniscient reason, with a special mission; and in this way he saves a bit of his own dignity. The Russian writer Belinsky, for instance, made use of Hegel during a certain phase of his life, to deify czardom. I realized that my freedom of maneuver remained intact only as long as I lived abroad behind the screen of diplomatic service, and yet I was threatened with

---

* Russian for: "Allah gives the situation!" (Tr.)

sliding because we are drawn into compromise almost without our being aware of it. My support was none other than Tiger. Like Penelope, he ripped what he was weaving and treated his political speeches as no more than a comic opera set to the music of impeccable orthodoxy. At the same time he swore that another, a humanist revolution would follow, and it was for this, his revolution, that we ought to work. A tender friend, he was very demanding of those he loved: what was allowed to inferior beings was not for people whose salvation he cared about. He put me on my guard against those unfortunates (especially pro-government Catholics) who were condemned in advance to become tools of the secret police.

He also advised me to stay as far away as possible from the literary milieu. Writers, with few exceptions, he did not take seriously. He thought they lacked the intellectual training for their new status, and for that reason had to sink to the rank of common lackeys. Of course he heartily despised "Zhdanovism," but he found it understandable that the phenomena of decay in Western literature and art had to provoke an equally lifeless attack. Whoever bears the taint of bad style deserves no better. For him the artificial sweetness in the works of French Communists corresponded to the decadent traits of the French literary language. He encouraged me to write about that taint. Only one contemporary French writer found grace in his eyes —a Thomist, Etienne Gilson—and he was an enemy, because anything that smacked of Aristotle was a personal insult to that admirer of Plato.

Tiger forbade me to publish certain poems. For example, the poem I wrote after a stopover in Detroit. After being taken up to the twentieth floor by the hotel porter, I sat in my plush and overheated room, near the radio trickling music, and looked down at the neons below me, the garages, the traffic—metal fish circulating in an aquarium—and was so powerfully struck by the universal blunting of human desires here that an image crossed my mind of a man being sucked out from inside as one sucks out an egg through a straw. And from that image came a poem about man torn from himself, about alienation. No political motives prompted me. Tiger, however, was of the opinion that the specialists in anti-Americanism would be too pleased by the work and would pervert my intention by reading into it a zeal to bend to Party directives.

Tiger was contradictory, someone will object. But only for those who have never found themselves inside a magic circle. Perhaps, too, my attempt to present his tricks and leaps is awkward; the word never exactly fits the serpent's undulations or the cat's soft fur. His grimaces, snorts, shouts, the whole theater, I always looked upon as but temporary disguises of the real Tiger. The real Tiger was one with the real, the deeper, me, revealed through poetry. Poetry is a constant self-negation; it imitates Heraclitian fluidity. And only poetry is optimistic in the twentieth century, through its sensual avidity, its premonitions of change, its prophecies with many meanings. Even if we leave no immortal works behind us, the discipline itself is worthy of praise. Tiger ·shrugged off my populist nostalgia with impatience; yet in bestowing upon me the glorious title of dialectician, he was alluding favorably to my origins; that is, to feudal vestiges unencumbered by petty-bourgeois habits. This meant, more or less, that he would not have thought well of me had I eliminated the tension born of the conflict between thesis and antithesis; in other words, had I either lapsed into the comfort of moral intransigency or attached myself solely to the present by writing for the Party. But poetic discipline is impossible without piety and admiration, without faith in the infinite layers of being that are hidden within an apple, a man, or a tree; it challenges one through becoming to move closer to what *is*. Such was my inner castle, a castle of prayer, and our friendship was secured by my resistance.

All the same, ordinary human despair must be given its just due. From Paris I went to Poland, where I spent my vacation. The whole country was bursting with suppressed hatred for its rulers and their Russian employers. The Normans after the conquest of England could not have been more isolated from

the population than the new privileged caste (I, by the very cut
of my clothes, carried the mark of that caste), and more than
once I noticed fear in the eyes of those who passed me in the
street. Terror is not, as Western intellectuals imagine, monumental; it is abject, it has a furtive glance, it destroys the fabric
of human society and changes the relationships of millions of
individuals into channels for blackmail. In addition, Poland's
economy, a captive of ideological requirements, made one's
hair stand on end. It brought to mind Gulliver's observations
about the land of the Balnibarbi, administered by the enlightened Academy of Projectors, where "the people [at the top]
are too much taken up in their own speculations to have regard
to what passed here below," and where "the people in the streets
walked fast, looked wild, their eyes fixed, and were generally
in rags."

No wonder, then, that Paris, after such a vacation, was not
very gay, nor was that morning when my plane, because of a
slight defect in the motor, stopped in New Brunswick, Canada,
after a night flight over the ocean—even though the green
landscape at dawn delighted me as I breathed in the fragrance
of the spruce forests. I fell into a crisis that was to drag out
over whole months, made more painful because there was no
one with whom I could share my burden. An American could
not have understood such strange modern conflicts. In official
Washington there resided only one poet, though one, it must
be said, of high caliber: St.-John Perse. It was he to whom I
confided my misery. It seems I bored him terribly. The author
of *Anabasis*, ensconced in his lofty solitude of a voluntary exile,
looked upon the moral tempests and struggles of his contemporaries as one regards the ebb and flow of the sea. I attempted,
nonetheless, to squeeze the opinion out of him about literature
as action, about a writer's responsibility when he sees that he
can get through the net of censorship only at the cost of daily
concessions. I spoke badly. I stammered. In that glittering light
(sun, neon, the chirping of birds—cardinals, their red like the

red in the seventeenth-century paintings of De La Tour) Europe lost the weight of existence, and I tried in vain to explain my turmoil.

No one will blame me, perhaps, for having sought out authorities. That was my purpose when, instead of going straight from New York to Washington one day, I turned off for Princeton. Princeton to me meant two streets. On one lived Christian Gauss, the Professor Emeritus of French Literature; he and Mrs. Gauss, old Parisians, had been contemporaries and friends of Oscar Miłosz. On the other stood Albert Einstein's little house. My irony and sarcasm only somersaulted on the surface; they did not destroy my childlike enthusiasm for people and human affairs. My nature demanded that I bend my knee before something or someone—to praise. Einstein's white mane, his gray sweatshirt with the fountain pen clipped to the front of it at the neck, his soft voice, the serene gestures of his hands in front of an old wooden statuette of the Madonna, everything about him appealed to my father complex, my yearning for a protector and leader. I felt remorseful toward him because of the disgrace of what had happened during the first Congress in Defense of Peace, held in Wrocław, Poland, in 1948: fear of the Russians prevented his appeal from being read—it called for the creation of a world government to control atomic energy. I was grateful for his melancholy smile, proof that he understood, that he did not condemn people who are powerless in spite of their good will.

To tell the truth, Einstein could not have helped me. In the problem that interested me, he was moving upon uncertain ground. As an exile he had no fondness for that condition, and he reacted more on an emotional level: "You had better stick to your country." His advice did not surprise me because I had repeated the same thing to myself often enough. To justify it he fell back on his optimism: one should not be hasty; the terror and the absurdity of dogmas will not last forever; no, they certainly have to end sometime. Despite all my veneration for him, a little ironical imp in me tore him from the pedestal that people had erected to this successor of Newton, and I saw him as one of many, part of a certain generation of Europeans. He was a humanitarian; his mind had been formed in an era when nothing could have shaken the prevailing assumption that man is a reasonable creature, and that if he falls into madness it is only temporary. The criterion for that era had been the individual man, who dominated the collectivity, who was safeguarded by inviolable law and empowered to protest by the ballot. But for my generation man was already the plaything of demonic powers born not in himself but in an interhuman space created by both him and his fellow-man. So I walked out of the little house on Mercer Street and my car door banged shut, and I drove past the mileage signs numbly, a stranger to my own body. All of us yearn naïvely for a certain point on the earth where the highest wisdom accessible to humanity at a given moment dwells, and it is hard to admit that such a point does not exist, that we have to rely only upon ourselves.

Nevertheless, in the fall of 1950 I said farewell to America. That was probably the most painful decision of my life—though none other was permissible. During my four-and-a-half-year stay, I had grown attached to the country and wished it the best. Its overheated civilization may have sometimes irritated me, but at the same time I had never come across so many good people ready to help their neighbor, a trait that could be all the more valued by this newcomer from the outer shadows, where to jump at one's neighbor's throat was the rule. Yes, but even if I had consented to a separation from Tiger—Tiger, already a professor in Warsaw, I mention here only as a symbol of *all* hope, of that hope to which his undulating leaps gave assent; that whoever proposes Marxism to mankind takes in hand a scorpion whose tail is filled with the dialectical poison—even if I had wanted to cancel my share in the community the easy way, old-fashioned honor would never have permitted me to flee in such a manner. To announce that I intended to stay in

America and obtain a position at some university would have been too simple and, therefore, ugly. For an average American my behavior would look insane, but I did not deceive myself either, and when I embarked in New York my teeth were chattering.

Tiger 2

———◆———

SO ONCE AGAIN the action shifts to Europe. The sequel is somewhat too sensational for my taste, and I am reluctant to deal in exposures because I would have to cater to gossip-mongering and probe the minds of a few old Communists so tragically experienced that they were inclined to save me, despite my unorthodoxy, for the future. (Besides, I won them over completely: rarely did anyone return from America then.) I also would have to delve into the psychology of other men, corrupted absolutely by absolute power. They turned my loyalty into a laughingstock, and in Warsaw I felt like a fool who, of his own free will, had walked into a den of bandits armed to the teeth. And yet, I do not regret anything today. I would not call that trip a mistake, because for my despair to come to a head I needed to see for myself Poland's Stalinist nightmare, and the cynics, who were too sure that now I would not escape their clutches, freed me from all moral obligations. My family was still abroad. Thanks to the help of those old Communists I spoke about earlier (I will never know what the real intentions of those former inmates of Stalin's prisons were), I arrived in France for a short stay at the beginning of 1951. I broke with the government at once. Paris obviously was linked in some special way with my destiny.

Despite the unheard-of complications of what could have been the plot of a detective story, there is a simple key that makes everything clear. Every man has only a limited supply of energy. In exceptionally difficult decisions he uses up his entire supply, so that he cannot move a step further. Simone Weil analyzed this many times in her writings. She says: "It is naïve on our part to be surprised when, having decided to do something, we do not stick to our decision. Something impelled us to undertake that decision, but that something was not strong enough to propel us all the way to accomplishment; it also happens that the very act of deciding exhausts the incentive, so that we cannot even begin to accomplish what we decided."

I would prefer not to go into those trials lest I be mistaken for an adventurer (although my Father Prefect would have said I was running true to form). At any rate, the figures on the chessboard had shifted. First Tiger had been in the Western camp and I in the Eastern, then both of us in the Eastern, and now our positions were reversed completely. Yet during that time, while our destinies were being forged, did we ever cease to be ourselves? Would we not have embraced one another, forgetting about frontiers guarded by the sword and the inscription *Cuius regio eius religio?* We were only intellectuals, who always deceive the prince in power because his goal is never their goal. And even if our outer successes have sometimes been enviable, our lot in this century of conformity is the worst of all.

Tiger was named Professor of Philosophy at the Party Institute in Warsaw for the forming of political cadres, and was soon appointed Professor at the University as well, but for several years the Party refused to admit him. He was anxious to gain entrance because it is bad to be modeled clay; one must be the hand that models. He himself was to blame, however; his personality did not submit easily to training. The rite is gloomy, and without the full gravity of its participants there could be no "odor of brimstone." Ideas were too quickly associated in Tiger's mind, and this annoyed others who were unable to keep up; his sense of humor led him to grimace in the least suitable part of a speech, when every other face wore a stony expression; he came to his lectures at the University wearing a bow tie, which was politically suspect, or he picked some well-thought-of personage as the subject for one of his pantomimes. At any rate, beneath his bows and his Oriental politeness they detected something alien.

Very soon his old hatred for strong-armed dunces returned. His dream of making men into philosophers ran up against the inertia of matter. But he had to keep his hatred in check, and only in his allegorical parables, reserved for a small circle of attached disciples, did he give vent to it. His parable about the two missionaries in central Africa is not hard to decipher: They had been debating with each other for a long time—one asserted that apes can be converted to Christianity; the other argued that they cannot. Tiger seemed to think that they cannot.

In 1950, he went to Moscow on a university-group excursion. He returned livid with fear. Until then, he had had no direct contact with Russian life, and it must have been no small shock if he talked about it only in monosyllables. After that he no longer spoke the name of his Eastern neighbor; he called it "Persia" instead. In Orwellian Poland, although the terror never went as far as in Russia during Stalin's last years, people saved themselves from mental illness by forming ties of uncompromisingly loyal friendship. Tiger's small group paid homage to his talents for psychotherapy. At once author and performer, he improvised whole serial-novels, adding new characters constantly. The metaphors were usually aimed at oppression and injustice; but they were colorful enough so that the closeness to reality did not spoil the game. Thus, Tiger told about a potentate named Bermanidez,* who lived in South America. He was an owner of factories and mines whose laborers worked sixteen hours a day. Even seven-year-old children (in rags) were harnessed to wheelbarrows. Bermanidez, an art lover, possessed a splendid collection of French Impressionists. In his presence one did not discuss trivial subjects, only aesthetics, such as the technique of Renoir or Monet. Bermanidez also owned a network of efficiently organized houses of prostitution where the

---

*Allusion to Jakub Berman, the most influential *éminence grise* and high official during the Stalinist era in Poland. (Tr.)

highest dignitaries, both lay and clerical, were admitted free of charge. The slightest whims were gratified there, including the strange caprice of a certain violet-robed dignitary: the girls had to dress in school uniforms and sit on benches. "How are you, little girls!" the venerable client would greet them as he ascended the platform. After their polite chorus in response, he would begin his lecture, in the middle of which he threw himself at one of them. Later, Bermanidez went bankrupt and his highly placed associates no longer recognized him on the street. But Tiger permitted him to keep his villa ("We are not cruel") and a cheaper car in place of his Rolls-Royce.

Sometimes science fiction crept into his parables. One of them goes like this: time machines have already been perfected and it is now possible to travel into every past epoch. Such expeditions stimulate great interest and the Party imposes strict regulations. Permission to journey into the recent past is hard to get—only members of the Central Committee can spend their vacations in pre-1939 Poland; those who are less resistant might be harmed by making comparisons. Passports to Ancient Rome or the Middle Ages are dispensed to citizens of lower rank. Ever since someone "chose freedom" on the Gobi Desert in the thirteenth century, however, only group excursions have been organized. Tiger suspected that most of the brilliant scholars of whom humanity is proud have simply been citizens of the future, "choosing freedom" during a tourist trip of this sort. They disguised their greater knowledge in concepts accessible to their new environment.

Thanks to his malicious humor, which devastated the "now," Tiger in his inner self was free. If not for those conventicles of trustworthy friends, the Marxist professor would probably have ended up a schizophrenic. Was he a Marxist? Yes, but let us betray a dreadful secret here: "Marxists" probably do not exist at all, for the term covers very different and often contradictory positions. Tiger played with the absurdities of official doctrine like a juggler tossing balls into the air. Yet he did not lose his sense of direction, or cease to burst out angrily against the apes who were capable of taking from Marx only what happened to please their ape minds.

He was not a materialist: the word "materialist," as he used it, was an insult. He set the human world, the historical world, so strongly against the immovable laws of the natural sciences, he so steeped himself in that world, so savored its wonders (barely intuited by his contemporaries), that all those dullards who changed Marxism into a kind of reworked Darwinism made him furious. It was the tightly interwoven texture of human phenomena that attracted him, that sort of aerial house ceaselessly erected by man over indifferent and mechanical nature. Even a small detail like the one noted down by ancient historians—that men in Egypt urinated in a squatting, not standing, posture—delighted him because it bore witness to changing customs, of which only man is capable. Yet the realm of the human is constantly invaded from without by a foreign element —terrifying and humiliating because it reminds us of our animality: death. Tiger was so obsessed with death that he would turn over the pages of a book quickly in order to avoid the picture of some unsuitable philosopher: "unsuitable" meant he died young. Tiger had meditated too long on man's uniqueness, however, for death to close the account. He used to say: "Only idiots doubt the immortality of the soul."

Salvation. It is impossible if we wear ourselves out trying to swim against the historical current, because then we fall victim to illusions. But if we swim with the current, what kind of conditions must be met? Both fear and the will to dominate nourished Tiger's personal faults of scheming and vindictiveness. Passionate in his attachments, he was ready to destroy his enemies by convincing himself he was destroying vermin. Yet he truly loved the Good; he would not have killed even a fly. And the puzzle of an ethic unsupported by some immovable Ten Commandments, of just rules painfully arrived at every day amid general instability, worried him, it seems, more and more. The gatherings of his small circle of friends were devoted to the question: What is permissible and what is not? It is permissible to remove an old-generation professor (vermin) from the department, but it is not permissible to imprison him or to deprive him of the possibility of earning his living.

Antitotalitarian to the core, Tiger had to humiliate himself and lie because he had persuaded himself that in the last analysis his deceit served the truth. The physical appearance of a professor of philosophy at Moscow University had left a strong impression on him. "Only prolonged slapping in the face could have given his skin that color." Tiger's pain at times reached such an intensity that he used to ask his friends: "Tell me, but tell me the truth; has it happened? Has my skin turned that color? Does it show?"

While Tiger so dubiously prospered in Warsaw, I was trying to make the best of my fall in Paris; for the lot of a refugee is such a fall, and I would recommend it to no one unless he is blessed with the health of a horse, the vitality of an alligator, and the nerves of a hippopotamus. Objectively, I did not have a chance: Western Europe does not know how to feed her own intellectuals, let alone the citizens of "second-rate"—in her outdated way of speaking—countries. My own face (rather the worse for wear) could scarcely pretend to virginal purity. A writer, who fled from a country where Tomorrow was being born (if the system is bad, then it is good enough for Eastern barbarians) was guilty of a *social blunder*. His status in Parisian society wavered between that of a pickpocket and that of a swindler. When I began to publish in French, every Stalinist journal, along with their sympathizers, was able to use it against me; but what humiliated me even more was their silent suspicion. I armored myself with my pride, with my disdain for ignoramuses and the *idées générales* rolling off their tongues, but such armor is seldom invulnerable.

At the same time, both the tone and the content of my writings provoked the Polish émigrés of the Right, who had wanted to get their hands on me even before the war, and set them off on a hot chase after "the dangerous Communist," which lasted for several years. This primitive thinking was precisely the reason why Tiger was opposed to parliamentary democracy; and indeed it can be threatening if every article in the so-called free press is immediately utilized as a denunciation to the police. Instead of irritating people with one's impudence, it would have been safer to sit quietly; however, the impulses that guide our fate have little to do with tact. I had been stifled too long by the gag of censorship for my anger not to break loose. To make sense out of my new condition, I could only write the truth about Stalinism. Besides, I did not forget that I had a duty, I did not forget that evening in Warsaw when an abyss opened up in front of me; when I heard people of supposedly impeccable orthodoxy saying to me: "One has the right to escape only if he finds a way to fight." So I rubbed my jaw after each blow and continued on my own way. And a voice kept repeating, "You are noble."

Alas, the voice clearly mocked. I was like a passenger in the time-vehicle from Tiger's parable, landing (there is a difference between visiting a place and living there) in a past era; little did it matter that it was somewhat closer than the Gobi Desert of the thirteenth century. Four hundred thousand novels about every possible erotic combination lay in the windows of Paris bookstores like medieval crossbows and swords on exhibit in a museum. The war in Indochina seemed like something from the era of Napoleon III. McCarthyism in America revived a spectacle of ignorance that was familiar to me from some previous incarnation. When the translation of my book *The Captive Mind* appeared in New York, press clippings from Alabama, Georgia, and South Carolina made me wince: a local journalist identified me as an ally, while I had believed that by coming out against human degradation, by this alone, I was already on the side of his Negroes. What scale can we use to weigh our deeds, if they are intercepted and mutilated beyond recognition, not only there, on the other side of the Elbe, but here as well? It is our intentions that will either damn us or save us. Yet it is doubtful whether one should protest the injury by throwing oneself in front of a train of prisoners and allowing oneself to be crushed under the wheels. Call it weakness or call it prudence, this is what caused my dread of defeat. The official anti-Communism of the West was false, as is every frozen thought, but many a time its representatives closed their eyes to what they did not wish to see in my works. In that Tower of Babel, language was confounded because the levels of consciousness were different. I had to consent in advance to defeat, which is dangerous because then we are tempted to exult in our inner readiness to accept the cross.

But the voice mocked, and that was lucky. Had it not been for that voice I could have easily forgotten Tiger; lofty, pure-hearted, I could have gotten rid of the antinomy and slipped back into the past. I rejected the demonism which Tiger, even while suffering, still savored; nonetheless I kept up my dialogue with him, with his warnings and curses. History's course is not something to be discarded easily. Yet if we do not agree to submit, we ought to have no more certainty than a vague hope. One of my American reviewers wrote that since I criticize both East and West, the only road left to me is Gandhi's, but his conclusion was not entirely correct.

Many of my contemporaries may regard such thrashing about as the neurotic unhinging of a modern Hamlet. Their jobs and their amusements prevent them from seeing what is really at stake. I was not a philosopher. Events themselves threw me into my century's towering philosophical pressures, into the vortex of its hardest and most essential questions. Perhaps these exceeded my grasp, but they mobilized all my energies.

Westerners like to dwell in the empyrean of noble words about spirit and freedom; but it is not often that they ask someone whether he has enough money for lunch. There were very few people in Paris who cared about my corporeal frame, but the kindness of those few is all the more dear to me now. Sixty cigarettes a day, hours of circling around a table, nights of insomnia, all this proved that I did not have the nerves of a hippopotamus and that the hatred of Leftist *bien pensants* as well as of Rightist émigrés, the prescribed calumnies in the

Warsaw press, the meals on borrowed francs, did not exactly make me happy. My frugal needs were my only virtue. I could have worked even strung up from a rafter by one foot. When someone finally manages to get out of that pit and sees his books published in various languages, he would not be telling the truth if he ascribed it to his own merits. I was led by a Hand. I know nothing about it except that, by inspiring those who befriend us, it acts too miraculously for us to have any doubt of its existence.

The classic result of all sudden ruptures and reversals is the rumination on one's own worthlessness and the desire to punish oneself, known as *delectatio morosa*. I would never have been cured of it had it not been for the beauty of the earth. The clear autumn mornings in an Alsatian village surrounded by vineyards, the paths on an Alpine slope over the Isère River, rustling with dry leaves from the chestnut trees, or the sharp light of early spring on the Lake of Four Cantons near Schiller's rock, or a small river near Périgueux on whose surface kingfishers traced colored shadows of flight in the July heat—all this reconciled me with the universe and with myself.

But it was not the same as it had been in America; it was not only nature that cured me. Europe herself gathered me in her warm embrace, and her stones, chiseled by the hands of past generations, the swarm of her faces emerging from carved wood, from paintings, from the gilt of embroidered fabrics, soothed me, and my voice was added to her old challenges and oaths in spite of my refusal to accept her split and her sickliness. Europe, after all, was home to me. And in her I happened to find help: the country of the Dordogne is like a Platonic recollection, a prenatal landscape so hospitable that prehistoric man, twenty or thirty thousand years ago, selected the valley of the Vézère for his abode (was he, too, moved by a Platonic recollection of Paradise?). And while I climbed the hills of Saint-Emilion near a place where only yesterday the villas of Roman officials had stood, I tried to imagine, gazing out over the brown furrows of earth in the vineyards, all the hands that had once toiled here. Something went on inside me then. Such transformations are, of course, slow, and at first they are hidden even from ourselves. Gradually, though, I stopped worrying about the whole mythology of exile, this side of the wall or that side of the wall. Poland and the Dordogne, Lithuania and Savoy, the narrow little streets in Wilno and the Quartier Latin, all fused together. I was like an ancient Greek. I had simply moved from one city to another. My native Europe, all of it, dwelled inside me, with its mountains, forests, and capitals; and that map of the heart left no room for my troubles. After a few years of groping in the dark, my foot once again touched solid ground, and I regained the ability to live in the present, in a "now" within which past and future, both stronger than all possible apocalypses, mingle and mutually enrich each other.

I know I should not try to crowd a multitude of faces, books, landscapes, victories, and defeats into a pallid schema, drained of the changing colors of days and hours. Yet how insistently one dominant motif ran through those days and hours is borne out by a lengthy work in verse which I began at the end of 1955.* Both its austere style and its contents are far from graceful, but grace is not always indicated. Artists crave being, a communion with the divine promise inside creation. For them, processions of armies, social struggles, the chaos of dying regimes and emergent political systems simply happen on the outside. For others, those battles and that chaos are reality itself. As for me, whatever I accomplished that was worthwhile was due precisely to the clash of these two attitudes within myself, so that perhaps what tossed me across borders and oceans was not only a spirit of adventure and not only indecisiveness. Faithful to Tiger, I endeavored to speak a language deliberately stripped of post-Romantic ornament, and to disentangle my own enigma and ultimately that of my generation. If I were to squeeze from that poem the most vital part, the argument (though poetry can never be reduced to prose) would run something like this: Immobility

* *Traktat poetycki* (*Treatise on Poetry*), published by Kultura, Paris, 1957. (Tr.)

or resistance to the historical changes that time brings with it in the name of unchangeable moral commandments and a stable structure of the universe is deserving of respect. However, those who armor themselves in this way risk punishment, because sooner or later the Spirit of History will appear, "His face large as ten moons, a chain of freshly cut heads around his neck." Then they will fall on their knees in front of him and will identify him with the Spirit of the Earth, "who gathers the legs of dead beetles into a soft clod from which a hyacinth sprouts"; that is, they will identify him with the mathematical necessity to which all of nature is subject. But nature's kingdom is not our home; we belong to it, and yet we do not belong. In nature's kingdom necessity is the only good; not so for us. In our kingdom, the process of becoming is history, and it obeys quite different laws. It grows out of ourselves, out of even our smallest deeds. Unfortunately, our adaptation to historical fluidity has not passed beyond the stage of awkward beginnings, but to liberate ourselves from her magnetism we must reinforce her, not turn away from her.

Woe to those who suddenly discover historical time unprepared, as an illiterate would discover chemistry. But woe also to those who deceive themselves by their obedience to an unchanging moral claim, because for them historical time, which demands of us constant renewal, is but fog and delusion. Even their art will be inert, for it has not been toughened in the purgatorial fires—and man's unavoidable contradictions are his purgatory.

This argument, presented too abstractly here, was not abstract for me because I took it from my own most personal experiences. A refusal of peace, of only private happiness: my departure from America was perhaps an escape from Cythera. In memory of my Latin teacher, Adolf Rożek, who sometimes visited my dreams, I ended my poem with a farewell line from Horace about Venus directing choirs under the rising moon. But I also settled accounts with the slaves of Progress: they tremble before the judgment of history because they have set it up as the highest instance of morality and aesthetics. They strain on tiptoe to peek at tomorrow but they are never tall enough, and the future never distributes good and bad points the way we expect. If our standards were contained in time instead of being invented by ourselves, history would crush us with its rigid, formal weight. But it is perverse, and it forces us, both in politics and in art, to thrust our demands into the future; in other words, to take a risk.

I finished my *Treatise on Poetry* in 1956 shortly before the revolutionary upheavals in Poland and Hungary. It appeared soon afterward in Paris. I never expected that a little book which was difficult would appeal to anyone or that it would merit the highest of awards. The latter came in a letter from Warsaw, and there could have been no better crown of laurel, for the letter was from Tiger. I had always assumed that even my more successful works need not have warranted his approval but that if he were to disapprove strongly of something, I would certainly, after thinking it over, have to admit he was right. On the other hand, something that failed to win his complete approval could not pretend to perfection. But Tiger's letter was also a reward for my dark night of the soul, when I refused simply to slip out of the antinomy between the divine and the historical that was poisoning my life. He, too, was poisoned by it, in spite of the reassurances he had given himself at the beginning. And our brotherhood was now put on a new footing at a higher turn of the intellectual spiral.

Tiger, though, let me down with his articles in the Warsaw press. They came out at a time when he could have removed his mask and spoken out on behalf of his own humanistic revolution. But it was other, younger Tigers who lunged out from behind the lianas of censorship, while he paced at the rear guard as if to cover the retreat of the Stalinists. I was sorry for his pusillanimity, for his incessant caution, his pussyfooting, as if he feared to stop his game because he might fall to pieces. But at the same time his tactics boded ill: if he was so restrained, it meant that the time was not ripe and there was no real "thaw"

in the offing, only a short-lived fever. But I think I did him
an injustice. Tiger may have been skeptical, but he was also
ashamed to copy the skillful ones who maneuvered a hundred-
and-eighty-degree turn and who overnight began to assert the
opposite of what they had asserted up to that moment. Had he
previously just lied and nothing more, doubtless he would have
had no scruples. But his subterfuges were always in keeping
with his vocation for tracking game, whatever we call that game
—probably it was only our elusive morality.

I read the news of Tiger's sudden death of a heart attack
as I was skimming through the papers one summer afternoon
in 1958. As usual when someone vanishes who, simply because
he existed, assured us of some kind of full union and reciprocity,
there was nothing to do but stare at the green leaf fluttering in
the wind. Nothing has yet been found to confront the elementary fact of death, nothing beyond the words of Ecclesiastes:
"For there shall be no lasting remembrance of the wise man no
more than of the fool, for the times to come shall cover all
things with oblivion." Later, I found out that in the period before his death he had been reading only two books: Proust's
Remembrance of Things Past and Hegel's *Aesthetics*. He joked
that Hegel was so difficult he had made him sick. His joke
was, I think, more of a confession than anyone realized. Tiger
was killed by his game. The heart, too quickly consumed by the
game, is unable to keep up with the mind, straining to discern
the will of God in the current of history.

If, unlike Tiger, I tried to console myself with advice from
the Sermon on the Mount—"Do not worry about tomorrow,
for tomorrow will take care of itself"—it does not give me the
right to boast. On the contrary. Tiger took much upon himself
for me, and his presence, whether near or far, acted on me like
a gadfly; he stung me, excited me, would not let me fall asleep.
He did not fulfill himself in written works, but we cannot gauge
the meaning of such an individual to society—what Socratic
rays, what encouragements that lead others to practical results.
I maintain that had Tiger not existed, several of his friends (both

in Poland and abroad) would have acted differently, and since they command various rostrums, the country where he was born would be poorer by one significant component.

With Tiger's death, my book comes to a close. The final chapter, although it treats of a person who was very near to me, is of a practical nature, since this is not a book of feelings. The example of our conflicts and reconciliations, the option standing before us, was meant to crown all that I have tried to say about my part of Europe, the Eastern part. We were not like the Russians, because there was no blessed patriotic cloud to obscure our consciousness. While we sought escape in justifications, we could not escape into the most convenient one, which the power of one's own country always affords, even though acquired at an indecent cost. Neither he nor I were deceived into thinking that the relative smallness of our country could be obviated. Perhaps I, coming from a linguistically heterogeneous area, understood, even better than he, the lasting consequences of defeat and the original sin weighing on Polish Communists, who disdained a past that absorbed every peasant child who went to school.

We were also different from Western Leftists because they were still tending a legend. For us, months and years of that legend had carved our very flesh. Their beliefs protected their ignorance of the geography and history of countries only a few hours away by air, and they thought they could find out enough about the labyrinthine complexities of human communities by reading the encyclopedia, like Flaubert's incorrigible Bouvard and Pécuchet. They had grown up in an age of bourgeois individualism, and suddenly they were beating their breasts and taking up the public cause—for us they were only neophytes. We Easterners did not have bourgeois individualism behind us; we drew from our own heritage and thus honored a different tradition. When Tiger lived on Rue Cardinal Lemoine, he forced himself to be "progressive," only to learn later that for us their way would not work.

Neither his nor my option was the right one—but there was

no right one, if we grant that waiting on the sidelines is not a solution. Moreover, had we been citizens of any other people's democracy, we would have fallen into even worse ambushes. Poland, even during the darkest years, preserved some sort of sympathy for the defenseless, thanks to her chaotic liberal past, to Catholicism, to the hatred of long-time Communists for the old Tormentor who had slain their beloved leaders. Somewhere else I would probably have recollected Einstein's good advice in a jail cell, having been accused of some random crime such as collaboration with American intelligence—and I would have confessed, as long as they demanded it, that the real head of the American intelligence was Einstein. In any case, no one would have winked and sent me abroad a second time. And Tiger, in spite of all his precautions, would have found a *provocateur* among his trusted friends.

As far as possible in this book I have avoided simplifications, and although the autobiographical fragments are only a pretext, I doubt that I appear on these pages as a haloed figure. Maybe even a rather severe judgment about myself flashes through here and there. If so, there is no reason to embellish Tiger's portrait either. Not only my opinions about him count, after all; other people who knew him less well are also entitled to a hearing. His former students stare at me in disbelief when I stand up for him. But, they exclaim, with a shrug of the shoulders, he was a terrified man, a coward, a broken mirror! They are brutal. And since our neighbors always measure us by an external standard, I repeat, as a warning to myself, the words of my poem about the many "half-open lips that never managed to speak out what they wanted to."

I do not presume to know how typical the adventures I have described here are of certain milieus in Eastern Europe. But when I compare us with the inhabitants of calm and orderly countries, I would be inclined, in spite of all our misfortunes and sufferings, to call us happier in one respect. Neither new models of cars, nor travels, nor love affairs provide the elixir of youth. In grabbing our portion of amusements and pleasures, we expose ourselves to the vengeance of time, which dulls receptivity. We Easterners, on the other hand, precisely because we had to gaze into the hells of our century, made the discovery that the elixir of youth is not a delusion. No one brought himself willingly to look into those hells. Time that was compressed, speeded up, was not physiological time; it, too, avenged itself with a concentration camp, a bullet, or a heart attack. Nevertheless, it taught us the meaning of full commitment and exploded the barriers between the individual and the social, between style and institution, between aesthetics and politics. That miraculous elixir is nothing other than the certainty that there are no boundaries to the knowledge of what is human; that to puff ourselves up with self-importance is inappropriate because each of our achievements falls away into yesterday, and we are always pupils in an introductory class. I suspect that the individual who lives out his journey from childhood to old age against an almost unchanging background, whose habits are never disrupted by the ups and downs of the social order, is too susceptible to the melancholy of things that are simply here, yet are opaque. Thus twenty-year-olds, with a pout of boredom, repeat the deceptive aphorism: "There is nothing new under the sun."

Through defeats and disasters, humanity searches for the elixir of youth; that is, of life made into thought, the ardor that upholds belief in the wider usefulness of our individual effort, even if it apparently changes nothing in the iron working of the world. It may be that we Eastern Europeans have been given the lead in this search. By choosing, we had to give up some values for the sake of others, which is the essence of tragedy. Yet only such an experience can whet our understanding, so that we see an old truth in a new light: when ambition counsels us to lift ourselves above simple moral rules guarded by the poor in spirit, rather than to choose them as our compass needle amid the uncertainties of change, we stifle the only thing that can redeem our follies and mistakes: love.